Congreve

Comedies

The Old Bachelor
The Double-Dealer
Love for Love
The Way of the World

A CASEBOOK

EDITED BY

PATRICK LYONS

M

First published 1982 by
THE MACMILLAN PRESS LTD
London and Basingstoke
Companies and representatives throughout the world

Printed in

ISBN o 333 26456 8 (hc)
ISBN o 333 26457 6 (pbk)

CONTENTS

ACKNOWLEDGEMENTS

The editor of this volume is gratefully indebted to Professor J. C. Bryce of the University of Glasgow, who kindly transcribed material from his edition of Adam Smith's *Literary Criticism* (in preparation), and to Harden Jay of Trinity College, Dublin, for her conversation, liberal with learning and wit.

The editor and publishers wish to thank the following for permission to use copyright material: James Agate, review of *The Way Of The World*, Lyric Theatre (1924), reprinted in *The Contemporary Theatre* (1924), by permission of George G. Harrap & Co. Limited; Anne Barton, extract from Introductory Note to *Double Dealer* (1971), by permission of The Scolar Press Limited, and a programme note to the Royal Shakespeare Company's production of *The Way Of The World*, Aldwych Theatre, London, 1978, by permission of the author; F. W. Bateson, extract from *L. C. Knights and Restoration Comedy* by permission of the Editors of *Essays in Criticism*, vol. vii (1957); Bonamy Dobrée, extracts from the Introduction to *Comedies by William Congreve* (World's Classics edition by Bonamy Dobrée, 1925) by permission of Oxford University Press; Sir John Gielgud, extracts from *Stage Directions*, 1963, by permission of Heinemann Educational Books Limited; Anthony C. Gosse, article 'Plot and Character in Congreve's *Double Dealer*' from *Modern Language Quarterly* 29 (1968), by permission of the editor; Harriett Hawkins, extract from *Likenesses of Truth in Elizabethan and Restoration Drama* (1972), by permission of Oxford University Press; Norman N. Holland, extract from *The First Modern Comedies* by permission of Harvard University Press, Copyright © 1959 by the President and Fellows of Harvard College; Peter Holland, extracts from *The Ornament of Action* (1979), by permission of Cambridge University Press; Malcolm Kelsall, extract from Introduction to *Love for Love* (1969), by permission of Ernest Benn Limited; L. C. Knights, extracts from 'Restoration Comedy: The Reality and the Myth' in *Explorations*, by permission of the author; Clifford Leech, extracts from 'Congreve and the Century's End' in *Philological Quarterly*, vol. xli by permission of the journal; Harold Love, extract from *Congreve*

(1974), by permission of Basil Blackwell Publisher Limited; Kathleen M. Lynch, extract from *The Social Mode of Restoration Comedy* (1926); Kenneth Muir, extract from 'The Comedies of William Congreve' in *Restoration Theatre* (1965), edited by Harris and Russell Brown by permission of Edward Arnold (Publishers) Limited; William Myers, extracts from 'Plot and Meaning in Congreve's Comedies' in *William Congreve* (1972), by permission of Edward Arnold Limited; Maximilian E. Novak, extracts from *William Congreve* (1971), by permission of Twayne Publishers, a Division of G. K. Hall & Co., Boston; Sir Nigel Playfair, extract from *The Story of the Lyric Theatre, Hammersmith* (1925), by permission of the Executors of the Estate; Irving Wardle, review of Royal Shakespeare Company's production of *The Way Of The World*, Aldwych Theatre (1978), in *The Times* 30 January 1978, by permission of Times Newspapers Limited; Virginia Woolf, essay 'Congreve Comedies' from *The Moment and Other Essays* (1947), and review of *Love for Love* at the Lyric Theatre, by permission of the Author's Literary Estate and The Hogarth Press Limited.

GENERAL EDITOR'S PREFACE

The Casebook series, launched in 1968, has become a well-regarded library of critical studies. The central concern of the series remains the 'single-author' volume, but suggestions from the academic community have led to an extension of the original plan, to include occasional volumes on such general themes as literary 'schools' and genres.

Each volume in the central category deals either with one well-known and influential work by an individual author, or with closely related works by one writer. The main section consists of critical readings, mostly modern, collected from books and journals. A selection of reviews and comments by the author's contemporaries is also included, and sometimes comment from the author himself. The Editor's introduction charts the reputation of the work or works from the first appearance to the present time.

Volumes in the 'general themes' category are variable in structure but follow the basic purpose of the series in presenting an integrated selection of readings, with an Introduction which explores the theme and discusses the literary and critical issues involved.

A single volume can represent no more than a small selection of critical opinions. Some critics are excluded for reasons of space, and it is hoped that readers will pursue the suggestions for further reading in the Select Bibliography. Other contributions are severed from their original context, to which some readers may wish to turn. Indeed, if they take a hint from the critics represented here, they certainly will.

A. E. DYSON

A NOTE ON TEXTS

Each of Congreve's plays was first printed, at the time it was first performed, in Quarto format. For a collected library edition in 1710, Congreve renumbered the scenes within each Act according to French practice, indicating a new 'scene' whenever another character entered; the order of scenes remained unaltered. He also incorporated some minor revisions, with gains as well as losses: a few grammatical forms were slightly adjusted; some oaths were expunged to avoid offending censorious readers; mention of the Plyants' sexual restraint was omitted, as was reference to Sir Paul's chamber-pot (although Foresight's urinal survives intact); explicit broomsticks were added, to arm the maids whom Lady Wishfort summons to bastinado Sir Wilful to bed in his drunkenness.

Some older texts incorporated revisions made for performance during the later eighteenth century. The 1710 version was the basis for Bonamy Dobrée's edition (Oxford, 1925). Recent editors have usually preferred to base their texts on the Quarto versions, for the kind of reasons argued by Peter Holland (see his excerpt in section 1 of Part Three, below). The Quartos are followed in Montague Summers's Nonesuch edition (London, 1923) and, in the current standard edition, by Herbert Davis (Chicago, 1967). Davis also lists Congreve's later revisions in an appendix; David Mann's computerised concordance to the plays (Ithaca, N. Y., 1973) is keyed to Davis's edition.

In this Casebook, act and scene references follow the Quarto divisions, unless there is a note to the contrary. In criticism written before the Second World War, quotations appear in whatever form they were first given; in subsequent criticism, quotations (unless otherwise noted) have been amended to follow Davis's text. In regard to the styling of characters' names (e. g., Mirabel/Mirabell), the forms in twentieth-century critical material have been systematised to the modern convention.

P. L.

INTRODUCTION

Congreve's comedies have been easily ranked among the greatest achievements of English drama without any matching readiness to discuss their greatness. It is understandable that audiences should be content to express their enjoyment in laughter and applause. Less understandable is the way reproachful critics have been equally satisfied with their own noises, in the mealy-mouthed manner of the following examples:

If the comedies of Congreve did not rack him with remorse in his last moments, he must have been lost to all sense of virtue. (Lord Kames, 1763).*

The surface [of Congreve's comedies] is so dazzling that sometimes one forgets what is lacking beneath. (Henry Ten Eyck Perry, 1925).[1]

Neither of these comments actually tells you anything about Congreve. A grudging attribution of power to the plays is quickly stifled in moralising, and the trouble here is that the moralising is so evidently sham: neither writer seems to feel in the slightest way tainted by his exposure to the supposed depravity, so that the real subject of such writing can be seen as self-congratulation, a smug reflection on superiority. What is particularly disgraceful (or disheartening, according to how you see it) is the wearisome recurrence of this kind of comment down the years, as if there were a breed of writers like the monkey-folk peopling Kipling's jungle, who 'have no speech of their own, but use the stolen words which they overhear when they listen, and peep, and wait up above in the branches'. Failure of insight deserves only passing mention in a volume charting the shifts of critical

---

* The absence of a numbered source-reference for a critical writing discussed in this Introduction signifies that the work is excerpted in the ensuing selection. The references appropriate to other material will be found in the Notes, pp. 28-9 below.

perception over several centuries, where the tedious parade of empty decency, mouthing nothings, should have no place. But these examples are far from unique or isolated or particular to any past epoch: they turn up still. They may, however, be useful at the outset, requiring us to consider whether Congreve eludes criticism or critics choose to evade Congreve. This Introduction will examine, from a contemporary point of view, which aspects of Congreve's comedies have proved most accessible to criticism in the succeeding centuries from his time to ours.

Besotted with a woman 'harder to be understood than a Piece of Aegyptian Antiquity, or an Irish Manuscript', the extravagant hero of *Love for Love* rails in exasperation at her refusal to make innermost feeling public. However, in personal matters, Congreve preferred reticence to self-exposure. To his most recent, scrupulous, well-informed biographer, he remained 'a dim figure that has largely escaped us',[2] and what we do know of his life is noticeably lacking props on which critical understanding might be built. Even Congreve's will held discreetly to a secret: naming as his executor Francis, the second Duke of Marlborough, it largely succeeded in muting the potential scandal of Congreve's bequeathing most of his belongings to the Duchess,[3] a legacy Henrietta was to pass on in turn to the daughter she had borne by the retired dramatist in 1723. (This discretion must have solaced the Duke, for in 1729 he was one of the pall-bearers at Congreve's funeral; in default of concrete evidence, gossip did eventually tire, leaving the Duchess free to make circumspect arrangements to be buried close to the writer she had loved, rather than in the ducal plot.) Congreve's fondness for reticence was already evident while he was writing his comedies: Anne Bracegirdle, the actress for whom he wrote leading roles, and with whom he then spent much of his leisure (she was his landlady's sister), was particularly noted for being 'not unguarded in her private life', which was no more typical of the stars of the contemporary stage than it was to be of Hollywood in its heyday. When posthumous *Memoirs of the Life, Writings, and Amours of William Congreve Esq.* were advertised, with saucy promise of temptingly spicy revelations, Anne Bracegirdle confronted Edmund Curll, its rascally publisher and demanded to know what material would be used. According to the book's shameless preface: 'Upon being civilly told, there would be found several Essays, Letters, and Characters of that

Gentleman's writing, she with a most affected, contradictory, Dramatick-drawl, cry'd out *Not one single Sheet of Paper I dare to swear.*' She was right; and, like other biographies of Congreve, this one failed either to illuminate or besmirch its subject.

Congreve must have destroyed his private papers with systematic care. The letters which remain recommend patent medicine, report on a favourite dog, and throughout show kindly, considerate involvement in friendships, but throw small light on the ways of his creativity. Even with the sudden dwindling of his output in 1700, just when *The Way of the World* had revealed a height of power, his amiable correspondence continued unruffled. It has been suggested that he sulked in disappointment at the unfavourable reception the play is supposed to have received, but this speculation is contradicted by the tone of Congreve's dedication ('That it succeeded on the Stage, was almost beyond my Expectation'), and recent research, indicating a revival of the play in the following season, does suggest it won popularity,[4] that Congreve had no need to put a brave face on despair. It seems his critics must be content not to know Congreve's intimate feelings, without inferring from this ignorance that he cared about nothing at all.

Congreve's literary criticism may allow no glimpse into a private world, but it does harbour searching and profoundly serious pre-occupation with comedy. He comes nearest to exposing emotion in the dedication prefixed to the first edition (1694) of *The Double-Dealer* when he rages at 'snarling and barking' by 'Illiterate Criticks' who had raised 'Impotent Objections' to what he had designed as 'a true and regular Comedy'; for later editions he retained his analytic account of the play's cruxes, and added some lines from Terence to underline his own orthodoxy with classical precedent, but he excised his bad-tempered display of spleen. To take comedy seriously was no paradox. It is evident, in hindsight, that writers after Milton, until the time of Wordsworth, were at their most vital when they set out to entertain; when they aimed at grave solemnity, their language either froze into marmoreal stiffness (as in, for instance, *The Mourning Bride*, Congreve's lifeless venture into tragedy) or else sank into tasteless bathos. Fastidious concern for what comedy might achieve is a sign of Congreve's alertness to the artistic possibilities of the times.

It might seem that Congreve's personal background has relevance here. His childhood and adolescence were spent in Ireland. Ireland has shaped and supplied comic writers for England since Congreve's time, providing Swift, Sterne and Joyce, as well as almost every dramatist whose plays have lasted, from Farquhar, Goldsmith and Sheridan to Wilde, Shaw and Beckett. Clowning is one way to bridge the distances an outsider may feel when faced with the habitual reflexes of an alien community, especially if that community treats his own as inferior, and English comedy has thrived and gained edge on the extra awareness of insecurity the displaced Irish could bring. Yet Ireland's claim on Congreve is doubtful: he insisted that he was born in Yorkshire, and parish records for 1670 confirm this. He departed from Ireland almost a refugee; before he could complete his degree, civil commotions during the Jacobite War (following James II's loss of the throne in England in 1688) had obliged Trinity College Dublin to close temporarily, and Congreve had left for England,[5] first staying with a dying grandfather in Staffordshire, then settling with his family in London. Even if memories of political and social upheaval in Dublin might have fostered some nervous basis for the illnesses which were to bedevil Congreve, that would hardly have escaped Swift, who attributed Congreve's ailments to excessive meals and wine during his Dublin student-days.

Once in London, Congreve readily became at home, negotiating his own way among its literary factions. He collaborated in setting up the theatre at Lincoln's Inn Fields which was directly controlled by the actors themselves, and he was active in attracting writing talent to this independent company and in supporting new writers. Free from both the unease of exile and the self-advertising bluster that was the mark of his friend John Vanbrugh, his critical writings show a fastidious temper applying itself, with assurance, to examine a world it knows well. All Congreve's plays won him acclaim, and all were written by the end of his twenties. After 1700 Congreve wrote little but lived modestly in a circle of close and – his correspondence suggests – dear friends, out of the public eye.

Huge and immediate fame had come from Congreve's dramatic achievement, not from any other assertion of personality, and that may be how his name came to stand for excellence in drama rather than for more idiosyncratic qualities. Panegyrics from Dryden and other contemporaries illustrate how the young dramatist was taken as an epitome of the best the stage had seen since the theatres had reopened at the restoration of the monarchy. The tendency among his champions to present Congreve more as a literary institution than as an individual was, ironically, to be reinforced when attacks on the theatre took Congreve as one of its chief representatives. By the 1690s, the monarchy was again established securely enough for at least indirect attacks on its policy to be tolerable, and reviling the theatre (which had been outlawed during the Puritan rule of the interregnum, and then reopened on the return of Charles II) became one way to oppose government without head-on confrontation. Congreve's plays did not rely on topicality, having clearly absorbed what admiration for the drama of the preceding decades could teach, and so he stood as a useful living target for all the monarchy had fostered since its restoration. It was by such logic that his detractors collaborated almost casually in regarding as 'Restoration' plays, comedies Congreve wrote during William of Orange's reign, grouping them with plays written in earlier, different times, by playwrights who had already quit the stage when Congreve was a child of seven, living overseas in Ireland.

Tagging Congreve as another exponent of 'Restoration Comedy' is misleading, blurring his own originality in presuming him to be yet one more (later) representative of its (often rapacious) libertine code. The label is not unhelpful, however, in pointing to where he started. One obvious difference between Congreve and later dramatists, even such near-contemporaries as Farquhar and Steele, is his lack of interest in unfolding a straightforward story. Instead (as he recognised, comparing his mode of construction to the layout of a formal garden), his comedies develop through contrasts, parallels and counterpoints, not along a simple linear procession of narrative. This was characteristic of Restoration comedy proper, and of course familiar too from earlier seventeenth-century plays – those of Shakespeare and Jonson, for instance. For his underlying structure Congreve drew on that model which first emerged in Etherege's *She Wou'd If She Cou'd* (1668), and which brought coherence into Restoration comedy. Its fundamental motif is a contrast between two categories of character, 'truewits and witwouds', (witwouds = witless people who aspire to wit), between cool, collected masterminds and blabber-mouthed fools. This has some resemblance to Ben Jonson's habit of contrasting confidence-tricksters and their dupes; however, in Restoration comedy the milieu is not the low-life underworld which interested Jonson but one of rank and breeding, and the goal of the characters becomes that of distinction and happiness through love.

The point of these wit-comedies is clear once it is recalled that, in the seventeenth century, wit meant far more than a capacity for snappy repartee; extending to cover the exercise of judgement, it included self-awareness along with an alert understanding of the tricky choices met in moulding satisfaction from life. Disguise, deceit and intrigues that often verge on paranoia supply the action, plotting and counter-plotting multiply in schemes of attack and defence. As they circle hungrily about the truewits, the witwouds vainly over-estimate their own value, constantly misjudge human relations, and provide one kind of dramatic interest as obstacles in the love-chases of the truewits. Their machinations never succeed, because witwouds assert to excess their claims to belong (thereby betraying how unfounded the claims are) and so are easily recognised and checked under the sharper, satiric observation of the truewits; and the truewits thereby confirm their own membership of an élite inner circle. But the truewits' very skills in satire provoke further dramatic tension, less easily resolved. What they find in the witwouds are negative images, defining for them what they could not wish to be, a parade of warnings reflecting how they do not wish to live. The various witwouds seem to test each of life's roles and to exhaust life's possibilities, until all appear futile and worthless. In the end the truewits are pushed to decide between alternatives which their own experience and observation have proved equally absurd, reaching a stalemate position, where love seems as fraught with folly and emptiness as does lovelessness. The plays' endings make no definite promise of happiness; they close inconclusively, in hesitation and recoil, leaving the future open and unspoken.

By the 1680s mechanical repetition of the formula was common, and it had been debased as hacks padded it with coarse farce. Congreve's freshness shows in his attention to devices which had added resonance in the finest of the earlier plays, particularly those of Etherege and Wycherley. Among the truewit group these writers had included isolated figures trapped in a social network who had come to view the satisfactions their world offered as hollow, giving them only a spur to satirical side-comments. In their loneliness, such characters add a sense of the paralysing, self-defeating aspects of self-consciousness. This emerges in Horner, towards the close of Wycherley's *The Country Wife* (1675), is sketched in Etherege's Medley, in *The Man of Mode* (1676), obvious in Scandal in *Love for Love*, and part of the melancholy that weaves through all of Congreve's comedies. It is an aspect, too, of the misanthropy in Heartwell's surliness, in Maskwell's contempt and in the sourness Valentine uncovers during his feigned madness.

These figures are developments from Manly, the misanthropic truewit Wycherley placed at the centre of *The Plain Dealer* (1677). Disgusted at social pretences, Manly yearns for escape in a more primitive way of living 'where honest downright barbarity is professed, where men devour one another like generous hungry lions and tigers, not like crocodiles' [ii]. The brutality lingering in this vision of happiness tells that, in society, natural aggression is (perhaps mercifully) trammelled by hypocrisy, so hinting that Manly's fantasy is actually delusion. There is further self-delusion in his egocentrically presumptive desire to conduct close relationships entirely on his own terms, with enslaving fidelity to his opinions and wishes; and as disappointments (inevitably) follow, he avoids recognising his own self-regarding error through outbursts of pathologically ugly rage:

> Her love! – a whore's, a witch's love! But what, did she not kiss well, sir? – I'm sure I thought her lips – but I must not think of 'em – but yet they are such I could still kiss – grow to – and then tear them off with my teeth, grind 'em into mammocks, and spit 'em in her cuckold's face. [*The Plain Dealer*, IV i]

In *The Way of the World* Lady Wishfort's more ridiculous passions touch similar extremes, veering to escapism in her fatuous plan to become a shepherdess with Mrs Marwood for pastoral companion, demanding that life be loyal to her widly extravagant fantasies, then unleashing her anxieties and disappointments in coarse abuse of her servants. She re-enacts in parody the yearnings for peace and retreat, the needs for trust, and the angers which move other, cleverer characters. What Wycherley had studied as manic, singular oddity becomes a more pervasive malaise, as Congreve's handling shifts and widens the angle of vision on his predecessor's material.

Congreve's distinctive enlargement of scope appears, too, in his treatment of those characters who, although intelligent enough to be truewits, submit themselves to the sway of passion and actually watch themselves lapse into folly. Some of their slips cause tolerably little harm, and can be as amusing as the quarrel between Mrs Foresight and Mrs Frail in which each exposes her own weakness until mutual need for secrecy and security leagues them together in conspiracy. Others are less fortunate: Mrs Fainall's resignation to lovelessness has painful aspects. Similar studies of knowing self-betrayal had been included in earlier comedy, notably by Etherege with Belinda and Mrs Loveit in *The Man of Mode* (1676), but his vision was relentlessly tough. As she rants at Dorimant for infidelity she had expected, what most stings Mrs Loveit to fury is knowing how ridiculous her rage makes her, seeing herself as a fit object for that reductive laughter which Hobbes described as 'sudden glory'; what most hurts is the blow to pride, as she anticipates his triumphant relish over her humiliation. Congreve, however, ranges over a greater variety of the implications laughter can carry. In the opening of *The Double-Dealer* the discussion as to whether or not jokes should be laughed at challenges the audience to find more complex responses to what follows than simple mirth. Further investigations of laughter probe both the playwright and his audiences.

I am as willing to laugh, as any body, and as easily diverted with an Object truly ridiculous: but at the same time, I can never care for seeing things that force me to entertain low thoughts of my own Nature. I dont know how it is with others, but I confess freely to you, I could never look long upon a Monkey, without very Mortifying Reflections.   [Letter to Dennis, 1695]

Those Characters which are meant to be ridicul'd in most of our Comedies are of Fools so gross, that in my humble Opinion, they should rather disturb than divert the well-natur'd and reflecting Part of an Audience; they are rather Objects of Charity than Contempt; and instead of moving our Mirth, they ought very often to excite our Compassion. This reflection mov'd me to design some Characters, which should appear ridiculous not so much thro' a natural Folly (which is incorrigible, and therefore not proper for the Stage) as thro' an affected Wit. . . .   [Dedication, *The Way of the World*, 1700]

Whereas earlier Restoration comedies had made elderly characters either simply pompous or simply voraciously lustful, ready targets for the automatically insulting reflexes of youthful mockery, Congreve brings them closer to horror-comedy by introducing a measure of pathos. As they brag about allure which they patently lack, or boast of fidelity in spouses who are openly deceiving them, the prattle sounds as anxious as it is funny; they retain sufficient nagging perception to urge on their efforts to persuade themselves that time hasn't altogether ruined their hopes and their chances, sensing that it already has.

In his presentation of truewit lovers, Congreve also alters the ground plan of earlier comedies. It had been usual to trace a gradual awakening of love between couples who meet in the course of the play; Congreve instead starts out with couples who are not strangers to each other, and who are already each other's match. In each play the central couple is different, but each couple has everything to lose from the beginning, as others exhibit to them the instability of passion and make love look like folly or empty fiction that can't endure. What is at stake is more than

intellectual integrity or social esteem, as rashness and doubt alternate in
the endeavours to reconcile worthwhile loving with worthwhile living:
their worlds are without the possibility of adventure, or the unexpected
surprise that was possible in earlier plays (it is always ridiculous people
who are surprised in Congreve's plays), and they are quite simply
gambling on their only possible chance of success.

Congreve's plays, then, are balanced constructions, built with finesse
and emotional subtlety, making demands on the judgement. Attacking
the theatre as a covert way to attack the government (he had almost
landed in prison again), the Rev. Jeremy Collier had no interest in these
qualities. He took the line that in displaying immorality the theatre
encourages it. Vanbrugh and others had flatly (though not altogether
convincingly) denied the charge, but Congreve probed its basis as an
argument, seeing at once that it denied an audience or dramatist any
capacity to exercise judgement. The tactics of Congreve's reply were to
turn Collier's underlying assumption back on its proponent, and treat
him as a stage fool with no judgement. Collier's simple equation
identified the dramatist and his audience with the characters in plays;
then all he had to do was extract all the remarks and scenes which he
could construe to be immoral, and denounce the theatre's supporters for
countenancing immorality. Congreve did not stop at pointing out that
Collier here was also exhibiting immoralities in quoting what he
deemed depraved; he fastened particularly on careless misquotations,
arguing that the divine must be judged as worse than those he
denounced for the initial immoralities because he had gone on to invent
new indecencies all his own. To apply Collier's logic to Collier, he
substituted Collier's name for his own, in a passage which had damned
Congreve, so that (like a fool on stage) Collier could be judged through
his own words: ' . . . his Pen has such a Libertine Stroke that 'tis
question whether the Practice or the Reproof be the more Licentious.
He teaches those Vices he would correct . . . .' Congreve showed how
Collier was already a joke.

Congreve's conclusion implies further reason for tackling Collier in
this way, making fun of him. He suggests that immorality (such as civic
disorder, rioting, suicide) is the common outcome of widespread
unhappiness, so that morality must benefit when public happiness is
augmented, as (for example) through the pleasures that theatre
provides. Nothing is ameliorated by censorious denunciation because
grumpiness does not enhance life; but a joke that appeals to judgement
is its own justification: in a society where judgement is grown-up, all the

arts exert moral force by their sheer presence and energy. While it would be pleasing to think that Queen Anne's government bore this in mind when they licensed Congreve and Vanbrugh to manage the Haymarket Theatre 'for better reforming the Abuses and Immorality of the Stage', the phrase was more probably intended as a sop to other reformists than as a jocular snub to Collier. Government documents rarely aspire to comic form.

Although Congreve's Lord Froth makes himself ridiculous by protesting 'there is nothing more unbecoming a Man of Quality, than to Laugh: Jesu, 'tis such a Vulgar Expression of the Passion! every Body can laugh', this very doctrine was to prevail on the eighteenth-century stage.[6] It was part of the new sentimental trend, which worshipped virtue-in-distress. During the last years of Congreve's life, sentimental comedies became the ruling fashion, and in these plays love's misfortunes merit only pathos without laughter; humour was tolerated when it was at the expense of servants, because that was reassuring for the new middle-class audience, far from secure about their own social standing. This was clearly at odds with the more democratic spirit in Congreve's comedies, where it is laughable to laugh at social inferiors. It is therefore, initially, surprising that his comedies should have remained so popular. What can be said is that they were already famous, as well as distinctively different from newer work. Thus, they were at once uncommon and celebrated, so audiences could take them as a kind of test. Whether or not audiences cared for the judgement exercised in Congreve's comedy, they could judge themselves to be cultured for being present, and beamingly appreciate their own discernment in displaying such good taste. (After all, if you outlaw laughter, you don't care whether or not you understand the jokes).

Reviews in the new journals came to dwell largely on performances of individual roles, often comparing these with performances by earlier actors,[7] as if the very actors were watched only to be measured, tried and tested. Frequently, actors selected one of Congreve's plays for a 'benefit' (a performance of a play chosen by a member of the company, who would then receive a percentage of the night's profits), as if to prove excellence by undertaking what was most demanding. Pope's remarks on dramatists significantly avoid direct comment on Congreve, and instead include him as the subject for a question which could belong in some viva voce examination quizzing social acumen:

> Tell me if Congreve's fools are fools indeed?

Attempted answers often reveal more temerity than shrewdness. Dennis's heavy-handed flattery (1721) comes perilously close to self-description, identifying fools as recognisable pests. The reviewer for the *London Chronicle* in 1758 (probably the dramatist Arthur Murphy) interprets wit to mean facility in catching people's attention with pithy, glittering remarks, claiming this to be such a good thing that you can never have too much of it, outrageously side-stepping Congreve's more modest arguement (in his *Letter to Dennis*) that characters require 'heightening' to become sufficiently distinctive on the stage. Confused judgement was possible because plays of the sentimental genre did pretend to transpose polite society directly onto the stage, so that what had simply been theatrical swagger might appear proper in social conduct. Up in Glasgow in the 1760s, Adam Smith's students learned how 'the whole of Congreve's wit' might be seen in the utterances of two fools, an 'affected lady' and Witwoud himself; at least they noticed the kind of language used – 'ridiculous similes' – and their fascination with grotesque physiognomy may not be brutality but a vestige of the Puritan's liking for his own portrait 'warts and all'. Novelists seized on the fashion for talking about Congreve to display taste, and frequently introduced reference to his plays, obliquely in echoes and directly as the topic of discussions, to provide a touchstone for character.[8] For instance, in *Evelina* (1778) the characters are at the theatre to banter and flirt; as they bandy clichés, *Love for Love* plainly matters to them only as another opportunity for chatter about each other.

Still holding sway in the later eighteenth century, the sentimental movement began to impose its vision further, distorting the performances of Congreve's plays. *Love for Love* suffered in the deletion of Valentine's off-hand dismissal of his bastard at Twickenham and of his risqué proposition during Mrs Frail's morning visit. In this version, Angelica's hesitation in accepting his love could only appear as heartless trifling with a man admirable for his propriety: in mollifying passing taste, the tensions in judgement are made to seem mere nonsense. (This, of course, assists Lord Orville's chaste pursuit of Evelina, at the expense of Congreve's play). To gratify the liking for tearful pathos, acting styles altered too. Horace Walpole could then envisage the venomous, covert love-scenes between Maskwell and Lady Touchwood as played for *comédie larmoyante:* as touching portrayals of distress in private life. To preserve respectability appropriate to his fame, Congreve's comedies were further and further altered to become a compendium of respectable attitudes (which rarely provide the staple of drama) and, as they became less and less stage-worthy, they were less and less staged. The production of 1842 which replaced Mrs Marwood with a male character can hardly have been *The Way of the World* in more than name.[9]

Apparent concern to define how Congreve's comedy was distinctively different from what was current turns out to be an excuse to use him as a vehicle for self-expression. Goldsmith and Sheridan were only interested in using him as a battering-ram to force space in the theatre for their own new brand of comedy. Samuel Johnson candidly admitted, when writing his account of Congreve in *Lives of the Poets*, that it had been many years since he had actually read the comedies. Drawing therefore on his powers of memory, his comment took shape under his more private obsessions and, lacking the immediacy of his *Preface to Shakespeare*, grew from the distorting anguish of his self-examinations. Projecting his own worries, Johnson expanded on false claims that Congreve had actually been born in Ireland but was too vain to acknowledge his origins; guilt over his snobbish repudiation of his own background haunted Johnson, who had refused to serve on his father's market-stall at Lichfield when he was twelve, and who was to return there in old age to make token penance with a stint serving on another stall. As intolerant of fools, and as deft with aggressive jibes as the very characters he berates for being 'intellectual gladiators', Johnson's own recurrent remorse after he had talked for victory made Congreve's wits victims of his self-disapproval. And Johnson's constant shame at failing to achieve that self-improvement he searched after in prayers and religious meditations qualifies his charge that perusal of Congreve's plays 'will make no man better'.

Its energies sapped as crude black-and-white moralising prevailed, the nineteenth-century theatre was weakened for all but melodrama, pantomime and farce, and Congreve's comedies were little staged. Perversely, this won them favour among critics holding the romantic

belief that artists are society's outcasts possessed of a vision not of this
earth; ceasing to have physical presence on the stage, the plays acquired
a kind of extra-terrestrial being which had its own appeal. Hazlitt was
not displeased if *The Way of the World* 'is an essence almost too fine; and
the sense of pleasure evaporates in an aspiration after something that
seems too exquisite ever to have been realised'. Romantic paradise was
childhood untroubled by sexuality ('angel infancy' was Wordsworth's
phrase), and praising Congreve for rarified stylishness banished
contemplation of his probing into adult emotions. Here is the tactic
Lamb adopted to circumvent charges that Congreve's characters
constitute an affront to public decency:

They break through no laws, or conscientious restraints. They know of none.
They have got out of Christendom into the land – what shall I call it? – of
cuckoldry – the Utopia of gallantry, where pleasure is duty and the manners
perfect freedom. It is altogether a speculative scene of things, which has no
reference to the world that is.

To defuse what might offend or startle those who never think of sex
when thinking of England, Lamb's own camp style simply charms away
out of sight all Congreve's explorations into the perilous fate which
attends escapism. Indifferent as an airy cherub to any of the painful
distinctions in Congreve's comedy ('we should sit unconcerned at the
issues'), Lamb daintily transforms all he touches until it furthers his
ideal of the theatre as a playground where moral concerns and matters
of feeling can be as uncomplicated as they would be for mischievous
children.

Horrified Victorians, attacking such easy acceptance of Congreve's
plays, were equally unscrupulous in twisting Congreve to their
purposes, though they lacked Lamb's honesty, never daring to admit
that 'we indict our dreams'. In Thackeray's outrageously untrue
biographical sketch, fiction is presented as fact, his novelistic skill
deployed wildly, first to invent and then to flesh out in detail what seems
a grotesque effigy of some enemy. Congreve is supplied with ridiculous
red shoes of Thackeray's manufacture, with a shocking string of
amorous conquests fantasised by Thackeray, along with a generous
state pension which would have come in handy during Congreve's lean
years, and have spared Swift the persistent nagging of influential
politicians necessary (as he confided in his *Journal to Stella*) to obtain

even the meagre stipend which the state proved less eager to pay than it had been to promise to Congreve. Superficially more respectable – at least abstaining from the overt malice of character-assassination – Macaulay championed Collier's denunciation of Congreve with showy complacence. Casually overlooking the absurdities which (as Congreve had demonstrated) vitiated that argument, and quite unperturbed by blemishes he noticed in its surface, Macaulay extolled Collier's book for 'so many bursts of that peculiar eloquence which comes from the heart and goes to the heart'. With this elevated self-assurance Macaulay provided himself ample license to ignore what had been said and to decide himself what actually was meant. Thus, where Congreve had rebutted Collier with mock-pedantry for his laborious attempt to demonstrate that the inclusion of a clerical buffoon named Prig in a comedy cast a desperate slur on the entire clergy, Macaulay could find Collier right and Congreve falsely self-righteous because young, and happily betray his own lack of humour in a patronising cluck. If its sheer indifference to the written word disqualifies Macaulay's comments as literary criticism, it does illustrate how Congreve's fame could be detached and then arbitrarily recycled to people Macaulay's dubious picture of a civilisation in decline. As his peculiar eloquence relied on Victorian readiness to mistake fiction for history, regardless of accuracy, Macaulay unscrupulously gave to Congreve the status of a character in a novel.[10]

More appreciative critics also held their distance. As much as Wilde may have admired and even (as he claimed) wished to rival Congreve, he never specified why.[11] (Indeed, they have little affinity under the skin: what ultimately propels Wilde's characters is dandyish self-admiration; his heroes and heroines have more in common with foppish witwouds than with Congreve's tense, urgent truewits.) Meredith's praise adds little detail to what had been said earlier, and is in the main Hazlitt's rhapsody on Millamant rephrased as if she were about to walk into one of Meredith's own novels. Meredith's theoretical context does, however, give this added meaning, as demonstration of his more general contention that 'where women are on the road to an equal footing with men . . . Comedy flourishes'. He does focus, refreshingly, the spiritedness and energy Congreve gave his female characters, who equal his men in astuteness and often outstrip them in poise and command. Congreve was a noted supporter of at least two women playwrights, Mary Pix and Catharine Trotter, whose work he admired and encouraged.[12] But this did not reflect the prevailing mood of his times.

There was then a growing sense that women should be protected and sheltered (as Lady Wishfort hoped to shield her daughter by giving her only female dolls, and by pretending the chaplain was female because dressed in a skirted cassock) – a shift away from feminism to dwell instead on femininity, associating women with softness, and evolving that sentimental view of women which Meredith properly deplored for its arrogant denial that women are capable of independent judgement.[13] Meredith's slant does, then, bring to light an important aspect of Congreve's work, but erroneously associates it with the spirit of the age. His unreliable explanation for a valid perception suggests that the genesis of Congreve's comedies is not susceptible to understanding on the model of Victorian novels.

In arguing that comic art could have significant merit, Meredith's was a lone voice. Nineteenth-century criticism reinforced the sense that what was serious should be solemn, which left to comedy the status of escapism, close to triviality. In practical terms, the theatre had been impelled to devalue entertainment, to draw comedy's teeth. This is apparent in Lamb's recommendation that Congreve be played in the style the actor Palmer had used with Sheridan, so that no passion would be felt, underlining instead 'the downright *acted* villainy of the part, so different from the pressure of conscious wickedness – the hypocritical assumption of hypocrisy'. Palmer's approach must have pleased Sheridan, who had provided his villain with asides that reach across the footlights, drawing the audience into his confidence with no other purpose than disarmingly gleeful relish at clever plotting. Far from the demands Congreve makes of the actor, this runs counter to his instructions, in the *Dedication* prefacing *The Double-Dealer*, for villainous soliloquies to be performed with villainous intent:

if he supposes any one to be by, when he talks to himself, it is monstrous and ridiculous to the last degree. . . . We ought not to imagine that this Man talks to us or to himself; he is only thinking, and thinking such Matter as were inexcusable Folly in him to speak.

Once Sheridan had defused villainy with clowning, the way was opened for the cheerfully lax conventions of music-hall and melodrama, where audiences could enjoy booing villains, noisily disregarding the sterner grasp on conventions which Congreve required in his tart insistence that we are conceal'd Spectators of the Plot in agitation, and the Poet finds it necessary to let us know the whole Mystery of his Contrivance; . . . and to that end is forced to make use of the expedient of Speech, no better way being yet invented for the Communication of Thought.

Although Wilde restored the mask of convention in apparently dead-pan indifference to the audience, his aim was not to restore its range to comedy. Developing from the poetics of French *symbolisme*, his plays were to make manifest imagination's power to freewheel outside human limitation, as if holding a tea-party when the cucumber sandwiches had already been scoffed, in fact populating Lamb's 'Utopia of gallantry'. To achieve this on stage, complications of circumstance took the place of plotting, while guyed clichés and relish in polishing bright aphorisms substituted for emotional impulses. Comment on revivals in the 1920s indicate how difficult it was to shake off this nineteenth-century legacy and find a style of performance suitable for Congreve, combining sparkle with more lethal bite.

This century has been fortunate in the diversity of theatrical experiment it has witnessed, and in the resulting virtuosity of performers and producers. Experimentalism has reached to revivals of Congreve's comedies, and reports of productions show a steady move away from fascination with the glittering surfaces towards exploring the tangled human impulses behind elaborate costumes and social masks. In an immodest programme-note for his own comedies *Crimes of Passion* (Royal Court, 1967), Joe Orton claimed that 'People are taken in by "the glittering style". It's not glitter. Congreve is the same. It's real – a slice of life. Nothing at all incredible.' It is true to say that at least three of Congreve's comedies have won back their place in the repertoire: *Love for Love* has even toured to Russia; both *The Way of the World* and *The Double-Dealer* have been screened in Britain on commercial television.[14]

In suggesting the relativism of our times, when shared assumptions are not to be expected, Orton's phrase – 'Nothing at all incredible' – also points to the direction critical comment on Congreve has increasingly followed. Instead of imposing the certainties of the times, critics have only had uncertainties to live with, and so have instead begun to tease out the internal laws of his comedies, to seek out his accomplishment in the way he works. This characterises the criticism of Bonamy Dobrée, Kathleen Lynch and, later, Virginia Woolf, who all belonged to the times when T. S. Eliot was proclaiming the impersonality of art, and W. B. Yeats was announcing that 'The Intellect of man is forced to choose/Perfection of the life or of the work'.

Although writing for *Scrutiny* may have impelled L. C. Knights to challenge whatever Bloomsbury championed, his criticism was not a revival of outworn moralising, but questioned the very basis of this approach: he asks whether its ease in accepting impersonality and relativism might not merely amount to slackness, an easy and uncaring doubt. American scholarship began to provide the basis for a strong reply. Studies such as Dale Underwood's work on Etherege[15] demonstrated with great thoroughness how closely and how carefully Restoration comedy had explored central issues in contemporary thought, drawing from the difficulties of scepticism its theatrical energies and the tensions that mark its best dramatic prose. The wealth of supporting detail in Norman N. Holland's extension of this approach to Congreve made it plain that here was a line of inquiry not to be dismissed. If it had sometimes seemed disreputable to take Congreve seriously (success on the stage did not necessarily endear him to the studious), it now became relatively blameless, for he had demonstrable substance. Now off the defensive, criticism was no longer obliged to be heavy-handed in relishing either his comedy or his theatricality.

No consensus has emerged in this, and what recent criticism shares is disagreement. Lady Touchwood has been found to be both a parody of a tragedy-queen and a vehicle for feeling; the ending of *Love for Love* has been taken as the miracle Angelica claims it to be, and as a more knowing fake; while the plotting of *The Way of the World* has been seen to have its own logic, as suited to the stage as to the study, it has still to be settled whether it is its oddity or its plausibility that makes it acceptable. Even reviews of the same production fail to concur: where Irving Wardle saw 'superlative treatment of the individual scenes', but a lack of continuity 'challenging the spectator to make sense of it', another reviewer writing on the aftermath of the same first-night admired how 'The great classic scenes . . . do not seem like "turns" in the smooth continuum'.[16] Congreve caught the relativism of his time in one tight phrase: 'some weep, and others laugh at one and the same thing'. Our times have so far released the energies his texts offer to the degree that they have been accepted as mirroring scepticism now.

NOTES

1. H. Ten Eyck Perry, *The Comic Spirit in Restoration Drama* (New Haven, Conn., 1925), p. 78.

2. John C. Hodges, *William Congreve: Letters and Documents* (London and New York, 1964), p. vii. Professor Hodges sifted what reliable information is available for his valuable biography *William Congreve, The Man* (London and New York, 1941).

3. Henrietta Churchill, 'the young Duchess', only child of the first Duke and Sarah ('the old Duchess'). By a special Act of Parliament she inherited the ducal title on her father's death in 1722 and conveyed it to her husband, Francis, Earl of Godolphin.

4. Robert Hume, *The Development of English Drama in the Late Seventeenth Century* (Oxford, 1976), esp. pp. 447 and 459.

5. It is not known for certain at what date Congreve left for England. He was in Staffordshire by Spring 1689, and in February that year Trinity gave leave of absence to those wishing to 'withdraw themselves . . . for their better security'. But Congreve *may* have left earlier, given the unrest prevailing in Dublin even before the English events of 1688.

6. The preference for 'sober and polite Mirth' advocated by Addison and Steele, amounting to a bias against laughter, tolerating only mild smiling, is expounded by Richard Boston, *An Anatomy of Laughter* (London, 1974), pp. 171–5, which cites Steele's approval of Terence's comedy *The Self-Tormentor* because it contained not one passage that could raise a laugh.

7. Year-by-year details of performance and reviews are given in Emmett L. Avery, *Congreve's Plays on the Eighteenth-Century Stage* (New York, 1951).

8. This topic is treated extensively by Robert Gale Noyes, 'Congreve and His Comedies in the Eighteenth-Century Novel', *Philological Quarterly*, XXXIX (1960), pp. 464–80.

9. Described in detail by Montague Summers in his Nonesuch Press edition, *The Complete Works of William Congreve* (London, 1923), III, pp. 7–8.

10. In claiming that Restoration society reacted against Puritan rule, replacing excessive strictness with extraordinary moral looseness, Macaulay is as inaccurate as he is over-neat. Interregnum legislation, such as the laws passed by Parliament in 1651 making adultery a capital crime, held significance for the Puritans: among the diversity of religious sects gathered under the Puritan umbrella, there was theological justification for a wide variety of sexual codes (including polygamy) and such legislation, whether or not it was actually enforced, aimed to impose some unity, at least in earthly practice.

If the Restoration is to be deemed a reaction against Interregnum ways, the reaction may well be seen as towards a new preoccupation with respectability. David Foxon has argued persuasively, in *Libertine Literature in England 1660–1745* (New York, 1964), pp. 45–51, that pornography began to appear at this time because of a new (voyeuristic) prudishness, which was not especially British but characteristic of Counter-Reformation Europe. Deflecting sexual impulses into fantasy, pornography could, like the rules and regulations of the counter-reformers, ease the strain on the individual to be responsible for sexual actions. This trend towards respectability is paralleled in Restoration concern for political security, which heightened in reaction to the turmoil of the Civil War times. Startling evidence for the Restoration as an era of great respectability appears in Peter Laslett's statistical study of illegitimacy in *The World We Have Lost* (London, 2nd edn 1971), pp. 138–45. From his examination of parish registers he shows that the proportion of all births which were actually illegitimate or occured during the first nine months of the parents' marriage was at its lowest in the period 1660–1710 and at its highest in the mid-Victorian period. Although Lawrence Stone, *The Family, Sex and Marriage in England, 1500–1800* qualifies the reading of some of Laslett's statistics (particularly in presenting evidence for knowledge of contraceptive methods in the late seventeenth century), there is still reason to see preoccupation with respect-ability in the reluctance to bear illegitimate children. It can be added here that Restoration comedy, at its best, pays heed to the psychological consequences of sexual conquest, and further differs from contemporary pornography in championing neither release nor repression.

11. *The Letters of Oscar Wilde*, edited by Rupert Hart-Davis (London, 1962), p. 500.

12. Congreve's championship of Mary Pix and Catharine Trotter is outlined by John C. Hodges, *Congreve the Man* (1941), pp. 60–1, and is expanded most interestingly by Fidelis Morgan, *The Female Wits* (London, 1981), which illustrates parallels between his work and plays by Pix and Trotter.

13. Collier's particular vehemence against 'immodest' remarks by female characters illustrates this development. He was clearly appealing to those women who, as Dryden noted in amusement, disliked *The Double-Dealer* because it 'exposed their Bitchery too much' (Letter to William Walsh, 12 December 1693).

14. Some notable productions are described by Kenneth Muir, 'Congreve on the Modern Stage', in Brian Morris (ed.), *William Congreve* (London, 1972).

15. Dale Underwood, *Etherege and the Seventeenth-Century Comedy of Manners* (New Haven, Conn., 1957). Professor Underwood's promised second volume, which was to have gone on to discuss Congreve, did not appear.

16. B. A. Young, *Financial Times* (30 Jan. 1978).

PART ONE

Congreve and his Contemporaries

1. COMMENT, 1693–1737

Bevil Higgons (1693)

Wit, like true Gold, refin'd from all Allay,
Immortal is, and never can decay:
'Tis in all Times and Languages the same;
Nor can an ill Translation quench the Flame:
For, tho' the Form and Fashion don't remain,
Th'intrinsick value still it will retain.
Then let each studied Scene be writ with Art;
And Judgement sweat to form the labour'd Part:
Each Character be just, and Nature seem;
Without th'Ingredient, Wit, 'tis all but Phlegm:
For that's the Soul, which all the Mass must move,
And wake our Passions into Grief, or Love.
But you, too Bounteous, sow your Wit so thick,
We are surpriz'd, and know not where to pick:
And while our Clapping does you Justice do,
Our selves we injure, and lose something new.
What may'nt we then, great Youth, of thee presage,
Whose Art and Wit so much transcend thy Age?
How wilt thou shine at thy Meridian height?
Who, at thy rising, give so vast a light.
When DRYDEN dying, shall the World deceive,
Whom we Immortal, as his Works, believe;
Thou shalt succeed, the Glory of the Stage,
Adorn and entertain the coming Age.

SOURCE: 'To Mr Congreve, on his Play, called, *The Old Batchelor*', verses prefixed to the first edition of the play (1693).

Thomas Southerne   (1693)

DRYDEN has long extended his Command,
By Right-divine, quite through the Muses Land,
Absolute Lord; and holding now from none,
But great *Apollo*, his undoubted Crown:
(That Empire settled, and grown old in Pow'r)
Can wish for nothing, but a Successor:
Not to enlarge his Limits, but maintain
Those Provinces, which he alone could gain.
His eldest *Wicherly*, in wise Retreat,
Thought it not worth his quiet to be great.
Loose, wandring, *Etherege*, in wild Pleasures tost,
And foreign Int'rests, to his hopes long lost:
Poor *Lee* and *Otway* dead! CONGREVE appears,
The Darling, and last Comfort of his Years:
May'st thou live long in thy great Masters smiles,
And growing under him, adorn these Isles:
But when – when part of him (be that but late)
His Body yielding must submit to Fate,
Leaving his deathless Works, and thee behind,
(The natural Successor of his Mind)
Then may'st thou finish what he has begun:
Heir to his Merit, be in Fame his Son.
What thou hast done, shews all is in thy Power;
And to Write better, only must Write more. . . .

SOURCE: extract from verses prefixed to *The Old Batchelor* (1693).

John Dryden   (1694)

Well then; the promis'd Hour is come at last;
The present Age of Wit obscures the past:
Strong were our Syres; and as they Fought they Writ,

Conqu'ring with Force of Arms, and Dint of Wit;
Theirs was the Giant Race, before the Flood;
And thus, when *Charles* Return'd, our Empire stood.
Like *Janus* he the stubborn Soil manur'd,
With rules of Husbandry the Rankness cur'd:
Tam'd us to Manners, when the Stage was rude;
And boistrous English Wit, with Art indu'd.
Our Age was cultivated thus at length;
But what we gain'd in Skill, we lost in Strength.
Our Builders were, with Want of Genius, curst;
The second Temple was not like the First:
'Till You, the best *Vitruvius*, come at length;
Our Beauties equal; but excel our Strength.
Firm *Dorique* Pillars found Your solid Base:
The fair *Corinthian* crowns the higher Space;
Thus all below is Strength, and all above is Grace.
In easie Dialogue is *Fletcher*'s Praise:
He mov'd the Mind, but had no Pow'r to raise.
Great *Johnson* did by Strength of Judgement please: [sc. Jonson]
Yet doubling *Fletcher*'s Force, he wants his Ease.
In diff'ring Talents both adorn'd their Age;
One for the Study, t'other for the Stage.
But both to *Congreve* justly shall submit,
One match'd in Judgement, both o'er-match'd in Wit.
In Him all Beauties of this Age we see;
Etherege his Courtship, *Southern*'s Purity;
The Satire, Wit, and Strength of Manly *Wicherly.*
All this in blooming Youth you have Atchiev'd;
. . .
Thy first Attempt an early Promise made;
That early Promise this has more than paid.
So bold, yet so judiciously you dare,
That your least Praise, is to be Regular.
Time, Place, and Action, may with Pains be wrought,
But Genius must be born; and never can be taught.
This is Your Portion; this Your Native Store;
Heav'n, that but once was Prodigal before,
To *Shakespear* gave as much; she could not give him more. . . .

SOURCE: extracts from 'To My Dear Friend, Mr Congreve, on his
Comedy, call'd *The Double-Dealer*': prefixed to the play (1694).

Colley Cibber   (re. 1695)

. . . the old Actors, in *Lincolns-Inn-Fields* began, with a new Comedy of Mr *Congreve*'s, call'd *Love for Love*; which ran with such extraordinary Success, that they had seldom occasion to act any other Play, 'till the End of the Season. . . . Mr *Congreve* was then in such high Reputation, as an Author, that besides his Profits, from his Play, they offer'd him a whole Share with them, which he accepted; in Consideration of which he oblig'd himself, if his Health permitted, to give them one new Play every Year. *Dryden*, in King *Charles*'s Time, had the same Share, with the King's Company; but he bound to give them two Plays every Season. This you may imagine he could not hold long, and I am apt to think, he might have serv'd them better, with one in a Year, not so hastily written. Mr *Congreve*, whatever Impediment he met with, was three Years before, in pursuance to his Agreement, he produc'd the *Mourning Bride*; and if I mistake not, the Interval had been much the same, when he gave them the *Way of the World*. But it came out the stronger, for the Time it cost him, and to their better Support, when they sorely wanted it. . . .

SOURCE: extract from *An Apology for the Life of Colley Cibber, Comedian* (1740).

Rev. Jeremy Collier   (1698)

. . . The business of Plays is to recommend Virtue, and discountenance Vice; To shew the Uncertainty of Humane Greatness, the Suddain Turns of Fate, and the Unhappy Conclusions of Violence and Injustice: 'Tis to expose the Singularities of Pride and Fancy, to make Folly and Falsehood contemptible, and to bring every Thing that is Ill under Infamy, and Neglect. This Design has been oddly pursued by the English Stage. Our Poets write with a different View. . . .

. . . Sometimes they don't stop short of Blasphemy . . .*Love for Love* has a strain like this . . . : Scandal solicits Mrs Foresight; She threatens to tell her Husband. He replies, *He will die a Martyr rather than disclaim his Passion.* Here we have Adultery dignified with the stile of Martyrdom: As if 'twas as Honourable to perish in Defence of Whoring, as to die for the Faith of Christianity. But these *Martyrs* will be a great while in burning, and therefore let no body strive to grace the Adventure, or encrease the Number. . . . Tattle would have carried off Valentine's Mistress. This latter, expresses his Resentment in a most Divine manner! *Tattle, I thank you, you would have interposed between me and Heaven, but Providence has laid Purgatory in your way.* Thus Heaven is debas'd into an Amour, and Providence brought in to direct the Paultry concerns of the Stage! Angelica concludes much in the same strain. *Men are generally Hypocrites and Infidels, they pretend to Worship, but have neither Zeal, nor Faith; How few, like Valentine, would persevere unto Martyrdom? &c.* Here you have the Language of the Scriptures, and the most solemn Instances of Religion, prostituted to Courtship and Romance! Here you have a Mistress made God Almighty, Ador'd with Zeal and Faith, and Worshipp'd up to Martyrdom! This if 'twere only for the Modesty, is strange stuff for a Lady to say of her self. . . . *Love for Love* will give us a farther account of this Authors Proficiency in the Scriptures. Our Blessed Saviour affirms himself *to be the Way, the Truth, and the Light* . . . . These expressions were remembred to good purpose. For Valentine in his pretended Madness tells Buckram the Lawyer; *I am Truth – I am Truth – Who's that, that's out of his way, I am Truth, and can set him right.* Now a Poet that had not been smitten with the Pleasure of Blasphemy, would never have furnish'd Frenzy with inspiration; nor put our Saviours Word in the Mouth of a Madman. . . .

Valentine in *Love for Love* is (if I may so call him) the Hero of the Play; this Spark the Poet would pass for a Person of Virtue, but he speaks too late. 'Tis true, He was hearty in his Affection to Angelica. Now without question, to be in Love with a fine Lady of 30 000 Pounds is a great Virtue! But then abating this single Commendation, Valentine is altogether compounded of Vice. He is a prodigal Debauchee, Unnatural and Profane, Obscene, Sawcy, and Undutiful; And yet this Libertine is crown'd for a Man of Merit, has his Wishes thrown into his Lap, and makes the Happy Exit. I perceive we should have a rare set of Virtues if these Poets had the making of them! How they hug a Vicious Character, and how profuse are they in their Liberalities to Lewdness. . . .

To sum up the Evidence. A fine Gentleman is a fine Whoring, Swearing, Smutty, Atheistical Man. . . . If there is any Sense stirring, They must have it, tho' the rest of the Stage suffer never so by the Partiality. And what can be the Meaning of this wretched Distribution of Honour? Is it not to give Credit and Countenance to Vice and to shame young People out of all pretences to Conscience and Regularity . . . ? How often is Learning, Industry, and Frugality ridiculed in Comedy? The rich Citizens are often Misers, and Cuckolds, and the Universities, Schools of Pedantry upon this score. In short, Libertinism and Profaneness, Dressing, Idleness, and Gallantry, are the only valuable Qualities. As if People were not apt enough of themselves to be Lazy, Lewd, and Extravagant, unless they were prick'd forward, and provok'd by Glory, and Reputation. . . .

I perceive the Laws of Religion and those of the Stage differ extreamly! The strength of [a Playright's] Defence lies in this choice Maxim, that the *Chief End of Comedy is Delight* . . . . To laugh without Reason is the Pleasure of Fools, and against it, of something worse. The exposing of Knavery, and making Lewdness ridiculous, is a much better occasion for Laughter. And with this submission I take to be the End of Comedy. And therefore it does not differ from Tragedy in the End, but in the Means. Instruction is the principal Design of both. The one works by Terror, the other by Infamy. . . . Indeed to make Delight the main business of Comedy is an unreasonable and dangerous principle: It opens the way to all Licentiousness, and Confounds the distinction between Mirth, and Madness. . . . And thus the worst Things are said, and the best abus'd; Religion is insulted, and the most serious Matters turn'd into Ridicule! . . . If Delight without Restraint, or Distinction, without Conscience or Shame, is the Supream Law of Comedy, 'twere well if we had less on't. Arbitrary Pleasure is more dangerous than Arbitrary Power. . . .

SOURCE: extracts from *A Short View of the Immorality and Profaneness of the English Stage* (1698), pp. 1, 60, 74, 76–7, 83,142–5, 156–7, 161–4. (Congreve's response to this censure is excerpted on page oo below).

John Dryden (1699, 1700)

4 March 1699 (new style)
. . . This Day was playd a reviv'd Comedy of Mr Congreve's calld the Double Dealer, which was never very taking; in the play bill was printed, – Written by Mr Congreve; with Severall Expressions omitted: What kind of Expressions those were you may easily guess; if you have seen the Monday's Gazette, wherein is the King's Order, for the reformation of the Stage: but the printing an Authours name, in a Play bill, is a new manner of proceeding, at least in England. . . .

12 March 1700 (new style)
. . . Congreves New Play [sc. *The Way of the World*] has had but moderate success; though it deserves much better. . . .

SOURCE: extracts from letters to Mrs Elizabeth Steward, in Charles E. Ward (ed.), *Letters of John Dryden* (Durham, N. C., 1942), pp. 113, 134.

Anonymous (1702)

Critick: . . . and tho' Mr *Congreve*'s Reputation arises from his first, third and fourth Play, yet I must needs say, that according to my taste, his second is the best he ever writ.
Ramble: If you mean the *Double Dealer*, you go against the Opinion of all the Town.
Critick: I can't help that; I'll follow my own Judgment as far as it will carry me, and if I differ from the Voice of the crowd, I shall value myself the more for my Sincerity: But you're mistaken, all the Town is not of that Opinion; some good Judges were of another; but without being byass'd or prejudic'd, I do take the *Double Dealer* to be among the most correct and regular Comedies: Mr *C.* intended it so, and it cost him unusual Labour to do't; but as he says, he has been at a

needless Expence, and the Town is to be treated at a cheaper rate: But with all Mr *Congreve*'s Merit, I don't take his Characters to be always Natural; even in the *Double Dealer* some are out of probability, one in his *Old Bachelor*, and several in *Love for Love* obsolete.

Sullen: We shall be glad you'll convince us of that; for as yet I have not heard that objected. . . .

. . .

Critick: . . . my Forces are so weaken'd already, I have not strength enough left to incounter such a gigantick Author.

Ramble: What, not *The Way o' the World*? as weak as I am, I dare appear against that.

Sullen: 'Tis not so easy a matter as you imagine: That Comedy cost Mr *Congreve* (as some say) two Years study.

Ramble: I have known better writ in a Month. . . .

. . .

Sullen: Shall we say nothing then to Mr *Congreve*?

Critick: Pray excuse me: I stand very well with that Gentleman at present, and shall be very sorry to incur his displeasure.

Ramble: Oh fie! this is partial –

Critick: Besides, he has done with the Stage, and is (in a poetical Sense) in the circumstances of the Dead: so let him sleep in peace.

SOURCE: extracts from *A Comparison between the Two Stages* (1702).

Royal Licence   (1704)

December 14, 1704

ANNE R. License for a New Company of Comedians.

WHEREAS We have thought fitt for the better reforming the Abuses, and Immoralty of the Stage That a New Company of Comedians should be Establish'd for our Service, under stricter Government and Regulations than have been formerly

We therefore reposing especiall trust, and confidence in Our Trusty and Welbeloved John Vanbrugh and Willm. Congreve Esqrs. for the due Execution, and performance of this our Will and Pleasure, do Give and Grant unto them the said John Vanbrugh, and Willm. Congreve full power and Authority to form, constitute, and Establish for Us, a Company of Comedians with full and free License to Act and Represent in any Convenient Place, during Our Pleasure all Comedies, Tragedys Plays, Interludes Operas, and to perform all other Theatricall and Musicall Entertainments whatsoever and to settle such Rules and Orders for the good Government of the said Company, as the Chamberlain of our Household shall from time to time direct and approve of GIVEN at our Court at St. James this 14th day of December in the third Year of Our Reign.

By her Majestys Command KENT

SOURCE: Public Record Office, LC 5/154, p. 35. (The licence was for the Theatre Royal in the Haymarket.)

John Dennis (1721)

To William Congreve, Esq.

SIR, I have lately heard, with some Indignation, that there are Persons who arraign the ridiculous Characters of our late Friend Mr *Wycherley*, for being forsooth too witty; mov'd, I suppose, by the wise Apprehension that they may be of dangerous Example, and spread the Contagion of Wit in this Witty and Politick Age; an Age so very Witty, and so very Politick, that it is always like to be an undetermin'd Question, whether our Wit has the Advantage of our Politicks, or our Politicks of our Wit.

As soon as I heard of this Accusation, I resolved to write a Defence of Mr *Wycherley*, and to direct this Defence to you, for the following Reasons: Because you had a true Esteem of Mr *Wycherley*'s Merit, as well as had your humble Servant; Because you are allow'd by all to be an undoubted Judge of the Matter in debate; and Because an express Vindication of Mr *Wycherley*'s ridiculous Characters, is an implicite one of some of your own.

The forementioned Persons pretend that Mr *Wycherley* is included in . . . Mr *Dryden*'s Preface to his Translation of *Fresnoy*. . . .

I know a Poet (says he) *whom out of Respect I will not name, who being too witty himself, could draw nothing but Wits in a certain Comedy of his: ev'n his Fools were infected with the Disease of their Author. They overflow'd with smart*

Repartees, and were only distinguish'd from the intended Wits by being call'd Coxcombs, tho' they did not deserve so scandalous a Name.

Thus far Mr Dryden, who in this Passage doth certainly reflect upon Mr *Wycherley*, and particularly upon his *Plain-dealer*. But having reason to believe, that this is wrongfully objected to him, I shall vindicate him against Mr *Dryden*, and all his Abettors; and make no doubt but I shall make it appear, that by this rash Censure, he has shewn himself no more a capable Judge of Comedy, than just to that Friendship which he profest to have for Mr *Wycherley*, or to that Regard which he ought to have had for his own Sentiments, and his own Sincerity. For, Sir, at this rate, what becomes of the Encomium which he has given to you before your *Double-dealer*? What could prevail upon him, in his Verses before that Play [excerpted above – Ed.], to tell you that you had

The Satire, Wit, and Strength of manly *Wycherley*?

What could he mean by commending you for having the Wit of Mr *Wycherley*, if that Wit is only a Disease, and serves to no purpose but to make you falsify your Characters? And why should he praise you for having Mr *Wycherley*'s Strength, when that Strength, according to him, must be Weakness it self? . . .

First, then, Mr *Wycherley*'s Coxcombs are really Coxcombs. And here we must observe that Fool and Wit are so far from being Terms that are incompatible or contradictory, that they are not so much as Terms of Opposition, there being several Persons who are call'd Wits, and who by the Vigour and Fire of their Constitutions are enabled sometimes to say what they call smart and witty things, who have not one grain of Judgment or Discernment to distinguish Right from Wrong, or Truth from Falshood; and that therefore the 523rd Reflection of *Rochefoucault* is certainly very Just: *On est quelque fois un sot avec l'Esprit, mais on ne l'est jamais avec du Jugement.* 'It may happen (says he) that a Man may be a Fool who has Wit, but he never can be so who has Judgment.' The Vanity of those whom they call Wits has made them pretend that there is a full Opposition between Wit and Fool, but the only true and full Opposition is between him that is a Fool, and him who is Wise. . . .

I desire in the next Place to observe, that as 'tis the Business of a Comick Poet to correct those Irregularities and Extravagances of Men's Tempers which make them uneasie to themselves, and troublesome and vexatious to one another, for that very Reason, your witty Fools are very just Subjects of Comedy, because they are more troublesome and shocking in Conversation to Men of Sense, than any other sort of Fools whatsoever. Such a Fool with all his smart Repartees, as Mr *Dryden* calls them, his snip snap, his hit for hit, and dash for dash, is but too often impertinent, impudent, insolent, opinionated, noisie, fantastical, abusive, brutal, perfidious; which shews the Solidity of that Reflection of *Rochefoucault* which is the 518th. *Il n'y a point des Sots si Incommodes que ceux qui ont de l'Esprit.* 'There are no Fools so troublesome as the Fools who have Wit.' . . .

SOURCE: extracts from *Letters on Milton and Wycherley* (1721), Letter IV; included in E. Niles Hooker (ed.), *The Critical Works of John Dennis*, II (Baltimore, 1943), pp. 230, 231, 232–3.

Jonathan Swift   (1711, 1729, 1730)

I

To Stella, 22 June 1711

I went late to-day to town, and dined with my friend Lewis. I saw Will. Congreve attending at the treasury, by order, with his brethren, the commissioners of the wine licenses. I had often mentioned him with kindness to lord treasurer [Robert Harley, Earl of Oxford]; and Congreve told me, that after they had answered to what they were sent for, my lord called him privately, and spoke to him with great kindness, promising his protection, &c. The poor man said, he had been used so ill of late years, that he was quite astonished at my lord's goodness, &c. and desired me to tell my lord so; which I did this evening, and recommended him heartily. My lord assured me he esteemed him very much, and he would be always kind to him; that what he said was to make Congreve easy, because he knew people talked as if his lordship designed to turn every body out, and particularly Congreve; which indeed was true, for the poor man told me he apprehended it. As I left my lord treasurer, I called on Congreve (knowing where he dined) and told him what had passed between my lord and me: so I have a worthy man easy, and that is a good day's work.

To Pope, 13 February 1729 (new style)

. . . But this renews the grief for the death of our friend Mr Congreve, whom I loved from my youth, and who surely, beside his other talents, was a very agreeable companion. He had the misfortune to squander away a very good constitution in his younger days, and I think a man of sense and merit like him, is bound in conscience to preserve his health for the sake of his friends, as well as of himself. Upon his own account I could not much desire the continuance of his life, under so much pain, and so many infirmities. Years have not yet hardened me, and I have an addition of weight on my spirits since we lost him, though I saw him so seldom, and possibily if he had lived on, should never have seen him more.

SOURCE: (a) Letter xxv, *Swift's Journal to Stella*, ed. Sir Harold Williams (Oxford, new edn 1974), II, p. 295; (b) extract from George Sherburn (ed.), *Correspondence* of *Alexander Pope* (Oxford, 1956), III, pp. 15–16.

II

For, as their Appetites to quench,
Lords keep a Pimp to bring a Wench;
So, Men of Wit are but a kind
Of Pandars to a vicious Mind,
Who proper Objects must provide
To gratify their Lust of Pride,
When weary'd with Intrigues of State,
They find an Idle Hour to Prate.
Then, shou'd you dare to ask a *Place*,
You Forfeit all your *Patron's* Grace,
And disappoint the sole Design,
For which he summon'd you to *Dine*.
    Thus, *Congreve* spent, in writing Plays,
And one poor Office, half his Days;
While *Montague*, who claimed the Station
To be *Maecenas* of the Nation,
For Poets open Table kept,
But ne'er consider'd where they Slept.
Himself, as rich as fifty *Jews*,

Was easy, though they wanted Shoes;
And, crazy *Congreve* scarce cou'd spare
A Shilling to discharge his Chair,
Till Prudence taught him to appeal
From *Paen*'s Fire to *Party* Zeal;
Not owing to his happy Vein
The Fortunes of his latter Scene,
Took proper *Principles* to thrive;
And so might ev'ry *Dunce* alive. . . .

SOURCE: extract from *A Libel on Doctor Delany and a Certain Great Lord* (1730).

Alexander Pope (1729, 1737)

I

To Gay, early in 1729 (new style)
. . . I never pass'd so melancholy a time, and now Mr *Congreve*'s death touches me nearly. It is twenty years that I have known him. Every year carries away something dear with it, till we outlive all tenderness, and become wretched Individuals again as we begun. . . .

SOURCE: extract from George Sherburn (ed.), *Correspondence of Alexander Pope* (Oxford, 1956), III, p. 3.

II

Some doubt, if equal pains or equal fire
The humbler Muse of Comedy require?
But in known Images of life I guess
The labour greater, as th'Indulgence less.
Observe how seldom ev'n the best succeed:

Tell me if Congreve's Fools are Fools indeed?
What pert low Dialogue has Farquhar writ!
How Van wants grace, who never wanted wit!   [Vanbrugh]
The stage how loosely does Astræa tread,   [Aphra Behn]
Who fairly puts all Characters to bed. . . .

SOURCE: extract from *The First Epistle of the Second Book of Horace* (1737), lines 282–91.

Voltaire (1733)

. . . The late Mr *Congreve* rais'd the Glory of Comedy to a greater Height than any English Writer before or since his Time. He wrote only a few Plays, but they are all excellent in their kind. The Laws of the Drama are strictly observ'd in them; they abound with Characters all which are shadow'd with the utmost Delicacy, and we don't meet with so much as one low, or coarse Jest. The Language is every where that of Men of Honour, but their Actions are those of Knaves; a Proof that he was perfectly well acquainted with human Nature, and frequented what we call polite Company. He was infirm, and come to the Verge of Life when I knew him. Mr *Congreve* had one Defect, which was, his entertaining too mean an Idea of his first Profession (that of a Writer), tho' 'twas to this he ow'd his Fame and Fortune. He spoke of his Works as of Trifles that were beneath him; and hinted to me in our first Conversation, that I should visit him upon no other Foot than that of a Gentleman, who led a Life of Plainness and Simplicity. I answer'd, that had he been so unfortunate as to be a mere Gentleman I should never have come to see him; and I was very much disgusted at so unseasonable a Piece of Vanity. . . .

SOURCE: extract from *Letters Concerning the English Nation*, No. XIX (London, 1733), pp. 188–9.

2. CONGREVE ON COMEDY AND ITS CRITICS

I On Composition and Convention (1694)

. . . I would not have any Body imagine, that I think this Play [*The Double-Dealer*] without its Faults, for I am Conscious of several, and ready to own them; but it shall be to those who are able to find them out. I confess I design'd (whatever Vanity or Ambition occasion'd that design) to have written a true and regular Comedy. . . . And now to make amends for the vanity of such a design, I do confess both the attempt, and the imperfect performance. Yet I must take the boldness to say, I have not miscarried in the whole; for the Mechanical part of it is perfect. That, I may say with as little vanity, as a Builder may say he has built a House according to the Model laid down before him; or a Gardiner that he has set his Flowers in a knot of such or such a Figure. I designed the Moral first, and to that Moral I invented the Fable, and do not know that I have borrow'd one hint of it any where. I made the Plot as strong as I could, because it was single, and I made it single, because I would avoid confusion, and was resolved to preserve the three Unities of the Drama, which I have visibly done to the utmost severity. . . . I heartily wish this Play were as perfect as I intended it, that it might be more worthy your [Charles Montague's] acceptance; and that my Dedication of it to you, might be more becoming that Honour and Esteem which I, with every Body, who are so fortunate as to know you, have for you. It had your Countenance when yet unknown; and now it is made publick, it wants your Protection.

And give me leave, without any Flattery to you, or Vanity in my self, to tell my Illiterate Criticks, as an answer to their Impotent Objections, that they have found fault with that, which has been pleasing to you. . . .

I have since the Acting of this Play hearkned after the Objections which have been made to it; for I was Conscious where a true Critick might have put me upon my defence. I was prepared for their Attack;

and am pretty confident I could have vindicated some parts, and excused others; and where there were any plain Miscarriages, I would most ingenuously have confess'd them. But I have not heard any thing said sufficient to provoke an Answer. Some little snarling and barking there has been, but I don't know one well-mouth'd Curr that has opened at all. That, which looks most like an Objection, does not relate in particular to this Play, but to all or most that ever have been written; and that is Soliloquy. Therefore I will answer it, not only for my own sake, but to save others the trouble, to whom it may hereafter be Objected.

I grant, that for a Man to Talk to himself, appears absurd and unnatural; and indeed it is so in most Cases; but the circumstances which may attend the occasion, make great alteration. It oftentimes happens to a Man, to have designs which require him to himself, and in their Nature, cannot admit of a Confidant. Such, for certain, is all Villany; and other less mischievous intentions may be very improper to be Communicated to a second Person. In such a case therefore the Audience must observe, whether the Person upon the Stage takes any notice of them at all, or no. For if he supposes any one to be by, when he talks to himself, it is monstrous and ridiculous to the last degree. Nay, not only in this case, but in any part of a Play, if there is expressed any knowledge of an Audience, it is insufferable. But otherwise when a Man in Soliloquy reasons with himself, and *Pro's* and *Con's*, and weighs all his Designs: We ought not to imaging that this Man either talks to us, or to himself; he is only thinking, and thinking such Matter, as were inexcusable Folly in him to speak. But because we are conceal'd Spectators of the Plot in agitation, and the Poet finds it necessary to let us know the whole Mystery of his Contrivance; he is willing to inform us of this Persons Thoughts, and to that end is forced to make use of the expedient of Speech, no other better way being yet invented for the Communication of Thought.

Another very wrong Objection has been made by some who have not taken leisure to distinguish the Characters. The Hero of the Play as they are pleas'd to call him, (meaning *Mellefont*) is a Gull, and made a Fool, and cheated. Is every Man a Gull and a Fool that is deceived? At that rate I'm afraid the two Classes of Men, will be reduc'd to one, and the Knaves themselves be at a loss to justifie their Title: But if an Open-hearted Honest Man, who has an entire Confidence in one whom he takes to be his Friend, and whom he has obliged to be so; and who (to confirm him in his Opinion) in all appearance, and upon several tryals has been so: If this Man be deceived by the Treachery of the other; must he of necessity commence Fool immediately, only because the other has proved a Villain? Ay, but there was Caution given to *Mellefont* in the first Act by his Friend *Careless*. Of what Nature was that Caution? Only to give the Audience some light into the Character of *Maskwell*, before his appearance; and not to convince *Mellefont* of his Treachery; for that was more than *Careless* was then able to do: He never knew *Maskwell* guilty of any Villany; he was only a sort of Man which he did not like. As for his suspecting his Familiarity with my Lady *Touchwood:* Let them examine the Answer that *Mellefont* makes him, and compare it with the Conduct of *Maskwell*'s Character through the Play.

I would have them again look into the Character of *Maskwell*, before they accuse any Body of weakness for being deceiv'd by him. For upon summing up the enquiry into this Objection, find they have only mistaken Cunning in one Character, for Folly in another.

But there is one thing, at which I am more concerned than all the false Criticisms that are made upon me; and that is, some of the Ladies are offended: I am heartily sorry for it, for I declare I would rather disoblige all the Criticks in the World, than one of the Fair Sex. They are concerned that I have represented some Women Vicious and Affected: How can I help it? It is the Business of a Comick Poet to paint the Vices and Follies of Humane kind; and there are but two Sexes that I know, *viz. Men*, and *Women*, which have a Title to Humanity: And if I leave one half of them out, the Work will be imperfect. I should be very glad of an opportunity to make my Complement to those Ladies who are offended: But they can no more expect it in a Comedy, than to be Tickled by a Surgeon, when he's letting them Blood. They who are Virtuous or Discreet, I'm sure cannot be offended, for such Characters as these distinguish them, and make their Beauties more shining and observ'd: And they who are of the other kind, may nevertheless pass for such, by seeming not to be displeased, or touched with the Satyr of this *Comedy*. Thus have they also wrongfully accused me of doing them a prejudice, when I have in reality done them a Service.

I have heard some whispering, as if they intended to accuse this Play of Smuttiness and Bawdy: But I declare I took a particular care to avoid it, and if they find any in it, it is of their own making, for I did not design it to be so understood. But to avoid my saying any thing upon a Subject, which has been so admirably handled before, and for their better instruction, I earnestly recommend to their perusal, the Epistle Dedicatory before the *Plain-Dealer*.

You will pardon me, Sir, for the freedom I take of making Answers to other People, in an Epistle which ought wholly to be sacred to you: But since I intend the Play to be so too, I hope I may take the more liberty of Justifying it, where it is in the right. I hear a great many of the Fools are angry at me, and I am glad of it; for I Writ at them, not to them. This is a bold confession, and yet I don't think I shall disoblige one Person by it; for no Body can take it to himself without owing the *Character*. . . .

SOURCE: extracts from the Dedication to Charles Montague, prefixed to first edition of *The Double-Dealer* (1694).

II   On Humour in Comedy (1695)

. . . To Define *Humour*, perhaps, were as difficult, as to Define *Wit*; for like that, it is of infinite variety. . . . And since I have mentioned *Wit* and *Humour* together, let me make the first Distinction between them, and observe . . . that *Wit is often mistaken for Humour.*

I have observed, that when a few things have been Wittily and Pleasantly spoken by any Character in a Comedy; it has been very usual for those, who make their Remarks on a Play, while it is acting, to say, *Such a thing is very Humorously spoken: There is a great Deal of Humour in that Part.* Thus the Character of the Person speaking, may be, Surprizingly and Pleasantly, is mistaken for a Character of *Humour*; which indeed is a Character of *Wit*. But there is a great Difference between a Comedy, wherein there are many things *Humorously*, as they call it, which is *Pleasantly* spoken; and one, where there are several Characters of *Humour*, distinguish'd by the Particular and Different Humours, appropriated to the several Persons represented, and which naturally arise, from the different Constitutions, Complexions, and Dispositions of Men. The saying of Humorous Things, does not distinguish Characters; For every Person in a Comedy may be allow'd to speak them. From a Witty Man they are expected; and even a *Fool* may be permitted to stumble on them by chance. Thô I make a Difference betwixt *Wit* and *Humour*; yet I do not think that Humorous Characters exclude Wit: No, but the Manner of *Wit* should be adapted to the *Humour*. As for Instance, a Character of a Splenetick and Peevish *Humour*, should have a Satyrical Wit. A Jolly and Sanguine *Humour*, should have a Facetious Wit. The Former should speak Positively; the Latter, Carelessly: For the former Observes, and shews things as they are; the latter, rather overlooks Nature, and speaks things as he would have them; and his *Wit* and *Humour* have both of them a less Alloy of Judgment than the others.

As *Wit*, so, its opposite, *Folly, is sometimes mistaken for Humour*.

Is any thing more common, than to have a pretended Comedy, stuff'd with such Grotesques, Figures, and Farce Fools? Things, that either are not in Nature, or if they are, are Monsters, and Births of Mischance; and consequently as such, should be stifled, and huddled out of the way, like *Sooterkins*; that Mankind may not be shock'd with an appearing Possibility of the Degeneration of a God-like *Species*. For my part, I am as willing to Laugh, as any body, and as easily diverted with an Object truly ridiculous: but at the same time, I can never care for seeing things, that force me to entertain low thoughts of my Nature. I dont know how it is with others, but I confess freely to you, I could never look long upon a Monkey, without very Mortifying Reflections, thô I never heard any thing to the Contrary, why that Creature is not Originally of a Distinct *Species*. As I dont think *Humour* exclusive of *Wit*, neither do I think it inconsistent with *Folly*; but I think the Follies should be only such, as Mens Humours may incline them to; and not Follies intirely abstracted from both Humour and Nature.

Sometimes, *Personal Defects are misrepresented for Humours*.

I mean, sometimes Characters are barbarously exposed on the Stage, ridiculing Natural Deformities, Casual Defects in the Senses, and Infirmities of Age. Sure the Poet must both be very Ill-natur'd himself, and think his Audience so, when he proposes by shewing a Man Deform'd, or Blind, to give them an agreeable Entertainment; and hopes to raise their Mirth, by what is truly an object of Compassion. . . .

External Habit of Body is often mistaken for Humour.

Affectation is generally mistaken for Humour.

But as these two last distinctions are the Nicest, so it may be most proper to Explain them, by Particular Instances from some Author of Reputation. *Humour* I take, either to be born with us, and so of a Natural Growth; or else to be grafted into us, by some accidental change in the Constitution, or revolution of the Internal Habit of Body; by which it becomes, if I may so call it, Naturaliz'd.

Humour is from Nature, *Habit* from Custom; and *Affectation* from Industry.

Humour, shews us as we *are*.

Habit, shews us, as we appear, under a forcible Impression.

Affectation, shews what we would be, under a Voluntary Disguise.

Thô here I would observe by the way, that a continued Affectation, may in time become a Habit.

The Character of *Morose* in the *Silent Woman*, I take to be a Character of Humour. . . .

Let us suppose *Morose* to be a Man Naturally Splenetick and Melancholly; is there any thing more offensive to one of such a Disposition, than Noise and Clamour? Let any Man that has the Spleen (and there are enough in *England*) be Judge. We see common Examples of this Humour in little every day. 'Tis ten to one, but three parts in four of the Company that you dine with, are Discompos'd and Startled at the Cutting of a Cork, or Scratching a Plate with a Knife: It is a Proportion of the same Humour, that makes such or any other Noise offensive to the Person that hears it; for there are others who will not be disturb'd at all by it. Well; But *Morose* you will say, is so Extravagant, he cannot bear any Discourse or Conversation, above a Whisper. Why, It is his excess of this Humour, that makes him become Ridiculous, and qualifies his Character for Comedy. If the Poet had given him, but a Moderate proportion of that Humour, 'tis odds but half the Audience, would have sided with the Character, and have Condemn'd the Author, for Exposing a Humour which was neither Remarkable nor Ridiculous. Besides, the distance of the Stage requires the Figure represented, to be something larger than the Life; and sure a Picture may have Features larger in Proportion, and yet be very like the Original. If this Exactness of Quantity, were to be observed in Wit, as some would have it in Humour; what would become of those Characters that are design'd for Men of Wit? I believe if a Poet should steal a Dialogue of any length, from the *Extempore* Discourse of the two Wittiest Men upon Earth, he would find the Scene but coldly receiv'd by the Town. But to the purpose.

The Character of Sir *John Daw* in the same Play, is a Character of Affection. He every where discovers an Affectation of Learning; when he is not only Conscious to himself, but the Audience also plainly perceives that he is Ignorant. Of this kind are the Characters of *Thraso* in the Eunuch of *Terence*, and *Pyrgopolinices* in the *Miles Gloriosus* of *Plautus*. They affect to be thought Valiant, when both themselves and the Audience know they are not. Now such a boasting of Valour in Men who were really Valiant, would undoubtedly be a *Humour*; for a Fiery

Disposition might naturally throw a Man into the same Extravagance, which is only affected in the Characters I have mentioned.

The Character of *Cob* in *Every Man in his Humour*, and most of the under Characters in *Bartholomew-Fair*, discover only a Singularity of Manners, appropriated to the several Educations and Professions of the Persons represented. They are not Humours but Habits contracted by Custom. Under this Head may be ranged all Country Clowns, Sailers, Tradesmen, Jockeys, Gamesters and such like, who make use of *Cants* or peculiar *Dialects* in their several Arts and Vocations. One may almost give a Receipt for the Composition of such a Character: For the Poet has nothing to do, but to collect a few proper Phrases and terms of Art, and to make the Person apply them by ridiculous Metaphors in his Conversation, with Characters of different Natures. Some late Characters of this kind have been very successful; but in my mind they may be Painted without much Art or Labour; since they require little more, than a good Memory and Superficial Observation. But true *Humour* cannot be shewn, without a Dissection of Nature, and a Narrow Search, to discover the first Seeds, from whence it has its Root and growth.

I should be unwilling to venture even on a bare Description of Humour, much more, to make a Definition of it, but now my hand is in, Ile tell you what serves me instead of either. I take it to be, *A singular and unavoidable manner of doing, or saying any thing, Peculiar and Natural to one Man only; by which his Speech and Actions are distinguish'd from those of other Men.*

Our *Humour* has relation to us, and to what proceeds from us, as the Accidents have to a Substance; it is a Colour, Taste, and Smell, Diffused through all; thô our Actions are never so many, and different in Form, they are all Splinters of the same Wood, and have Naturally one Complexion; which thô it may be disguised by Art, yet cannot be wholly changed: We may Paint it with other Colours, but we cannot change the Grain. So the Natural sound of an Instrument will be distinguish'd, thô the Notes expressed by it, are never so various, and the Divisions never so many. Dissimulation, may by Degrees, become more easy to our practice; but it can never absolutely Transubstantiate us into what we would seem: It will always be in some proportion a Violence upon Nature.

A Man may change his Opinion, but I believe he will find it a Difficulty, to part with his *Humour*, and there is nothing more provoking, than the being made sensible of that difficulty. Sometimes, one shall meet with those, who perhaps, Innocently enough, but at the

same time impertinently, will ask the Question; *Why are you not Merry?*
Why are you not Gay, Pleasant, and Cheerful? then instead of answering,
could I ask such one; *Why are you not handsome? Why have you not Black Eyes,
and a better Complexion?* Nature abhors to be forced.

The two Famous Philosophers of *Ephesus* and *Abdera*, have their
different Sects at this day. Some Weep, and others Laugh at one and the
same thing.[*]

I dont doubt, but you have observed several Men Laugh when they
are Angry; others who are Silent; some that are Loud: Yet I cannot
suppose that it is the passion of *Anger* which is in it self different, or more
or less in one than t'other; but that it is the *Humour* of the Man that is
Predominant, and urges him to express it in that manner. Demonstrations of pleasure are as Various; one Man has a Humour of retiring
from all Company, when any thing has happen'd to please him beyond
expectation; he hugs himself alone, and thinks it an Addition to the
pleasure to keep it Secret. Another is upon Thorns till he has made
Proclamation of it; and must make other people sensible of his
happiness, before he can be so himself. So it is in Grief, and other
Passions. Demonstrations of Love and the Effects of that Passion upon
several Humours, are infinitely different; but here the Ladies who
abound in Servants are the best Judges. Talking of the Ladies, methinks
something should be observed of the Humour of the Fair Sex; since they
are sometimes so kind as to furnish out a Character of Comedy. But I
must confess I have never made any observation of what I Apprehend
to be true Humour in Women. Perhaps Passions are too powerful in that
Sex, to let Humour have its Course; or may be by Reason of their
Natural Coldness, Humour cannot Exert it self to that extravagant
Degree, which it often does in the Male Sex. For if ever any thing does
appear Comical or Ridiculous in a Woman, I think it is little more than
an acquir'd Folly, or an Affectation. We may call them the weaker Sex,
but I think the true Reason is, because our Follies are Stronger, and our
Faults are more prevailing.

One might think that the Diversity of Humour, which must be
allowed to be diffused throughout Mankind, might afford endless
matter, for the support of Comedies. But when we come closely to
consider that point, and nicely to distinguish the Difference of

---

* [Ed.] Heraclitus of Ephesus (fl. c. 500 BC) and Democritus (460–370 BC)
were often termed, respectively, the 'weeping' and the 'laughing' philosophers.

Humours, I believe we shall find the contrary. For thô we allow every Man something of his own, and a peculiar Humour; yet every Man has it not in quantity, to become Remarkable by it: Or, if many do become Remarkable by their Humours; yet all those Humours may not be Diverting. Nor is it only requisite to distinguish what Humour will be diverting, but also how much of it, what part of it to shew in Light, and what to cast in Shades; how to set it off by preparatory Scenes, and by opposing other humours to it in the same Scene. . . .

. . . It were perhaps, the Work of a long Life to make one Comedy true in all its Parts, and to give every Character in it a True and Distinct Humour. . . .

SOURCE: extracts from *A Letter to John Dennis, concerning Humour in Comedy* (1695).

III Response to Jeremy Collier's Censure (1698)

. . . To reprimand him a little in his own Words, if these Passages produc'd by Mr *Collier* are obscene and profane, *Why were they rak'd in and disturb'd, unless it were to conjure up Vice, and revive Impurities? Indeed Mr* Collier *has a very untoward way with him; his Pen has such a Libertine Stroke, that 'tis a question whether the Practice or the Reproof be the more licentious.*

He teaches those Vices he would correct, and writes more like a Pimp than a P——. Since the business must be undertaken, why was not the Thought blanch'd, the Expression made remote, and the ill Features cast into Shadows? So far from this, which is his own Instruction in his own words, is Mr *Collier*'s way of Proceeding, that he has blackned the Thoughts with his own *Smut*; the Expression that was remote, he has brought nearer; and lest by being brought near its native Innocence might be more visible, he has frequently varied it, he has new-molded it, and stamp'd his own Image on it; so that it at length is become Current Deformity, and fit to be paid into the Devil's Exchequer.

I will therefore take the Liberty to exorcise this evil Spirit, and whip him out of my Plays, wherever I can meet with him. . . .

First, I desire that I may lay down *Aristotle*'s Definition of Comedy;

which has been the Compass by which all the Comick Poets, since his time, have steer'd their Course. I mean them whom Mr *Collier* so very frequently calls *Comedians*; for the Distinction between *Comicus* and *Comœdus*, and *Tragicus* and *Tragœdus* is what he has not met with in the long Progress of his Reading.

Comedy (says *Aristotle*) is an Imitation of the worse sort of People. Μίμησις φαυλοτέρων, *imitatio pejorum*. He does not mean the worse sort of People in respect to their Quality, but in respect to their Manners. This is plain, from his telling you immediately after, that he does not mean Κατὰ πάσον χαχίαν, relating to all kinds of Vice: there are Crimes too daring and too horrid for Comedy. But the Vices most frequent, and which are the common Practice of the looser sort of Livers, are the subject Matter of Comedy. He tells us farther, that they must be exposed after a ridiculous manner: For Men are to be laugh'd out of their Vices in Comedy; the Business of Comedy is to delight, as well as to instruct: And as vicious People are made asham'd of their Follies or Faults, by seeing them expos'd in a ridiculous manner, so are good People at once both warn'd and diverted at their Expence.

Thus much I thought necessary to premise, that by shewing the Nature and End of Comedy, we may be prepared to expect Characters agreeable to it.

Secondly, Since Comick Poets are oblig'd by the Laws of Comedy, and to the intent that Comedy may answer its true end and purpose above-mentioned, to represent vicious and foolish Characters: In Consideration of this, I desire that it may not be imputed to the Perswasion or private Sentiments of the Author, if at any time one of these vicious Characters in any of his Plays shall behave himself foolishly, or immorally in Word or Deed. I hope I am not yet unreasonable; it were very hard that a Painter should be believ'd to resemble all the ugly Faces that he draws.

Thirdly, I must desire the impartial Reader, not to consider any Expression or Passage cited from any Play, as it appears in Mr *Collier*'s Book; nor to pass any Sentence or Censure upon it, out of its proper Scene, or alienated from the Character by which it is spoken; for in that place alone, and in his Mouth alone, can it have its proper and true Signification. . . .

I cannot think it reasonable, because Mr *Collier* is pleas'd to write one Chapter of *Immodesty*, and another of *Profaneness*, that therefore every Expression traduc'd by him under those Heads, shall be condemn'd as obscene and profane immediately, and without any further Enquiry.

Perhaps Mr *Collier* is acquainted with the *deceptio visus*, and presents Objects to the View through a stain'd Glass; things may appear seemingly profane, when in reality they are only seen through a profane *Medium*, and the true Colour is dissembled by the help of a Sophistical Varnish: Therefore, I demand the Privilege of the *habeas Corpus* Act, that the Prisoners may have Liberty to remove, and to appear before a just Judge in an open and an uncounterfeit light.

Indeed there are few things which distinguish the manner of a Man's Breeding and Conversation, more visibly, than the Metaphors which he uses in Writing; I mean in writing from himself, and in his own Name and Character. A Metaphor is a similitude in a Word, a short Comparison; and it is used as a similitude, to illustrate and explain the meaning. The Variety of *Ideas* in the Mind, furnish it with variety of Matter for Similitudes; and those *Ideas* are only so many Impressions made on the Memory, by the force and frequency of external Objects.

Pitiful and mean Comparisons, proceed from pitiful and mean *Ideas*; and such *Ideas* have their beginning from a familiarity with such Objects. From this Author's poor and filthy Metaphors and Similitudes, we may learn the Filthiness of his Imagination; and from the Uncleanness of that, we may make a reasonable guess at his rate of Education, and those Objects with which he has been most conversant and familiar. . . .

I come now to his Chapter of the Immorality of the Stage.

His Objections here are rather Objections against Comedy in general, than against mine, or any bodies Comedies in particular. He says the Sparks that *marry up the Top-Ladies*, and are rewarded with Wives and Fortunes in the last *Acts*, are generally debauch'd Characters. In answer to this, I refer to my first and second Proposition. He is a little particular in his Remarks upon *Valentine*, in *Love for Love*. He says,

This Spark, the Poet would pass for a Person of Vertue; but he speaks too late.

I know who, and what he is, that always speaks too soon. Why is he to be pass'd for a Person of Vertue? Or where is it said that his Character makes extraordinary Pretensions to it! *Valentine* is in *Debt*, and in *Love*; he has honesty enough to close with a hard Bargain, rather than not pay his Debts, in the first *Act*; and he has Generosity and Sincerity enough, in the last *Act*, to sacrifice every thing to his Love; and when he is in danger of losing his Mistress, thinks every thing else of little worth. This, I hope, may be allow'd a Reason for the Lady to say, *He has Vertues*: They are such in respect to her; and her once saying so, in the last *Act*, is all the notice that is taken of his *Vertue* quite thro' the Play.

Mr *Collier* says, he *is Prodigal*. He was prodigal, and is shewn, in the first *Act* under hard Circumstances, which are the Effects of his Prodigality. That he is unnatural and undutiful, I don't understand: He has indeed a very unnatural Father; and if he does not very passively submit to his Tyranny and barbarous Usage, I conceive there is a Moral to be apply'd from thence to such Fathers. That he is *profane* and *obscene*, is a false Accusation, and without any Evidence. In short, the Character is a mix'd Character; his Faults are fewer than his good Qualities; and, as the World goes, he may pass well enough for the best Character in a Comedy; where even the best must be shewn to have Faults, that the best Spectators may be warn'd not to think too well of themselves. . . .

In *Love for Love, Valentine* says, *I am Truth.*

If the Reader pleases to consult the Fourth Act of that Comedy, he will there find a Scene, wherein *Valentine* counterfeits madness.

One reason of his Counterfeiting in that manner, is, that it conduces somewhat to the design and end of the Play. Another reason is, that it makes a Variation of the Character; and has the same effect in the Dialogue of the Play, as if a new Character were introduc'd. A third use of this pretended madness is, that it gives a Liberty to Satire; and authorises a Bluntness, which would otherwise have been a Breach in the Manners of the Character. Mad-men have generally some one Expression which they use more frequently than any other. *Valentine* to prepare his Satire, fixes on one which may give us to understand, that he will speak nothing but Truth; and so before and after most of his Observation says – *I am Truth*. For example, *Foresight* asks him

– *What will be done at Court?*

Val. *Scandal will tell you – I am Truth, I never come there.*

I had at first made him say, *I am Tom-tell-troth*; but the sound and meanness of the Expression displeas'd me: and I alter'd it for one shorter, that might signifie the same thing. What a Charitable and Christian-like Construction my dear Friend *Mr Collier* has given to this Expression, is fit only to be seen in his own Book; and thither I refer the Reader: I will only repeat his Remark as it personally aims at me – *Now a Poet that had not been smitten with the pleasure of Blasphemy, would not have furnish'd Frenzy with Inspiration,* &c. Now I say, a Priest who was not himself furnish'd with Frenzy instead of Inspiration, would never have mistaken one for the other. . . .

To what end has he made such a Bugbear of the Theatre? Why would he possess the Minds of weak and melancholick People with such frightful *Ideas* of a poor Play? Unless to sowre the humours of the People of most leisure, that they might be more apt to mis-employ their vacant hours. It may be there is not any where a People, who should less be debarr'd of innocent Diversions, than the People of *England*. I will not argue this Point; but I will strengthen my Observation with one Parallel to it from *Polybius*; That excellent Author, who always moralizes in his History, and instructs as faithfully as he relates; in his 4th Book, attributes the Ruin of *Cynethia* by the *Ætolians*, in plain Terms, to their degeneracy from their *Arcadian* Ancestors, in their neglect of Theatral and Musical Performances. The *Cynethians* (says my Author) had their Situation the farthest *North* in all *Arcadia*; they were subjected to an inclement and uncertain Air, and for the most part cold and ·melancholick; and, for this reason, they of all People should last have parted with the innocent and wholesome Remedies, which the Diversions of Musick administred to that sowrness of Temper, and sullenness of Disposition, which of necessity they must partake from the Disposition and Influence of their Climate; 'For they no sooner fell to neglect these wholesome Institution, when they fell into Dissentions and Civil Discords, and grew at length into such depravity of Manners, that their Crimes in number and measure surpass'd all Nations of the *Greeks* beside.'

He gives us to understand, that their *Chorus*'s on the Theatres, their frequent Assemblies of young People, Men and Women, mingling in Musical Performances, were not instituted by their Ancestors out of Wantonness and Luxury, but out of Wisdom; from a deliberated and effectual Policy, and for the Reasons above noted. Much more might be cited from *Polybius*, who has made a very considerable digression on this occasion.

The Application of what I have borrow'd, is very plain. Is there in the World a Climate more uncertain than our own? And which is a natural Consequence, Is there any where a People more unsteady, more apt to discontent, more *saturnine, dark*, and *melancholick* than our selves? Are we not of all People the most unfit to be alone, and most unsafe to be trusted with our selves? Are there not more Self-murderers, and melancholick Lunaticks in *England*, heard of in one Year, than in a great part of *Europe* besides? From whence are all our Sects, Schisms, and innumerable Sub-divisions in Religion? Whence our Plots, Conspiracies, and Seditions? Who are the Authors and Contrivers of these things? Not they who frequent the Theatres and Consorts of Musick. No, if they had, it may be Mr *Collier*'s Invective had not been levell'd that way; his *Gun-Powder-Treason* Plot upon Musick and Plays (for he says *Musick is as dangerous as Gun-powder*) had broke out in another Place, and all his False-Witnesses been summoned elsewhere.

SOURCE: extracts from *Amendments of Mr Collier's False and Imperfect Citations, &c.* (1698).

IV   On Retirement from the Theatre

Come, see thy Friend, retir'd without Regret,
Forgetting Care, or striving to forget;
In easy Contemplation soothing Time
With Morals much, and now and then with Rhime,
Not so robust in Body, as in Mind,
And always undejected, tho' declin'd;
Not wondering at the World's new wicked Ways,
Compar'd with those of our Fore-Fathers Days,
For Virtue now is neither more or less,
And Vice is only varied in the Dress;
Believe it, Men have ever been the same,
And all the Golden Age, is but a Dream.

SOURCE: extract from *A Letter to Viscount Cobham* (published posthumously in 1729).

PART TWO

Comment and Appraisal from Burke to Meredith

Edmund Burke   (1748)

. . . he who seems to have shared the Gifts of Nature as largely as he has abused them, was the celebrated Mr *Congreve*, who, to the charms of a lively Wit, solid Judgement and rich Invention, has added such Obscenity, as none can, without the greatest danger to Virtue, listen to; the very texture and groundwork of some of his Plays is Lewdness, which poison the surer, as it is set off with the Advantage of Wit. I know 'tis said in his Excuse, that he drew his Pictures after the times; but whoever examines his Plays will find, that he not only copied the ill Morals of the Age, but approved them, as may be seen in such Characters as he plainly proposes for Imitation; thus his *Angelica* in *Love for Love* (the chastest of all his Plays) he meant for a perfect Character, and such perhaps as he would have wished his own Mistress to have been; but the Rankness of her Ideas, and Expressions, in the Scene between her and old *Foresight*[1] (as well as in other parts of the Play), are scarce consistent with any *Male*, much less *Female* Modesty. Much of that Respect we pay the Sex is owing to the Opinion we have of their Innocence; but if a Lady lets her Lover understand she is as knowing as himself, a great Part of it must necessarily vanish. . . . the Satyr[2] contained in a lewd Picture, can never be so instructive as the foul Ideas it will raise, [cannot but be] pernicious; Prudence, and a regard to Decency require [such works] should be sedulously avoided. . . .

SOURCE: extract from article in *The Reformer*, No. 2, 4 February 1748 (new style).

NOTES

1. [Ed.] *Love for Love*, II i.
2. [Ed.] Satire is to be understood here.

Anonymous   (1758)

I

Covent-Garden, 11 October, 1758.   Yesterday evening was performed at the above theatre, the comedy of *Love for Love.*

Were I to give my own opinion, I should say, that this is the best comedy either antient or modern, that ever was written to please upon the stage; for while the most superficial judges admire it, it is impossible but the nicest, and most accurate, must approve.

It is written strictly up to the rules of the drama; yet it has all that variety of characters and incidents, which is pleaded in their excuse by those who deviate from them. What fault then can we find in it? Oh, says somebody, it has too much Wit. Well, that is a fault so seldom committed, I should think we might overlook it for once; but even in this case we can only say of Congreve, what Addison has already said of Cowley,

He'd pleas'd us more if he had pleas'd us less.

and it must be confessed indeed that Congreve was richer in wit, I mean in wit of the true sterling kind, than any man whatsoever; and in this particular he puts me in mind of a certain Dutch Jewess I once heard of, who had so many jewels that she stuck them in the heels of her shoes, for he has made all the personages in his comedies Wits, from the highest to the lowest; and in particular the character of Jeremy, in this play, is one of the wittiest that ever was writ. But, I don't know how it is, he has still taken care never to violate Nature; for tho' he has shewn her every where loaded with finery, it may be rather said to set her off to advantage, than disguise her; since her acquaintance might distinguish her at first sight.

Nor is there any Writer that has marked his characters so strongly, or so highly finished them, as Congreve. He seems indeed to have given in to the notion that vicious persons are the proper representations for a comic writer to make: and I remember Voltaire mentions it as an instance of his consummate knowledge in human nature that he has made all his characters speak the language of honest men, but commit the actions of knaves. I will not say that he copied his manners from the Great among whom he lived. . . .

II

Drury-Lane, 14 November, 1758. Yesterday evening at the above theatre was presented *The Way of the World*, a comedy, which for poignancy of wit; delicacy of humour; regularity of conduct; propriety of manners; and continuity of character; may (if ever work might) be reckoned a finished piece.

Mr Congreve had too intimate an acquaintance with human nature not to know that the generality of mankind have a much greater share of vices, than virtues, in their composition; and it is the business of a comic poet to turn the most glaring side outward. To this we owe his Fainal and Mirabel: two parts, the justness of which, Mr Havard and Mr Palmer made us conscious of; and yet all that can be said in their favour is that they are a couple of well-bred rascals. Mirabel indeed seems to be immoral upon principle; his vices are shewn as an ornament to his character. Fainal is vicious, but in a grosser way.[*]

It was at two characters in this comedy (Witwoud and Petulant) that Mr Pope seems to have levelled these lines,

> Observe how seldom even the best succeed,
> Tell me if Congreve's fools be fools indeed?

because the above-mentioned gentlemen happened to say as many good things as any in the piece. But if they cannot properly be called fools, in which light the author intended to shew them, they must certainly be called cox-combs, which are but a degree above them. And since the best things degenerated become the worst, why may we not say that an impertinent wit is the most disagreeable of fools.

Mr O'Brien has a peculiar tone of voice very fit for doing justice to a part of this kind; and the significancy of his looks and gestures add not a

---

* [Ed.] As mentioned in 'A Note on Texts' (p. 10), character-name spelling in this Casebook is editorially systematised in material written since *c.* 1900; forms used in earlier material are retained as first printed.

little to the pleasure of the spectators. However, the quickness of his parts does not seem to slacken his industry, and if he continues to mind his business, I think there is no doubt of his making a great actor.

It may not be universally known, perhaps, as he has not thought proper to give any intimation of the kind, that Mr Congreve took the plot of his *Way of the World* from the French. Yet the most unobserving reader will easily perceive upon looking over the Amorous Widow, a comedy translated from Dancourt, by Mr Betterton, that both those plays have taken their rise from the same original. However Mr Congreve was too great a Genius to submit to a servile copy; he has therefore by his refinement, additions, and alterations, given the thing quite a different air. How much superior is Lady Wishfor't to Lady Laycock? The author has invented a language on purpose for her; forged new manners, and in short left nothing wanting but what can only be given by such an actress as Mrs Clive. Lady Wishfor't is indeed a ridiculous character, but she shews a ridiculous woman of quality; whereas all the actresses that have hitherto performed the part have dressed themselves like mad women, and acted in the strain of an old nurse. A high fruze tower, a gaudy petticoat of one sort, and a gown of another, was sure to create a laugh; but Mrs Clive is not obliged to have recourse to any such pityful expedients. Accordingly she dresses the part in the pink of the present mode, and makes more of it than any actress ever did.

There is a strong tincture of affectation in the character of Millamant; which is so foreign to Mrs Pritchard's disposition, one of whose chief beauties is ease, and a close attention to nature, that it is not strange if this part should appear less becoming upon her than many others. Not withstanding which, her life and spirit is such, that, since Mrs Woffington's retirement from the stage, I do not see any actress, besides herself, in any degree equal to it. Mrs Yates does the part of Marwood incomparably well, and gives us great reason to regret that we have not the pleasure of seeing her oftener.

This is the last play that Mr Congreve ever writ; and it is said, that the cold reception which it met with from the public, on its first appearance, was the reason why he would never write another; but since that, they have acquired a juster notion of its value; and it gave me great pleasure to see such a crouded pit and boxes last night. Yates, in the character of Sir Wilful, hardly ever opened his mouth, but he set the house in a roar; and from the great satisfaction they expressed at the whole performance, it is evident, that however fond the town may be of those fantastical representations (which old Cibber aptly enough compares to dram-drinking) it is evident I say that their tastes are not yet so vitiated, but they have still a relish for some wholesome entertainments. . . .

SOURCE: review articles in *The London Chronicle*, 12–14 October and 14–16 November 1758. (The writer may have been Arthur Murphy, the playwright – Ed.)

Oliver Goldsmith (1760, 1766)

I

. . . Our theatres seem now to aim at glorious opposition; harlequin is set against harlequin, one dancing-master opposes another; the scene shifters, the singers, and even the drummers figure at each house by turns, and it is to be hoped soon that mere actors will thus become useless. The audience now sit uneasy at the sprightly sallies of Vanbrugh, or Congreve, and with impatience desire only to see the Invasion or the Fair.[1] These are the scenes that charm; to see the stage crowded with figures, to hear trumpets, crackers and tempests, these are what lift our souls into greatness, and even, for a while, steal us from ourselves. . . .

II

. . . as I was pretty much unacquainted with the present state of the stage, I demanded who were the present theatrical writers in vogue. . . . – 'Sir', returned my companion [a strolling player], 'the public think nothing about dialect, or humour, or character, for that is none of their business; they only go to be amused, and find themselves happy when they can enjoy a pantomime under the sanction of Jonson's or Shakespeare's name.' 'So then, I suppose', cried I, 'that our modern dramatists are rather imitators of Shakespeare than of nature?' – 'To say the truth', returned my companion, 'I don't know that they imitate anything at all; nor indeed does the public require it of them; it is not the composition of the piece, but the number of starts and attitudes that may be introduced into it, that elicits applause. I have known a piece with not one jest in the whole shrugged into popularity, and another saved by the poet's throwing in a fit of the gripes. No, sir, the works of Congreve and Farquhar have too much wit in them for the present taste; our modern dialect is much more natural.' . . .

SOURCE: I extract from *On the Present State of Our Theatres* (1760); II extract from ch. XVIII of *The Vicar of Wakefield* (1766).

NOTE

1. [Ed.] *Harlequin's Invasion* and *The Fair* were enjoying popularity as afterpieces at the time; Goldsmith considered the former unamusing and heavy-handed, and complained that the latter lacked 'even Pantomime probability to support it'.

Adam Smith (1762)

. . . The whole of Congreve's wit consists in the ridiculousness of his similes, as his comparing two persons bespattering one another to two apples roasting; or the young lady newly come to town, gaping with amazement, he compares her wide-open mouth to the gate of her father's house.[1] . . .

SOURCE: extract from Lecture 8 (delivered in 1762) of Smith's course of lectures on Rhetoric and Belles Lettres (MS notes taken by students, preserved in Glasgow University Library).

NOTE

1. [Ed.] The allusions here are to: (a) Witwoud in *The Way of the World*, IV i –
' . . . They could neither of 'em speak for Rage; and so fell a-splutt'ring at one another like two roasting Apples'; and (b) Belinda in *The Old Bachelor*, IV iii –

... And t'other did so stare and gape – I fansied her like the Front of her Father's Hall; her Eyes were two Jut-Windows, and her Mouth the great Door, most hospitably kept open, for the Entertainment of Travelling Flies.'

Henry Home, Lord Kames   (1762–63)

I

... Congreve defines humour to be 'a singular and unavoidable manner of doing or saying anything, peculiar and natural to one man only, by which his speech and actions are distinguished from those of other men'. Were this definition just, a majestic and commanding air, which is a singular property, is humour; as also a natural flow of correct and commanding eloquence, which is no less singular. Nothing just or proper is denominated humour; nor any singularity of character, words, or actions, that is valued or respected. When we attend to the character of an humorist, we find that it arises from circumstances both risible and improper, and therefore it lessens the man in our esteem, and makes him in some measure ridiculous. . . .

In Congreve's comedies, the action is often suspended to make way for a play of wit. . . . A play analysed, is a chain of connected facts of which each scene makes a link. Each scene, accordingly, ought to produce some incident relative to the catastrophe or ultimate event, by advancing or retarding it. A scene that produceth no incident, and for that reason may be termed *barren*, ought not to be indulged, because it breaks the unity of the action: a barren scene can never be [included], because the chain is complete without it. In *The Old Bachelor*, the 3d scene of act 2, and all that follows to the end of that act, are mere conversation-pieces, productive of no consequence. The 10th and 11th scenes, act 3 *Double Dealer*, the 10th, 11th, 12th, 13th and 14th scenes, act 1 *Love for Love*, are of the same kind. Neither is *The Way of the World* entirely guiltless of such scenes. It will be no justification, that they help to display characters: it were better, like Dryden, in his *dramatis personæ*, to describe characters beforehand, which would not break the chain of action. . . .

II

. . . How odious ought writers to be who thus spread infection through
their country, employing the talents they have from their Maker most
ungratefully against himself, by endeavouring to corrupt and disfigure
his creatures! If the comedies of Congreve did not rack him with
remorse in his last moments, he must have been lost to all sense of
virtue. . . .

SOURCE: I   extracts from *Elements of Criticism* (1762), vol. II, p. 44,
vol. III, pp. 258, 266–7; II   extract from *Elements* . . ., 2nd edition
with additions by the author (1763), vol. III, p. 400.

Horace Walpole   (1775–76)

. . . It is the proof of consummate art in a comic writer, when you seem
to have passed your time at the theatre as you might have done out of it
– it proves he has exactly hit the style, manners, and character of his
cotemporaries. . . . *The Double Dealer*, the ground-work of which is
almost serious enough for tragedy in private life, perplexes the
attention; and the wit of the subordinate characters is necessary to
enliven the darkness of the back-ground.

Congreve is undoubtedly the most witty author that ever existed.
Though sometimes his wit seems the effort of intention, and though an
effort, never failed; it was so natural, that, if he split it into ever so many
characters, it was a polypus that soon grew perfect in each individual.
We may blame the universality of wit in all his personages, but nobody
can say which ought to have less. It assimilated with whatever character
it was poured into: and . . . his gentlemen, ladies old or young, his
footmen, any of his coxcombs (for they are not fools but puppies) have as
much wit, and wit as much their own, as his men of most parts and
understandings. Not only Lady Wishfor't and Ben are characteristically
marked, but Scandal, Mrs Frail, and every fainter personage, are
peculiarly different from each other. . . . Witwoud is different from
Tattle, Valentine from Mellefont, and Cynthia from Angelica. That
still each play is unnatural, is only because four assemblages of different

persons could never have so much wit as Congreve has bestowed on them. We want breath or attention to follow their repartees; and are so charmed with what every body says, that we have not leisure to be interested in what any body does. We are so pleased with each person, that we wish success to all; and our approbation is so occupied, that our passions cannot be engaged. We even do not believe that a company who seem to meet only to show their wit, can have any other object in view. Their very vices seem affected, only to furnish subject for gaiety: thus the intrigue of Careless and Lady Pliant does not strike us more than a story that we know is invented to set off the talents of the relator. For these reasons, though they are something more, I can scarce allow Congreve's to be true comedies. No man would be corrected, if sure that his wit would make his vices or ridicules overlooked. . . .

The comic writer's art consists in seizing and distinguishing these shades, which have rendered man a fictitious animal, without destroying his original composition. The French, who have carried the *man of society* farther than other nations, no longer exhibit the naked passions. . . . Ambition circumvents, not invades; lust tempts, but does not ravish. Ill-nature whispers, rather than accuses. Husbands and wives can hate, without scolding. . . . The enemies of *sentimental comedy* (or, as the French, the inventors, called it, *comédie larmoyante*) seem to think that the great business of comedy is to make the audience laugh. A Scot, an Irishman, a Mrs Slipslop can always produce a laugh, at least from half the audience. For my part, I confess I am more disposed to weep than to laugh at such poor artifices. . . . What is finer than the serious scenes of Maskwell and Lady Touchwood in *The Double Dealer*? I do not take the *comédie larmoyante* to have been so much a deficience of pleasantry in its authors, as the effect of observation and reflection. Tragedy has been confined to the distresses of kings, princesses, and heroes; and comedy restrained to making us laugh at passions pushed to a degree of ridicule. In the former, as great personages only were concerned, language was elevated to suit their rank, rather than their sentiments; for real passion rarely talks in heroics. Had tragedy descended to people of subordinate stations, authors found the language would be too pompous. I should think that the first man who gave a *comédie larmoyante* rather meant to represent a melancholy story in private life, than merely to produce a comedy without mirth. If he had therefore not married two species then reckoned incompatible, that is tragedy and comedy, or, in other words, distress with a cheerful conclusion . . . he would have given a third species to the stage. . . .

SOURCE: extracts from 'Thoughts on Comedy, written in 1775 and 1776', in *Works* (posthumously published, 1798), II, pp. 316–18, 320–1.

Fanny Burney   (1778)

. . . The play was Love for Love; and though it is fraught with wit and entertainment, I hope I shall never see it represented again; for it is so extremely indelicate, – to use the softest word I can, – that Miss Mirvan and I were perpetually out of countenance, and could neither make any observations ourselves, nor venture to listen to those of others. This was the more provoking, as Lord Orville was in excellent spirits, and exceedingly entertaining.

When the play was over, I flattered myself I should be able to look about me with less restraint, as we intended to stay the Farce; but the curtain had hardly dropped, when the box-door opened, and in came Mr Lovel, the man by whose foppery and impertinence I was so much teazed at the ball where I first saw Lord Orville.

[The ladies are also joined by Lord Orville, Sir Clement Willoughby and Captain Mirvan, and after some general talk the play is discussed.]

. . . said Sir Clement, '. . . Pray, Ladies, how have you been entertained with the play?'

'Want of entertainment', said Mrs Mirvan, 'is its least fault: but I own there are objections to it, which I should be glad to see removed.'

'I could have ventured to answer for the Ladies', said Lord Orville, 'since I am sure this is not a play that can be honoured with their approbation.'

'What, I suppose it is not sentimental enough!' cried the Captain, 'or else it's too good for them; for I'll maintain it's one of the best comedies in our language, and has more wit in one scene, than there is in all the [other] plays put together.'

[Mr Lovel affects not to have given the play any attention, even to noting its title: 'one has so much to do, in looking about and finding out one's acquaintance . . . one merely comes to meet one's friends, and shew that one's alive'.]

. . . said the Captain, '. . . this is one of the best jokes I ever heard!

Come to a play and not know what it is! – Why I suppose you wouldn't have found it out, if they *fob'd* you off with a scraping of fidlers [*sic*] or an opera? – Ha! ha! ha! – why now, I should have thought you might have taken some notice of one *Mr Tattle* that is in this play?'

The sarcasm, which caused a general smile, made him colour: but, turning to the Captain with a look of conceit, which implied that he had a retort ready, he said, 'Pray, Sir, give me leave to ask, – what do you think of *one Mr Ben*, who is also in this play?'

The Captain, regarding him with the utmost contempt, answered in a loud voice, 'Think of him! – why I think he's a *man!* ' And then, staring full in his face, he struck his cane on the ground, with a violence that made him start. He did not, however, chuse to take any notice of this; but, having bit his nails some time, in manifest confusion, he turned very quick to me, and, in a sneering tone of voice, said, 'For my part, I was most struck with the *country* young lady, Miss Prue; pray what do *you* think of her, Ma'am?'

'Indeed, Sir', cried I, very much provoked, 'I think – that, is, I do not think any thing about her.'

'Well, really, Ma'am, you prodigiously surprise me! – *mais apparemment ce n'est qu'un façon de parler?* – though I should beg your pardon, for probably you do not understand French?'

I could almost have cried, that such impertinence should be levelled at me; and yet, chagrined as I was, I could never behold Lord Orville, and this man at the same time, and feel any regret for the cause I had given him of displeasure.

'The only female in the play', said Lord Orville, 'worthy of being mentioned to these ladies, is Angelica.'

'Angelica', cried Sir Clement, 'is a noble girl; she tries her lover severely, but she rewards him generously.'

'Yet, in a trial so long', said Mrs Mirvan, 'there seems rather too much consciousness of her power.'

'Since my opinion has the sanction of Mrs Mirvan's', added Lord Orville, 'I will venture to say, that Angelica bestows her hand rather with the air of a benefactress, than with the tenderness of a mistress. Generosity without delicacy, like wit without judgment, generally gives as much pain as pleasure. The uncertainty in which she keeps Valentine, and her manner of trifling with his temper, gives no very favourable idea of her own.'

'Well, my Lord', said Mr Lovel, 'it must, however, be owned that uncertainty is not the *ton* among our ladies at present; nay, indeed, I think they say, – though faith', taking a pinch of snuff, 'I hope it is not true – but they say, that *we* now are most shy and backward.'

The curtain then drew up, and our conversation ceased. . . . How strange it is . . . that this man, not contented with the large share of foppery and nonsense which he has from nature, should think proper to affect yet more! for what he said of Tattle and of Miss Prue, convinced me that he really had listened to the play, though he was so ridiculous and foolish as to pretend ignorance. . . .

SOURCE: extracts from *Evelina* (1778), Letter xx.

Richard Brinsley Sheridan   (1779)

DANGLE (*Reading*): *Bursts into tears and exit!* – What, is this a tragedy?

SNEER: No, that's a genteel comedy, not a translation – only taken from the French: it is written in a style which they have lately tried to run down; the true sentimental, and nothing ridiculous in it from the beginning to the end.

MRS DANGLE: Well, if they had kept to that, I should not have been such an enemy to the stage; there was certainly some edification to be got from those pieces, Mr Sneer!

SNEER: I am quite of your opinion, Mrs Dangle: the theatre, in proper hands, might certainly be made the school of morality; but now, I am sorry to say it, people seem to go there principally for their entertainment!

MRS DANGLE: It would have been more to the credit of the managers to have kept it in the other line.

SNEER: Undoubtedly, madam; and hereafter perhaps to have had it recorded, that in the midst of a luxurious and dissipated age, they preserved two houses in the capital, where the conversation was always moral at least, if not entertaining!

DANGLE: Now, egad, I think the worst alteration is in the nicety of the audience! – No *double-entendre*, no smart innuendo admitted; even Vanbrugh and Congreve obliged to undergo a bungling reformation!

SNEER: Yes, and our prudery in this respect is just on a par with the artificial bashfulness of a courtesan, who increases the blush upon her cheek in an exact proprotion to the diminution of her modesty. . . .

SOURCE: extract from *The Critic* (1779), Act I.

Samuel Johnson (1780)

. . . Neither the time nor place of his birth is certainly known: if the inscription upon his monument be true he was born in 1672. For the place, it was said by himself that he owed his nativity to England, and by every body else that he was born in Ireland. Southern mentioned him with sharp censure, as a man that meanly disowned his native country. The biographers assign his nativity to Bardsa, near Leeds in Yorkshire, from the account given by himself, as they suppose, to Jacob.

To doubt whether a man of eminence has told the truth about his own birth is, in appearance, to be very deficient in candour; yet nobody can live long without knowing that falsehoods of convenience or vanity, falsehoods from which no evil immediately visible ensues, except the general degradation of human testimony, are very lightly uttered, and once uttered are sullenly supported. Boileau, who desired to be thought a rigorous and steady moralist, having told a petty lie to Lewis XIV continued it afterwards by false dates; thinking himself obliged 'in honour', says his admirer, to maintain what, when he said it, was so well received. . . .

[In] the long-continued controversy between Collier and the poets . . . [the] cause of Congreve was not tenable: whatever glosses he might use for the defence or palliation of single passages, the general tenour and tendency of his plays must always be condemned. It is acknowledged with universal conviction that the perusal of his works will make no man better; and that their ultimate effect is to represent pleasure in alliance with vice, and to relax those obligations by which life ought to be regulated. . . .

Congreve has merit of the highest kind: he is an original writer, who borrowed neither the models of his plot nor the manner of his dialogue.

Of his plays I cannot speak distinctly, for since I inspected them many years have passed; but what remains upon my memory is that his characters are commonly fictitious and artificial, with very little of nature, and not much of life. He formed a peculiar idea of comick excellence, which he supposed to consist in gay remarks and unexpected answers; but that which he endeavoured, he seldom failed of performing. His scenes exhibit not much of humour, imagery, or passion; his personages are a kind of intellectual gladiators; every sentence is to ward or strike; the contest of smartness is never intermitted; his wit is a meteor playing to and fro with alternate coruscations. His comedies have therefore, in some degree, the operation of tragedies: they surprise rather than divert, and raise admiration oftener than merriment. But they are the works of a mind replete with images, and quick in combination.

SOURCE: extract from essay on Congreve in *Lives of the English Poets* (1780).

Elizabeth Inchbald   (1808)

. . . Were the characters in *Love for Love* as natural and as edifying as they are witty, it would be a perfect composition: but the conversation of many of the persons of this drama is either so immoral, or so tinctured with their occupations or propensities, that no such people now exist, and it is to be supposed, never, at any period, existed.

The presiding quality of characters may be too closely adhered to, as well as too much neglected, by an author. Men love, in general, to appear that which they are not – but as their peculiar tempers or callings are no doubt, at times, discoverable either in their language or manners, such peculiarities, to appear natural in imitation, should only be resorted to occasionally.

It were indeed to be wished that wicked men, like the men in this comedy, would hold discourse according to their evil natures; that the innocent and the unwary might know whom to shun – but to seem virtuous is the usual design of people devoted to vice.

From the charge of conspicuous faults or singularities the author has, however, exempted his two sincere lovers. For though Valentine and Angelica are both somewhat too gay to be good, yet compared with the company they keep, they are most respectable personages. . . .

SOURCE: extract from 'Remarks' prefacing Mrs Inchbald's edition of the play in her compendium *The British Theatre*, XIII (1808).

William Hazlitt   (1819)

. . . In turning over the pages of the best comedies, we are almost transported to another world, and escape from this dull age to one that was all life, and whim, and mirth, and humour. The curtain rises, and a gayer scene presents itself, as on the canvass of Watteau. We are admitted behind the scenes like spectators at court, on a levée or birth-day; but it is the court, the gala day of wit and pleasure, of gallantry and Charles II! What an air breathes from the name! what a rustling of silks and waving of plumes! what a sparkling of diamond ear-rings and shoe-buckles! what bright eyes (ah, those were Waller's Sacharissa's as she passed!), what killing looks and graceful motions! How the faces of the whole ring are dressed in smiles! how the repartee goes round! how wit and folly, elegance and awkward imitation of it, set one another off! Happy, thoughtless age, when kings and nobles led purely ornamental lives; when the utmost stretch of a morning's study went no farther than the choice of a sword-knot, or the adjustment of a side-curl; when the soul spoke out in all the pleasing eloquence of dress; and beaux and belles, enamoured of themselves in one another's follies, fluttered like gilded butterflies, in giddy mazes, through the walks of St James's Park. . . .

. . . Congreve's works are a singular treat to those who have cultivated a taste for the niceties of English style: there is a peculiar flavour in the very words, which is to be found in hardly any other writer. To the mere reader his writings would be an irreparable loss: to the stage they are already become a dead letter, with the exception of one of them, *Love for Love*. This play is as full of character, incident, and stage-effect, as almost any of those of his contemporaries, and fuller of wit than any of his own, except perhaps *The Way of the World*. It still acts, and is acted well. The effect of it is prodigious on the well-informed spectator. . . .

The Way of the World was the author's last and most carefully finished performance. It is an essence almost too fine; and the sense of pleasure evaporates in an aspiration after something that seems too exquisite ever to have been realised. After inhaling the spirit of Congreve's wit, and tasting 'love's thrice reputed nectar' in his works, the head grows giddy in turning from the highest point of rapture to the ordinary business of life; and we can with difficulty recall the truant Fancy to those objects which we are fain to take up here, *for better, for worse*. What can be more enchanting than Millamant and her morning thoughts, her *doux sommeils?* What more provoking than her reproach to her lover, who proposes to rise early, 'Ah! idle creature!' The meeting of these two lovers after the abrupt dismissal of Sir Wilful, is the height of careless and voluptuous elegance, as if they moved in air, and drank a finer spirit of humanity. . . . She is the ideal heroine of the comedy of high life, who arrives at the height of indifference to every thing from the height of satisfaction; to whom pleasure is as familiar as the air she draws; elegance worn as a part of her dress; wit the habitual language which she hears and speaks; love, a matter of course; and who has nothing to hope or fear, her own caprice being the only law to herself, and rule to those about her. Her words seem composed of amorous sighs – her looks are glanced at prostrate admirers or envious rivals.

> If there's delight in love, 'tis when I see
> That heart that others bleed for, bleed for me.

She refines on her pleasures to satiety; and is almost stifled in the incense that is offered to her person, her wit, her beauty, and her fortune. . . .

Congreve has described all this in his character of Millamant, but he has done no more; and if he had, he would have done wrong. He has given us the finest idea of an artificial character of this kind; but it is still the reflection of an artificial character. The springs of nature, passion, or imagination are but feebly touched. . . . The mere fine lady of comedy, compared with the heroine of romance or poetry, when stripped of her adventitious ornaments and advantages, is too much like the doll stripped of its finery. . . . Millamant is nothing but a fine lady;

and all her airs and affectation would be blown away with the first breath of misfortune. Enviable in drawing-rooms, adorable at her toilette, fashion, like a witch, has thrown its spell around her; but if that spell were broken, her power of fascination would be gone. For that reason I think the character better adapted for the stage: it is more artificial, more theatrical, more meretricious. . . .

Some how, this sort of acquired elegance is more a thing of costume, of air and manner; and in comedy, or on the comic stage, the light and familiar, the trifling, superficial, and agreeable, bears, perhaps, rightful sway over that which touches the affections, or exhausts the fancy. – There is a callousness in the worst characters in the *Way of the World*, in Fainall, and his wife and Mrs Marwood, not very pleasant; and a grossness in the absurd ones, such as Lady Wishfort and Sir Wilful, which is not a little amusing. . . . The description of Lady Wishfort's face is a perfect piece of painting. The force of style in this author at times amounts to poetry. Waitwell, who personates Sir Rowland, and Foible, his accomplice in the matrimonial scheme upon her mistress, hang as a dead weight upon the plot. They are mere tools in the hands of Mirabell, and want life and interest. Congreve's characters can all of them speak well, they are mere machines when they come to act. . . .

SOURCE: extracts from *Lectures on the English Comic Writers* (1819); reprinted in P. P. Howe (ed.), *Complete Works of William Hazlitt* (London, 1931) vol. VI.

Charles Lamb   (1822)

The artificial Comedy, or Comedy of manners, is quite extinct on our stage. Congreve and Farquhar show their heads once in seven years only, to be exploded and put down instantly. The times cannot bear them. Is it for a few wild speeches, an occasional licence of dialogue? I think not altogether. The business of their dramatic characters will not stand the moral test. We screw everything up to that. Idle gallantry in a fiction, a dream, the passing pageant of an evening, startles us in the same way as the alarming indications of profligacy in a son or ward in real life should startle a parent or guardian. We have no such middle emotions as dramatic interests left. We see a stage libertine playing his loose pranks of two hours' duration, and of no after-consequence, with the severe eyes which inspect real vices with their bearings on two worlds. We are spectators to a plot or intrigue (not reducible in life to the point of strict morality) and take it all for truth. . . . We have been spoiled with – not sentimental comedy but – a tyrant far more perni-cious to our pleasures which has succeeded to it, the exclusive and all-devouring drama of common life; where the moral point is everything; where, instead of the fictitious half-believed personages of the stage (the phantoms of old comedy) we recognise ourselves, our brothers, aunts, kinsfolk, allies, patrons, enemies – the same as in life – with an interest in what is going on so hearty and substantial, that we cannot afford our moral judgment, in its deepest and most vital results, to compromise or slumber for a moment. . . . We carry our fireside concerns to the theatre with us. We do not go thither, like our ancestors, to escape from the pressure of reality, so much as to confirm our experience of it; to make assurance double, and take a bond of fate. . . . All that neutral ground of character, which stood between vice and virtue . . . is broken up and disfranchised, as injurious to the interests of society. . . . We dread infection from the scenic representation of disorder; and fear a painted pustule. In our anxiety that our morality should not take cold, we wrap it up in a great blanket surtout of precaution against the breeze and sunshine.

. . . I do not know how it is with others, but I feel the better always for the perusal of one of Congreve's – nay, why should I not add even of Wycherley's – comedies. I am the gayer at least for it; and I could never connect those sports of a witty fancy in any shape with any result to be drawn from them to imitation in real life. They are a world of themselves almost as much as fairyland. Take one of their characters, male or female (with few exceptions they are alike), and place them in a modern play, and my virtuous indignation shall rise against the profligate wretch as warmly as the Catos of the pit could desire; because in a modern play I am to judge of the right and the wrong. The standard of *police* is the measure of *political justice*. The atmosphere will blight it, it cannot live here. It has got into a moral world, where it has no business, from which it must needs fall headlong; as dizzy and incapable of making a stand, as a Swedenborgian bad spirit that has wandered unawares into the sphere of one of Good Men, or Angels. But in its own world do we feel the creature is so very bad? The Fainalls and the

Mirabels, the Dorimants and the Lady Touchwoods, in their own sphere, do not offend my moral sense; in fact, they do not appeal to it at all. They seem engaged in their proper element. They break through no laws, or conscientious restraints. They know of none. They have got out of Christendom into the land – what shall I call it? – of cuckoldry, the Utopia of gallantry, where pleasure is duty, and the manners perfect freedom. It is altogether a speculative scene of things, which has no reference whatever to the world that is. No good person can be justly offended as a spectator, because no good person suffers on the stage. Judged morally, every character in these plays – the few exceptions only are *mistakes* – is alike essentially vain and worthless. The great art of Congreve is especially shown in this, that he has entirely excluded from the scenes – some little generosities in the part of Angelica perhaps excepted – not only anything like a faultless character, but any pretensions to goodness or good feelings whatsoever. Whether he did this designedly, or instinctively, the effect is as happy, as the design (if design) was bold. I used to wonder at the strange power which his *Way of the World* in particular possesses of interesting you all along in the pursuits of characters, for whom you absolutely care nothing – for you neither hate nor love his personages – and I think it is owing to this very indifference for any, that you endure the whole. He has spread a privation of moral light, I will call it, rather than by the ugly name of palpable darkness, over his creations; and his shadows flit before you without distinction or preference. Had he introduced a good character, a single gush of moral feeling, a revulsion of the judgment to actual life and actual duties, the impertinent Goshen would have only lighted to the discovery of deformities, which now are none, because we think them none. . . .

The whole is a passing pageant, where we should sit as unconcerned at the issues, for life or death, as at a battle of the frogs and mice. But like Don Quixote, we take part against the puppets, and quite as impertinently. We dare not contemplate an Atlantis, a scheme, out of which our coxcombical moral sense is for a little transitory ease excluded. We have not the courage to imagine a state of things for which there is neither reward nor punishment. We cling to the painful necessities of shame and blame. We would indict our very dreams.

Amidst the mortifying circumstances attendant upon growing old, it is something to have seen the *School for Scandal* in its glory. This comedy grew out of Congreve and Wycherley, but gathered some allays of the sentimental comedy which followed theirs. It is impossible that it should be now *acted*, though it continues, at long intervals, to be announced in the bills. . . . The highly artificial manner of Palmer in this character [Joseph Surface] counteracted every disagreeable impression which you might have received from the contrast, supposing them real, between the two brothers. You did not believe in Joseph with the same faith with which you believed in Charles. The latter was a pleasant reality, the former a no less pleasant poetical foil to it. The comedy . . . is incongruous; a mixture of Congreve with sentimental incompatibilities. . . .

SOURCE: extracts from 'On the Artificial Comedy of the Last Century' (1822), included in *Essays of Elia* (1823): see William Macdonald (ed.), *The Works of Charles Lamb* (London, 1903), I, pp. 281–6.

Thomas Babington Macaulay,
Lord Macaulay (1841)

. . . Whether a thing shall be designated by a plain noun substantive or by a circumlocution is a mere matter of fashion. Morality is not at all interested in the question. But morality is deeply interested in this, that what is immoral shall not be presented to the imagination of the young and susceptible in constant connection with what is attractive. . . . We will take, as an instance of what we mean, a single subject of the highest importance to the happiness of mankind, conjugal fidelity. We can at present hardly call to mind a single English play, written before the civil war, in which the character of a seducer of married women is represented in a favourable light. . . . On the contrary, during the forty years which followed the Restoration, the whole body of the dramatists invariably represented adultery, we do not say as a peccadillo, we do not say as an error which the violence of passion may excuse, but as the calling of a gentleman, as a grace without which his character would be imperfect. . . . In all this there is no passion and scarcely any thing that can be called preference. The hero intrigues, just as he wears a wig; because, if he did not, he would be a queer fellow, a city prig, perhaps a

Puritan. . . . Take Congreve; and compare Bellmour with Fondlewife, Careless with Sir Paul Pliant, or Scandal with Foresight. In all these cases, and in many more which might be named, the dramatist evidently does his best to make the person who commits the injury graceful, sensible, and spirited, and the person who suffers it a fool, or a tyrant, or both.

[Macaulay ascribes this demoralisation of the comic stage to the reaction under the Restoration against the 'overstrained austerity' of the Commonwealth Puritans and to the corrupting influence of a licentious Court: 'The comic poet was the mouthpiece of the most deeply corrupted part of a corrupted society.'[1] After a powerful passage in the high Macaulayan vein, Collier's *Short View of the Profaneness and Immorality of the English Stage* (1698) – excerpted in Part One above – comes under consideration.]

. . . We scarcely know any volume which contains so many bursts of that peculiar eloquence which comes from the heart and goes to the heart. Indeed the spirit of the book is truly heroic. . . . [Collier] was, however, so injudicious as to place among the outrageous offences which he justly arraigned some things which are really quite innocent, and some slight instances of levity which, though not strictly correct, could easily be paralleled from the works of writers who had rendered great services to morality and religion. Thus he blames Congreve, the number and gravity of whose real transgressions made it quite unnecessary to tax him with any that were not real, for using the words 'martyr' and 'inspiration' in a light sense; as if an archbishop might not say that a speech was inspired by claret, or that an alderman was a martyr to the gout. . . .

Congreve was precisely in that situation in which it is madness to attempt a vindication; for his guilt was so clear that no address of eloquence could obtain an acquittal. On the other hand, there were in his case many extenuating circumstances which, if he had acknowledged his error and promised amendment, would have procured his pardon. The most rigid censor could not but make great allowances for the faults into which so young a man had been seduced by evil example, by the luxuriance of a vigorous fancy, and by the inebriating effect of popular applause. . . . Congreve's answer was a complete failure. He was angry, obscure, and dull. . . . Collier had taxed him with profaneness for calling a clergyman Mr Prig, and for introducing a coachman named Jehu, in allusion to the King of Israel, who was known at a distance by his furious driving. . . . Congreve might with good effect have appealed to the public whether it might not be fairly presumed that, when such frivolous charges were made, there were no very serious charges to make. Instead of doing this, he pretended that he meant no allusion to the Bible by the name of Jehu, and no reflection by the name of Prig. . . . All that Congreve gained by coming forward on this occasion, was that he completely deprived himself of the excuse which he might with justice have pleaded for his early offences. . . .

SOURCE: extracts from 'Comic Dramatists of the Restoration' *Edinburgh Review*, LXXII, No. 146 (January 1841).

NOTE

1. [Ed.] For a discussion of moral attitudes before and after the Restoration, see note 10 of the Introduction (page 28 above).

William Makepeace Thackeray (1851)

. . . though he was also voted to be one of the greatest tragic poets of any day, it was Congreve's wit and humour which first recommended him to courtly fortune. And it is recorded that his first play, the *Old Bachelor*, brought our author to the notice of that great patron of English muses, Charles Montague, Lord Halifax[1] – who, being desirous to place so eminent a wit in a state of ease and tranquillity, instantly made him one of the Commissioners for licensing hackney-coaches, bestowed on him soon after a place in the Pipe Office, and likewise a post in the Custom House of the value of 600*l*.

A commissionship of hackney-coaches – a post in the Custom House – a place in the Pipe Office, and all for writing a comedy! Doesn't it sound like a fable, that place in the Pipe Office? . . .

Reading in these plays now, is like shutting your ears and looking at people dancing. What does it mean? the measures, the grimaces, the bowing, shuffling and retreating, the cavalier seul advancing upon those ladies – those ladies and men twirling round at the end in a mad galop, after which everybody bows and the quaint rite is celebrated.

Without the music we can't understand that comic dance of the last century – its strange gravity and gaiety, its decorum or its indecorum. It has a jargon of its own quite unlike life; a sort of moral of its own quite unlike life too. . . .

Congreve's comic feast flares with lights, and round the table, emptying their flaming bowls of drink, and exchanging the wildest jests and ribaldry, sit men and women, waited on by rascally valets and attendants as dissolute as their mistresses – perhaps the very worst company in the world. There doesn't seem to be a pretence of morals. At the head of the table sits Mirabel or Belmour (dressed in the French fashion and waited on by English imitators of Scapin and Frontin). Their calling is to be irresistible, and to conquer everywhere. Like the heroes of the chivalry story, whose long-winded loves and combats they were sending out of fashion, they are always splendid and triumphant – overcome all dangers, vanquish all enemies, and win the beauty at the end. Fathers, husbands, usurers are the foes these champions contend with. They are merciless in old age, invariably, and an old man plays the part in the dramas which the wicked enchanter or the great blundering giant performs in the chivalry tales, who threatens and grumbles and resists – a huge stupid obstacle always overcome by the knight. It is an old man with a money-box: Sir Belmour his son or nephew spends his money and laughs at him. It is an old man with a young wife whom he locks up: Sir Mirabel robs him of his wife, trips up his gouty old heels and leaves the old hunks. The old fool, what business has he to hoard his money, or to lock up blushing eighteen? Money is for youth, love is for youth, away with the old people. When [Mirabel] is sixty, having of course divorced the first Lady Millamant, and married his friend Doricourt's granddaughter out of the nursery – it will be his turn; and young Belmour will make a fool of him. All this pretty morality you have in the comedies of William Congreve, Esq. They are full of wit. Such manners as he observes, he observes with great humour; but ah! it's a weary feast, that banquet of wit where no love is. It palls very soon; sad indigestions follow it and lonely blank headaches in the morning.

. . . He writes as if he was so accustomed to conquer, that he has a poor opinion of his victims. Nothing's new except their faces, says he: 'every woman is the same'. He says this in his first comedy, which he wrote languidly in illness, when he was an 'excellent young man'. . . .

What a conquering air there is about [him]! What an irresistible Mr Congreve it is! Sinner! of course he will be a sinner, the delightful rascal!

Win her! of course he will win her, the victorious rogue! He knows he will: he must – with such a grace, with such a fashion, with such a splendidly embroidered suit. You see him with red-heeled shoes deliciously turned out, passing a fair jewelled hand through his dishevelled periwig, and delivering a killing ogle along with his scented billet. . . .

SOURCE: extracts from *English Humourists of the Eighteenth Century*, a series of lectures first delivered 1851; published with author's revisions 1853, pp. 58–9, 66–7, 69–70, 74–5, 77.

NOTE

1. [Ed.] Charles Montague (1661–1715), to whom Congreve dedicated *The Double-Dealer*, was created Baron Halifax (1700) and then Earl of Halifax (1714); he is not to be confused with George Savile (1633–95), created Baron Savile (1668) and then Marquess of Halifax (1682), whose title died with him. Thackeray's recital of the official patronage bestowed on Congreve does indeed 'sound like a fable' when compared with Swift's verses castigating Montague's pretensions to be a Maecenas (see Part One, above.)

George Meredith   (1877)

. . . Question cultivated women whether it pleases them to be shown moving on an intellectual level with men, they will answer that it does; numbers of them claim the situation. Now, Comedy is the fountain of sound sense; not the less perfectly sound on account of the sparkle: and Comedy lifts women to a station offering them free play for their wit, as they usually show it, when they have it, on the side of sound sense. . . . In Congreve's *Way of the World*, Millamant overshadows Mirabel, the sprightliest male figure of English comedy. . . . Is it not preferable to be the pretty idiot, the passive beauty, the adorable bundle of caprices, very feminine, very sympathetic, of romantic and sentimental fiction? Our women are taught to think so. . . . The heroines of Comedy are like women of the world, not necessarily heartless for being clear-sighted: they seem so to the sentimentally reared only for the reason that they use their wits, and are not wandering vessels cruising for a captain or a pilot. Comedy is an exhibition of their battle with men, and that of men with them: and as the two, however divergent, both look on one object, namely, Life, the gradual similarity of their impressions must bring them to some resemblance. The Comic poet dares to show us men and women coming to this mutual likeness. . . .

Congreve's *Way of the World* is an exception to our other comedies, his own among them, by virtue of the remarkable brilliancy of the writing, and the figure of Millamant. The comedy has no idea in it, beyond the stale one, that so the world goes; and it concludes with the jaded discovery of a document at a convenient season for the descent of the curtain. A plot was an afterthought with Congreve. By the help of a wooden villain (Maskwell) marked Gallows to the flattest eye, he gets a sort of plot in *The Double-Dealer*. His *Way of the World* might be called The Conquest of a Town Coquette, and Millamant is a perfect portrait of a coquette, both in her resistance to Mirabel and the manner of her surrender, and also in her tongue. The wit here is not so salient as in certain passages of *Love for Love*, where Valentine feigns madness or retorts on his father, or Mrs Frail rejoices in the harmlessness of wounds to a woman's virtue, if she 'keeps them from air'. In *Way of the World*, it appears less prepared in the smartness, and is more diffused in the characteristic style of the speakers. Here, however, as elsewhere, his famous wit is like a bully-fencer, not ashamed to lay traps for its exhibition, transparently petulant for the train between certain ordinary words and the powder-magazine of the improprieties to be fired. . . . Judging him by his wit, he performed some happy thrusts, and taking it for genuine, it is a surface wit, neither rising from a depth nor flowing from a spring.

On voit qu'il travaille à dire de bons mots.

. . . This is the sort of wit one remembers to have heard at school, of a brilliant outsider; perhaps to have been guilty of oneself, a little later. It was, no doubt, a blaze of intellectual fireworks to the bumpkin squire, who came to London to go to the theatre and learn manners.

Where Congreve excels all his English rivals is in his literary force, and a succinctness of style peculiar to him. . . . The flow of boudoir Billingsgate in Lady Wishfort is unmatched for the vigour and pointedness of the tongue. It spins along with a fine ring, like the voice of Nature in a fury, and is, indeed, racy eloquence of the elevated fishwife.

Millamant is an admirable, almost a lovable heroine. It is piece of genius in a writer to make a woman's manner of speech portray her. You feel sensible of her presence in every line of her speaking. . . . An air of bewitching whimsicality hovers over the graces of this Comic heroine, like the lively conversational play of a beautiful mouth. But in wit she is no rival of Célimène [in Molière's *Le Misanthrope*]. What she utters adds to her personal witchery, and is not further memorable. She is a flashing portrait, and a type of the superior ladies who do not think, not of those who do. In representing a class, therefore, it is a lower class, in proportion that one of Gainsborough's full-length aristocratic women is below the permanent impressiveness of a fair Venetian head. . . .

There has been fun in Bagdad. But there never will be civilisation where Comedy is not possible; and that comes of some degree of social equality of the sexes. I am not quoting the Arab to exhort and disturb the somnolent East; rather for cultivated women to recognise that the Comic Muse is one of their best friends. They are blind to their interests in swelling the ranks of the sentimentalists. Let them look with their clearest vision abroad and at home. They will see that where they have no social freedom, Comedy is absent: where they are household drudges, the form of comedy is primitive: where they are tolerably independent, but uncultivated, exciting melodrama takes its place and a sentimental version of them. . . . But where women are on the road to an equal footing with men, in attainments and liberty – in what they have won for themselves and what has been granted them by a fair civilisation – there, and only waiting to be transplanted from life to the stage, or the novel, or the poem, pure Comedy flourishes. . . .

SOURCE: extracts from 'On the Idea of Comedy and the Uses of the Comic Spirit', a lecture delivered at the London Institution, 1 February 1877 and subsequently published as *Essay; On Comedy* . . . (1897); reprinted in *Works of George Meredith* (Memorial Edition): XXIII, *Miscellaneous Prose* (London, 1910), pp. 14–15, 17–21, 31–2.

PART THREE

Twentieth-Century Studies

1. GENERAL STUDIES ON CONGREVE'S ART

Bonamy Dobrée   The Style of Congreve
(1925)

The most evident pleasure we obtain from the drama is in the interplay of character, by the colours woven together to make up an objective view of humanity; but though in this . . . Congreve must be ranked with the masters, he does not take a very high place among them. His first piece, *The Old Bachelor*, has all the obviousness of Jonson without the especial creative purpose that made it necessary: Bluffe is a version of Bobadill, Fondlewife is modelled on Kitely; we detect patches of Brome, we scent the influence of Marston. Congreve had learned much from the old masters, but he had not yet made them his own, nor entered into the Restoration inheritance. As characterisation the play adds nothing to our riches; we are still in a late Elizabethan world. In *The Double-Dealer* there is a new set of contrasts that are almost too striking, of the harsh unredeemed villains with the rightly named Froths, and with the candid Cynthia. *Love for Love* again is a return, not to Jonson, but to the purest Wycherley. *The Way of the World*, however, soars above all, and the characterisation becomes subtle and individual; too subtle almost, since even Pope was constrained to ask 'Tell me if Congreve's fools are fools indeed'. For here Congreve broke through the rules he had laid down in that happy piece of constructive criticism, the *Letter Concerning Humour in Comedy*, and made his people three-dimensional. The greatest triumph, of course, is Millamant, many-faceted, spontaneous, who hides her feeling beneath her gaiety, and is so well set off against Lady Wishfort, Mrs Marwood, and Mrs Fainall, not containing within herself the springs that move those others, but alive with the possibility of containing them.

Characterisation, however, is not a solely dramatic element: as an ingredient it is equally important in the novel; but what we may hazard as being specifically dramatic is the changes of speed, of movement, which constitute the rhythm of a piece. You can have 'great still novels' like those of Richardson, you cannot have a play that those adjectives will suit. It may even be said that a dramatic moment is definitely that where the rhythm changes, of which the knocking at the gate in *Macbeth* may be taken as one *locus classicus*, and Cleopatra's 'Peace! Peace! Dost thou not see my baby at my breast That sucks the nurse asleep?' as another, in the reverse direction. For, as in physical life, it is not motion that we feel, but change of motion. In the drama this varying of speed may be achieved by the introduction of new persons, by changes of tempo, or by the quality of the phrasing. . . .

. . . Of all these methods Congreve was a master, producing results of delicious beauty. When his works were reprinted, he made the addition or loss of a person upon the stage constitute a new scene, not to borrow a French habit, but to emphasise the change of tempo, and to allow each scene to be itself a separate jewel. To give only one example of how, by phrasing alone, he could alter the speed, it will be enough to point out the staggering finale of *The Double-Dealer*. The play has been proceeding at a glorious and ever-increasing pace; until the last moment we are borne along in a tremendous rush; it seems incredible that the curtain should not come down upon a tumult: but then:

BRISK   This is all very surprizing, let me perish!
LADY FROTH   You know I told you Saturn looked a little more angry than usual.

This shows his strength: we are suddenly pulled up sharp. A technically similar, but in tone vastly different, ending to *The Way of the World* illustrates his grace, like that of a pigeon, which hurtling through the air with closed wings, opens them to alight on the selected branch. It is all done by phrasing; for it is in prose that Congreve most surely excels. . . .

. . . Stage prose, like pulpit, or even law-court prose, is not to be judged in the same way as chamber prose, or that written for the inward ear. Browne so enthralling to murmur to oneself; Swift so delightful to read to one's friend; Gibbon so effective and amusing to quote, would empty box and gallery alike; while the grandiose periods of Burke sent the Mother of Parliaments to dinner. For stage prose must be easy to say at once rapidly and loud; it must suit the human lungs working under specialised conditions. The weight must always be brought naturally, and rather obviously, onto the important word. . . .

. . . In his prose plays Dryden never seemed quite sure of his rhythm, and, perhaps through fear of slipping into the 'other harmony' of verse, often ran too many unstressed syllables together. He here lacked the splendid assurance of his critical and controversial essays, as much as he did the irresistible march of his verse. But Congreve learned something of flexibility from him, and how to deal with runs; as he learned, it may be, a certain swing from Etherege, and how to introduce the note of lyrical sadness into comedy:

Did you not tell me there was no credit to be given to faces? That women nowadays have their passions as much at will as they have their complexions, and put on joy and sadness, scorn and kindness, with the same ease as they do their paint and patches. – Are they the only counterfeits?

[*The Man of Mode,* v 2]

Etherege more nearly approaches Congreve for a sensitive ear than any other dramatist of the period, but he had not the rich polyphonic mastery of vowels; while Wycherley, giant as he was, something neglected his surface in the bigger scale of his conceptions. . . .

If one were to have to select the two lines that best exhibit Congreve's flavour, one might do worse than choose the sentence that ushers in Millamant for the first time:

Here she comes i'faith, with her fan spread and streamers out, and a shoal of fools for tenders – Ha, no, I cry her mercy.   [*Way of W.,* II 4]

The beauty of that needs no insistence; the delicate play of the vowels, the dancing rhythm, with the sharp uptake at the end attended with the entirely new sound of 'cry', sweep us away with their effect of spontaneity. And see, too, a little later in the same scene, how skilfully he can now play on one note, recurring to the same word:

Beauty the lover's gift – Lord, what is a lover that it can give? Why one makes lovers as fast as one pleases, and they live as long as one pleases, and they die as soon as one pleases: and then, if one pleases, one makes more.

'How it chimes, and cries tink in the close, divinely!' The reiteration never gives the ear the smallest bother, because, said as they must be to gain the full meaning, the phrases only gather their weight upon 'pleases' in the last instance, the stresses otherwise playing all around it. At last the voice fatefully pounces upon the word, as a hawk, after several feints, lands upon a predestined prey. . . .

SOURCE: extracts from Introduction to *Comedies by William Congreve* ('World Classics' edition, Oxford, 1925), pp. xvi–xxi, xxvi–xxvii.

Virginia Woolf   'Speed, Stillness and Meaning' (1937)

The four great plays through which Congreve is immortal take up very little space, and can be bought very cheaply; but they can be seen very seldom, and to read them, silently and in solitude, is to do them an injustice. The best way to repair that injustice is to consider them with the author's help more critically, if more coldly, than we are able when the words are embodied on the stage. Congreve, the man of mystery, the man of superb genius who ceased to use his genius at his height, was also, as any reader may guess from almost any page, of the class of writers who are not so entirely submerged in their gift but that they can watch it curiously and to some extent guide it even when they are possessed by it. Whatever he has to say in a letter, in a dedication, in a prologue about his art is worth listening to with all our ears. Let us then put to him some of the questions that the remembrance of his plays has left over in the mind before we allow the Tattles and the Foresights, the Wishforts and the Millamants to sweep us off our feet.

First there is the old grievance which, though it sounds elementary, must always have its say: the grievance that is summed up in the absurd names he gives his characters – Vainlove, Fondlewife, and the rest – as if we were back again in the age of mummer and cart, when one humour to one character was all the audience could grasp or the actor express. To that he replies, '. . . the distance of the stage requires the figures represented to be something larger than the life', a warning to the reader to suppress the desire for certain subtleties which the playwright cannot satisfy, a reminder that the imponderable suggestions which come together on silent feet in fiction are denied the playwright. He must speak; the speaking voice is the only instrument allowed him. That introduces a second question: they must speak, but why so artificially? Men and women were never so witty as he makes them; they never speak so aptly, so instantly, and with such a wealth of figure and imagery as he would have us believe. And to that he replies, 'I believe if a poet should steal a dialogue of any length, from the extempore discourse of the two wittiest men upon earth, he would find the scene but coldly receiv'd by the town'. People on the stage must be larger than life because they are further from us than in the book; and cleverer than life because if he set down their actual words we should be bored to distraction. Every writer has his selection to make; his artifice to enforce; these are the playwright's. These are the methods by which he puts us in the frame of mind needed for his purpose.

Still there remains another grievance which is not so elementary nor so easily laid to rest; and that is, of course, the plot. Who can remember the plot when the book is shut? Who has not been teased by its intricacies while the book is open? As everybody is agreed something must happen, and it matters very little what happens if it serves to make the characters more real, or more profound, than they would otherwise have been; a plot should put the characters on the rack and show them thus extended. But what are we to say when the plot merely teases and distorts the character, and distracts us from any more profound enjoyment than that of asking who is behind that door, who is behind that mask? To this Congreve the critic gives us no satisfactory answer. Sometimes, as in the preface to *The Double-Dealer*, he prides himself that he has maintained 'the unities of the drama'. But a certain doubt declares itself elsewhere. In the dedication to *The Way of the World* he envies Terence. Terence, he points out, had 'great advantages to encourage his undertaking for he built most on the foundations of Menander; his plots were generally modelled and his characters ready drawn to his hand'. Either then, one must conclude, the old weather-worn plots which slip into the mind so smoothly that we scarcely notice them – the legendary, the prehistoric – are the only tolerable ones, or we are forced to suppose that the plot-making genius is so seldom combined with the genius for creating character that we must allow even Shakespeare to fail here – even Shakespeare sometimes lets the plot dictate to the character; suffers the story to drag the character out of its natural orbit. And Congreve, who had not Shakespeare's miraculous fecundity, who could not cover up the farfetched and the mechanical with the abundance of his imagination and the splendour of his poetry, fails here. The character is squeezed to fit the situation; the machine has set its iron stamp upon live flesh and blood.

But, now that we have dismissed the questions that hang about an unopened book, let us submit ourselves to the dramatist in action. The dramatist is in action from the very first word on the very first page. There are no preliminaries, no introductions; the curtain rises and they are in the thick of it. Never was any prose so quick. Miraculously pat, on the spot, each speaker caps the last, without fumbling or hesitation; their minds are full charged; it seems as if they had to rein themselves in, bursting with energy as they are, alive and alert to their finger-tips. It is we who fumble, make irrelevant observations, notice the chocolate or the cinnamon, the sword or the muslin, until the illusion takes hold of us, and what with the rhythm of the speech and the indescribable air of tension, of high breeding that pervades it, the world of the stage becomes the real world and the other, outside the play, but the husk and cast-off clothing. To attempt to reduce this first impression to words is as futile as to explain a physical sensation – the slap of a wave, the rush of wind, the scent of a bean field. It is conveyed by the curl of a phrase on the ear; by speed; by stillness. It is as impossible to analyse Congreve's prose as to distinguish the elements – the bark of a dog, the song of a bird, the drone of the branches – which make the summer air. But then, since words have meaning, we notice here a sudden depth beneath the surface, a meaning not grasped but felt, and then come to realise something not merely dazzling in this world, but natural, for all its wit; even familiar, and traditional. It has a coarseness, a humour something like Shakespeare's; a toppling imagination that heaps image upon image; a lighting swiftness of apprehension that snatches a dozen meanings and compacts them into one.

And yet it is not Shakespeare's world; for just as we think, tossed up on the crest of some wonderful extravagance of humour, to be swept into poetry we come slap against hard common sense, and realise that here is a different combination of elements from the poet's. There is tragedy – Lady Touchwood and Maskwell in *The Double-Dealer* are not comic figures – but when tragedy and comedy collide it is comedy that wins. Lady Touchwood seizes her dagger; but she drops it. A moment more and it would have been too late. Already she has passed from prose to rant. Already we feel not that the scene is ridiculous, for there is passion there; but that it is unsafe. Congreve has lost his control, his fine balance is upset; he feels the ground tremble beneath him. Mr Brisk's comment, 'This is all very surprising, let me perish,' is the appropriate one. With that he finds his feet and withdraws.

The world that we have entered, then, in Congreve's comedies is not the world of the elemental passions. It is an enclosure surrounded with the four walls of a living-room. Ladies and gentlemen go through their figures with their tongues to the measure dictated by common sense as precisely as they dance the minuet with their feet; but the image has only a superficial rightness. We have only to compare Congreve's comedy with Goldsmith's or with Sheridan's, let alone with Wilde's, to be aware that if, to distinguish him from the Elizabethans, we confine him to a room, not a world, that room is not the drawing-room of the eighteenth century, still less is it the drawing-room of the nineteenth century. Drays roar on the cobbles beneath; the brawling of street hucksters and tavern rioters comes in at the open windows. There is a coarseness of language, an extravagance of humour, and a freedom of manners which cast us back to the Elizabethans. Yet it is in a drawing-room, surrounded by all the fopperies and refinements of the most sophisticated society in the world, that these ladies and gentlemen speak so freely, drink so deeply, and smell so strong. It is the contrast, perhaps, that makes us more aware of the coarseness of the Restoration dramatists than of the Elizabethan. A great lady who spits on the floor offends where a fishwife merely amuses. And perhaps it was for this reason that Congreve incurred first the majestic censure of Dr Johnson and then the more supercilious contempt of the Victorians who neglected, Sir Edmund Gosse informs us, either to read him or to act him. More conscious than we are of the drawing-room, they were quicker repelled perhaps by any violation of its decencies.

But however we may account for the change, to reach *The Way of the World* through *The Old Bachelor*, *The Double-Dealer* and *Love for Love* is to become more and more at loggerheads with Dr Johnson's dictum: 'It is acknowledged, with universal conviction, that the perusal of his works will make no man better; and that their ultimate effect is to represent pleasure in alliance with vice, and to relax those obligations by which life ought to be regulated.' On the contrary, to read Congreve's plays is to be convinced that we may learn from them many lessons much to our advantage both as writers of books and – if the division is possible – as livers of life. We might learn there, to begin with, the discipline of plain speech; to leave nothing lurking in the insidious shades of obscurity that can be said in words. The phrase is always finished; nothing is left to dwindle into darkness, to sound after the words are over. Then, when we have learnt to express ourselves, we may go on to observe the indefatigable hard work of a great writer: how he keeps us entertained because something is always happening, and on the alert because that something is always changing, and by contrasting laughter and seriousness, action and thought, keeps the edge of the emotions always sharp. To ring so many changes and keep up so rapid a speed of movement might well be enough, but in addition each of these characters has its own being, and each differs – the sea-dog from the fop, the old eccentric from the man of the world, the maid from the mistress. He has to enter into each; to leave his private pigeon-hole and invest himself with the emotions of another human being, so that speech meets speech at full tilt, each from its own angle.

A genius for phrase-making helps him. Now he strikes off a picture in a flash: '. . . there he lies with a great beard, like a Russian bear upon a drift of snow'. Now in a marvellous rush of rapid invention he conveys a whole chapter of guttersnipe life.

That I took from washing of old gauze and weaving of dead hair, with a bleak blue nose, over a chafing dish of starv'd embers, and dining behind a traverse rag, in a shop no bigger than a bird cage.   [*Way of W.*, v]

Then, again, like some miraculous magpie he repeats the naïve words, follows the crude emotions, of a great gawky girl like Miss Prue. However it is done, to enter into such diverse characters is, the moralists may note, at any rate to forget your own. Undoubtedly it is true that his language is often coarse; but then it is also true that his characters are more alive, quicker to strip off veils, more intolerant of circumlocutions than the ordinary run of people. They are reduced to phrase-making oftener than we could wish, and fine phrases often sound cynical; but then the situations are often so improbable that only fine phrases will cover them, and words, we must remember, were still to Congreve's generation as delightful as beads to a savage. Without that rapture the audacity of his splendid phrases would have been impossible.

But if we have to admit that some of the characters are immoral, and some of the opinions cynical, still we must ask how far we can call a character immoral or an opinion cynical if we feel that the author himself was aware of its immorality and intended its cynicism? And, though it is a delicate matter to separate an author from his characters and detach him from their opinions, no one can read Congreve's comedies without detecting a common atmosphere, a general attitude that holds them together for all their diversity. The stress laid on certain features creates a common likeness as unmistakable as the eyes and nose of a family face. The plays are veined through and through with satire. 'Therefore I would rail in my writings and be revenged', says Valentine in *Love for Love*. Congreve's satire seems sometimes, as Scandal says, to have the whole world for its butt. Yet there is underneath a thinking mind, a mind that doubts and questions. Some hint thrown out in passing calls us back to make us ponder it: for instance, Mellefont's 'Ay, My Lord, I shall have the same reason for happiness that your Lordship has, I shall think myself happy'. Or, again, a sudden phrase like 'There's comfort in a hand stretched out to one that's sinking' suggests, by its contrast, a sensibility that trembles on the edge of tears. Nothing is stressed; sentiment never broadens into sentimentality; everything passes as quickly as a ray of light and blends as indistinguishably. But if we needs must prove that the creator of Sir Sampson Legend and old Foresight had not only a prodigious sense of human absurdity and a bitter conviction of its insincerity but as quick a regard for its honesty and decency as any Victorian or Dr Johnson himself, we need only point to his simplicity. After we have run up the scale of absurdity to its sublime heights a single word again and again recalls us to common sense. 'That my poor father should be so very silly' is one such comment, immensely effective in its place. Again and again we are brought back to sanity and daylight by the sound of a voice speaking in its natural tones.

But it is the Valentines, the Mirabells, the Angelicas, and the Millamants who keep us in touch with truth and, by striking a sudden serious note, bring the rest to scale. They have sharpened their emotions upon their wits. They have flouted each other; bargained; taken love and examined it by the light of reason; teased and tested each other almost beyond endurance. But when it comes to the point and she must be serious, the swiftest of all heroines, whose mind and body seem equally winged, so that there is a rush in the air as she passes and we exclaim with Scandal, 'Gone; why, she was never here, nor anywhere else', has a centre of stillness in her heart and enough emotion in her words to furbish out a dozen pages of eloquent disquisition. 'Why does not the man take me? Would you have me give myself to you over again?' The words are simple, and yet, after what has already been said, so brimming with meaning that Mirabell's reply, 'Ay, over and over again', seems to receive into itself more than words can say. And this depth of emotion, we have to reflect, the change and complexity that are implied in it, have been reached in the direct way; that is by making each character speak in his or her own person, without addition from the author or any soliloquy save such as can be spoken on the stage in the presence of an audience. No, whether we read him from the moralist's angle or from the artist's, to agree with Dr Johnson is an impossibility. To read the comedies is not to 'relax those obligations by which life ought to be regulated'. On the contrary, the more slowly we read him and the more carefully, the more meaning we find, the more beauty we discover.

Here perhaps, in the reflections that linger when the book is shut and *The Way of the World* is finished, lies the answer to the old puzzle why at the height of his powers he stopped writing. It is that he had done all that was possible in that kind. The last play held more than any audience could grasp at a single sitting. The bodily presence of actors and actresses must, it would seem, often overpower the words that they had to speak. He had forgotten, or disregarded, his own axiom that 'the distance of the stage requires the figures represented to be something larger than the life'. He had written, as he says in the dedication, for 'the *Few*', and 'but little of it was prepar'd for that general taste which seems now to be predominant in the palates of our audience'. He had come to despise his public, and it was time therefore either to write differently or to leave off. But the novel, which offered another outlet, was uncongenial; he was incorrigibly dramatic, as his one attempt at fiction shows. And poetry, too, was denied him, for though again and again he brings us to the edge of poetry in a phrase like 'You're a woman, One to whom Heav'n gave beauty, when it grafted roses on a briar', and suggests, as Meredith does in his novels, the mood of poetry, he was unable to pass beyond human idiosyncrasy to the more general statement of poetry. He must move and laugh and bring us into touch with action instantly.

Since these two paths then were blocked, what other way was there for a writer of Congreve's temperament but to make an end? Dangerous as it is to distinguish a writer from his work, we cannot help but recognise a man behind the plays – a man as sensitive to criticism as he was skilled in inflicting it on others; for what is his defiance of the critics but deference to them? A scholar too with all the scholar's fastidiousness; a man of birth and breeding for whom the vulgar side of fame held little gratification; a man, in short, who might well have said with Valentine, 'Nay, I am not violently bent upon the trade', and sit, handsome and portly and sedate as his portrait shows him, 'very gravely with his hat over his eyes', as the gossips observed him, content to strive no more.

But indeed he left very little for the gossips to feed upon; no writer of his time and standing passed through the world more privately. Voltaire left a dubious anecdote; the Duchess of Marlborough, it is said, had an effigy of him set at her table after his death; his few discreet letters provide an occasional hint: 'Ease and quiet is what I hunt after'; 'I feel very sensibly and silently for those whom I love' – that is all. But there is a fitness in this very absence of relics as though he had consumed whatever was irrelevant to his work and left us to find him there. And there, indeed, we find something beyond himself; beyond the many figures of his fertile and brilliant imagination; beyond Tattle and Ben, Foresight and Angelica, Maskwell and Lady Wishfort, Mirabell and Mellefont and Millamant. Between them they have created what is not to be confined within the limits of a single character or expressed in any one play – a world where each part depends upon the other, the serene, impersonal, and indestructible world of art.

SOURCE: 'Congreve's Comedies', essay first published in *Times Literary Supplement* (1937); included in *Collected Essays*, 1 (London, 1966), pp. 76–84.

L. C. Knights   'Tendency Wit' (1937)

Henry James – whose 'social comedy' may be allowed to provide a standard of maturity – once remarked that he found Congreve 'insufferable',[1] and perhaps the first thing to say of Restoration drama – tragedy as well as comedy – is that the bulk of it is insufferably dull. . . .

In the matter of sexual relations Restoration comedy is entirely dominated by a narrow set of conventions. The objection that it is only certain characters, not the dramatists themselves, who accept them can be more freely encountered when the assumptions that are expressed most frequently have been briefly illustrated.

The first convention is, of course, that constancy in love, especially in marriage, is a bore. . . . And the convention is constantly turning up in Congreve. 'There is no creature perfectly civil but a husband', explains Mrs Frail, 'for in a little time he grows only rude to his wife, and that is the highest good breeding, for it begets his civility to other people' [*Love for Love*, I i]. 'Marry her! Marry her!' Fainall advises Mirabell, 'Be half as well acquainted with her charms, as you are with her defects, and my life on't, you are your own man again' [*The Way of the World*, I i]. And Witwoud: 'A wit should no more be sincere than a woman constant; one argues a decay of parts, as t'other of beauty' [ibid.]. Appetite, it seems (and this is the second assumption), needs perpetually fresh stimulus. . . . 'Would anything but a madman complain of uncertainty?' asks Congreve's Angelica, for 'security is an insipid thing, and the overtaking and possessing of a wish, discovers the folly of the chase' [*Love for Love*, IV i]. And Fainall, in *The Way of the World*, speaks for a large class when he hints at a liking for sauce – a little gentleman's relish – to his seductions: 'I'd no more play with a man that slighted his ill fortune than I'd make love to a woman who under-valued the loss of her reputation' [I i]. Fainall, of course, is what he is, but the attitude that makes sexual pleasure 'the bliss', that makes woman 'delicious' – something to be savoured – as well as 'damned' and 'destructive', demands, for its support, 'the pleasure of a chase'.[2]

> Would you long preserve your lover?
> Would you still his goddess reign?
> N⸢ ⸣er let him all discover,
> Never let him much obtain.   [*Old B.*, II]

Restoration comedy used to be considered outrageously outspoken, but such stuff as this, far from being 'outspoken', hovers on the outskirts of sexual relations, and sees nothing but the titillation of appetite (''Tis not the success', Collier observed, 'but the manner of gaining it which is all in all').[3] Sex is a hook baited with tempting morsels;[4] it is a thirst quencher;[5] it is a cordial;[6] it is a dish to feed on;[7] it is a bunch of grapes;[8] it is anything but sex. (This, of course, explains why some people can combine a delighted approval of Restoration comedy with an un-balanced repugnance for such modern literature as deals sincerely and realistically with sexual relationships.)

Now the objection referred to above was that sentiments such as these are not offered for straightforward acceptance. Many of them are attributed to characters plainly marked as Wicked (Maskwell, for example, is the black-a-vised villain of melodrama), or, more frequently, as trivial, and the dramatist can therefore dissociate himself. He may even be engaged in showing his audience the explicit, logical consequences of the half-unconscious premises on which they base their own lives, saying, as Mr Dobrée has it, 'Here is life lived upon certain assumptions; see what it becomes'. To this there are several answers. The first is that reflections of the kind that I have quoted from are indistinguishable in tone and style from the general epigrammatic stock-in-trade (the audience was not altogether to be blamed if, as Congreve complained, they could not at first 'distinguish betwixt the character of a Witwoud and a Truewit'); and they are largely 'exhibited', just as all the self-conscious witticisms are exhibited, for the sake of their immediate 'comic' effect. One has only to note the laughter of a contemporary audience at a revival, and the places where the splutters occur, to realise how much of the fun provides a rather gross example of tendency wit.[9] The same attitudes, moreover, are manipulated again and again, turning up with the stale monotony of jokes on postcards, and the play that is made with them demands only the easiest, the most superficial, response. But it is, after all, useless to argue about the degree of detachment, the angle at which these attitudes and assumptions are presented. As soon as one selects a particular comedy for that exercise one realises that all is equally grist to the mill and that the dramatist (there is no need, here, to make distinctions) has no coherent attitude of his own. A consistent artistic purpose would not be content to express itself in a style that allows so limited, so local an effect. . . .

. . . Even Congreve, by common account the best of the comic writers, is no exception. I have said that his verbal pattern often seems to be quite unrelated to an individual mode of perceiving. At best it registers a very limited mode. Restoration prose is all 'social' in its tone, implications and general tenor, but Congreve's observation is *merely* of the public surface. And Congreve, too, relies on the conventional assumptions. In *The Way of the World*, it is true, they are mainly given to the bad and the foolish to express: it is Fainall who discourses on the pleasures of disliking one's wife, and Witwoud who maintains that only old age and ugliness ensure constancy. And Mirabell who is explicitly opposed to some aspects of contemporary manners, goes through the common forms in a tone of rather weary aloofness: 'I wonder, Fainall, that you who are married, and of consequence should be discreet, will suffer your wife to be of such a party.' But Congreve himself is not above raising a cheap snigger –

> Ay there's my grief; that's the sad change of life,
> To lose my title, and yet keep my wife.   [*Way of W*., II i]

– and, above all, the characters with some life in them have nothing to fall back on: nothing, that is, except the conventional, and conventionally limited, pleasures of sex. Millamant, who says she loathes the country and hates the town, expects to draw vitality from the excitement of incessant solicitation:

I'll be solicited to the very last, nay, and afterwards . . . I should think I was poor and had nothing to bestow, if I were reduced to an inglorious ease, and freed from the agreeable fatigues of solicitation. . . . Oh, I hate a lover that can dare to think he draws a moment's air, independent of the bounty of his mistress. There is not so impudent a thing in nature, as the saucy look of an assured man, confident of success. The pedantic air of a very husband has not so pragmatical an air.

Everyone seems to have found Millamant intelligent and attractive, but her attitude is not far removed from that expressed in

> Would you long preserve your lover:
> Would you still his goddess reign?

and she shares with characters who are decidedly not attractive a disproportionate belief in 'the pleasure of the chase'. Which is not surprising in view of her other occupations and resources; visiting, writing and receiving letters, tea-parties and small talk make up a round that is never for a moment enlivened by the play of genuine intelligence. As Vanbrugh's Lady Brute remarks: 'After all, a woman's life would be a dull business, if it were not for the men. . . . We shou'd never blame Fate for the shortness of our days; our time would hang wretchedly upon our hands' [*The Provok'd Wife*, III iii]. And although Congreve recognises, at times, the triviality of his characters –

You had the leisure to entertain a herd of fools; things who visit you from their excessive idleness; bestowing on your easiness that time which is the encumbrance of their lives. How can you find delight in such society?

[Mirabell, in *Way of W.*, II i]

– it is to the world whose confines were the Court, the drawing-room, the play-house and the park (a world completely lacking the real sophistication and self-knowledge that might, in some measure, have redeemed it) that he limits his appeal.

It is, indeed, hard to resist the conclusion that 'society' – the smart town society that sought entertainment at the theatres – was fundamentally bored. . . .

. . . The criticism that defenders of Restoration comedy need to answer is not that the comedies are 'immoral', but that they are trivial, gross and dull.

SOURCE: excerpts from 'Restoration Comedy: The Reality and the Myth', *Scrutiny*, VI No. 2 (1937); reprinted in *Explorations* (London, 1946), pp. 131, 141–2, 142–3, 145–7, 148.

NOTES

[These have been reorganised and renumbered from the original – Ed.]

1. Henry James, *Letters*, I, p. 40.

2. *The Old Bachelor*, I i; III 8 ('O thou delicious, damned, dear, destructive woman!'); IV i.

3. Jeremy Collier, *A Short View of the Profaneness and Immorality of the English Stage* (1698; 5th edn, 1738), p. 116. [Excerpted in Part One, above – Ed.]

4. ' 'Tis true you are so eager in pursuit of the temptation, that you save the devil the trouble of leading you into it: nor is it out of discretion that you don't swallow the very hook yourselves have baited, but . . . what you meant for a whet turns the edge of your puny stomachs' (*The Old Bachelor*, I i). 'Strike Heartwell home, before the bait's worn off the hook. Age will come. He nibbled fairly yesterday, and no doubt will be eager enough to-day to swallow the temptation' (ibid., III i).

5. 'What was my pleasure is become my duty: and I have as little stomach to her now as if I were her husband. . . . Pox on't! that a man can't drink without quenching his thirst' (The *Double-Dealer*, III i).

6. 'You must get you a mistress, Rhodophil. That indeed is living upon cordials; but as fast as one fails, you must supply it with another (*Marriage à la Mode*, I i).

7. 'Because our husbands cannot feed on one dish, therefore we must be starved' (ibid., III i).

8. 'The only way to keep us new to one another, is never to enjoy, as they keep grapes, by hanging them upon a line; they must touch nothing, if you would preserve them fresh' (ibid., v i).

9. The Freudian 'censor' is at times projected in the form of the stage puritan. The plays written soon after the Commonwealth period appealed to Royalist prejudices by satirising the 'seemingly precise'; and even later, when 'the bonfires of devotion', 'the bellows of zeal', were forgotten, a good deal of the self-conscious swagger of indecency seems to have been directed against 'our protestant husbands', city merchants, aldermen and the like; the 'daring' effect was intensified by postulating a shockable audience somewhere – not necessarily in the theatre. Not that the really obscene jokes were merely bravado: Collier quite rightly remarked that 'the modern poets seem to use smut as the old ones did Machines, to relieve a fainting situation' (*A Short View* . . ., op. cit., p. 4).

F. W. Bateson L. C. Knights and Restoration Comedy (1957)

. . . Mr Knights denies any seriousness to the plays. While recognising that 'there is a place in the educational process for, say, La Rochefoucauld', he cannot detect in Restoration comedy a similar 'tough strength of disillusion'. The plays seem to him to be confined to 'a miserably limited set of attitudes'. Dorimant's intrigues in *The Man of Mode* are, he asserts, 'of no more human significance than those of a barn-yard cock'; and Restoration comedy as a whole lacks 'the essential stuff of human experience'. Moreover, the plays have 'no significant relation with the best thought of the time', and the unreal sexual conventions that they appeal to – that constancy is a bore, 'the pleasure of the chase', etc. – contrast unfavourably with 'such modern literature as deals sincerely and realistically with sexual relationships'.

Most of these objections seem to me to derive from a misunderstanding of what comedy can or should attempt. There is a concealed premise in Mr Knight's assumptions as to what constitutes non-trivial literature, which comes out when he says, in the essay's first sentence: 'Henry James – whose "social comedy" may be allowed to provide a standard

of maturity – once remarked that he found Congreve "insufferable".'
James's judgement, a casual comment apparently in one of his letters, is
intended to carry more force than it very well can. Naturally James
thought Congreve insufferable. Congreve would have thought James
insufferable. And why should James's 'social comedy' provide a
standard of the comically serious? How would Shakespeare's or
Molière's comedies fare if they were judged by such a criterion?
Underlying Mr Knight's more specific objections to Restoration
comedy there is always the lurking implication that Wycherley and
Congreve *ought* to have written like James or D. H. Lawrence, or at any
rate (Mr Knights was writing while the seventeenth-century Dissoci-
ation of Consciousness was still booming) like an Elizabethan or
Jacobean dramatist.

Ought they? It is the crucial issue. Or is literature necessarily limited
and directed by the processes of history to different dramatic forms at
different times? Now if Eliot's dictum is accepted, as I suppose it must be
(it is an unconcealed premise in Mr Knights's own *Drama and Society in
the Age of Jonson*), that a 'radical change in poetic form' is almost always
the 'symptom' of some very much deeper change in society and in the
individual' (*The Use of Poetry and the Use of Criticism*), it surely follows
that any deep change in society and in the individual's relation to
society will be reflected or expressed in a radical change in the
dominant literary form. The depth of the social and individual changes
brought about by the Civil War will not be disputed. The first question,
then, to be asked of Restoration comedy, in order to determine a
properly relevant approach to it, is not whether it is like James or
Shakespeare, but in what respects it is the appropriate dramatic
expression of the social revolution of the mid-seventeenth century. Until
this question has been answered the strictly literary issues do not arise at
all. Mr Knights begs it when he contrasts the 'rich common language'
available to an Elizabethan dramatist with the 'mechanical' antitheses
of Congreve. Rich in what currency? And the same fallacy seems to be
present in Mr Knights's comparison of Halifax's *Character of Charles II* –
and later of some sentences from Burnet – with passages from *Love for
Love* and *The Way of the World*. Can dramatic prose *ever* be usefully
compared with that appropriate to historical or political commentary?
It is no criticism of chalk that it isn't cheese. The question is whether it is
good or bad chalk.

I have not the learning, nor is this the place, to attempt a
comprehensive critical account of the Restoration comedy of manners.

All that I can hope to do is to suggest a perhaps more relevant approach
to these plays. The sexual impropriety is still, of course, the real bone of
contention. The seventeenth century distinguished between low
comedy, which was merely meant to make an audience laugh, and high
or 'genteel' comedy, which used the laugh as a form of social comment –
ridendo corrigere mores. A defence of Restoration comedy must demonstrate that its sex jokes have a serious social function. I think it can
be shown that they have and that the plays, at their best, need fear no
comparison even in Mr Knights's eyes, with 'such modern literature as
deals sincerely and realistically with sexual relationships'. But if the
demonstration is to be effective it will be necessary to analyse the
Restoration treatment of sex in some detail.

Here, then, as an elementary test-case, is part of a seduction scene
between two minor characters in *Love for Love* – Tattle, who is described
in the list of *dramatis personae* as a 'half-witted beau,' and Miss Prue, 'a
silly awkward country girl.' Tattle has just explained to Prue that, if she
is to be thought well-bred, she must learn how to lie; her words must
contradict her thoughts, though her actions should also contradict her
words.

PRUE   O Lord, I swear this is pure! – I like it better than our old-fashioned
country way of speaking one's mind; – and must not you lie too?

TAT.   Hum! – Yes; but you must believe I speak truth.

PRUE   O Gemini! well, I always had a great mind to tell lies; but they
frighted me, and said it was a sin.

TAT.   Well, my pretty creature; will you make me happy by giving me a
kiss?

PRUE   No, indeed; I'm angry at you.   [*Runs and kisses him.*]

TAT.   Hold, hold, that's pretty well: – but you should not have given it me,
but have suffered me to take it.

PRUE   Well, we'll do't again.

TAT.   With all my heart. – Now then, my little angel!   [*Kisses her.*]

PRUE   Pish!

TAT.   That's right – again, my charmer!   [*Kisses again.*]

PRUE   O fy! now I can't abide you.

TAT.   Admirable! that was as well as if you had been born and bred in
Covent Garden all the days of your life; – And won't you show me, pretty miss,
where your bed-chamber is?

PRUE   No, indeed, won't I; but I'll run there and hide myself from you
behind the curtains.

TAT.   I'll follow you.

PRUE Ah, but I'll hold the door with both hands, and be angry; – and you
shall push me down before you come in.

TAT. No, I'll come in first, and push you down afterwards. [III i]

The episode is not one of Congreve's high spots, but its theatrical
potentialities should be obvious. In the hands of a competent actor and
actress the scene can be very funny indeed. In what, however, does the
fun consist? First of all, I suppose, in the reversal – painless and in a way
satisfying – of the auditor's normal rational expectations. On the stage
are two human beings – looking, in spite of the beau's oddities and girl's
country ways, very much like you and me – and a sort of lesson is
apparently in progress. Tattle, the would-be seducer, is instructing Prue
in the way a well-bred woman will receive the advances of a young man
like himself. Part of the reversal of our expectations is, of course, the
unusualness of the subject for a lesson, part of it is the contrast between
Prue's uncouth speech and manners with her unerring knowledge of
what she wants, but the big surprise, I suppose, is the girl's innocently
enthusiastic progress, under her teacher's approving eyes, from kisses to
copulation. So the human beings are not so human after all! But Prue is
enjoying herself so much that the audience finds itself involuntarily
sharing in the sudden topsy-turvy values. Nevertheless the scene is not,
as Lamb tried to argue in the Elia essay 'On the Artificial Comedy of the
Last Century', an excursion into an amoral fairyland, the land of
cuckoldry, a Utopia of gallantry. [Excerpted in Part Two above – Ed.]
For the effectiveness of the dramatic paradoxes depends upon the
audience's continuous awareness that it is *not* in fairyland. Prue is an
adolescent girl, and if she goes on as she seems determined to do she will
soon find herself 'in trouble'. As the seduction proceeds to its final
physical conclusion the tension between reality and what had at first
seemed just a *façon de parler*, a mere make-believe parody of an ordinary
lesson, mounts and mounts until the audience's laughter is replaced by
an incredulous gasp. Is it all just an elaborate joke, or is Congreve going
to take Prue at her word? The Nurse's interruption a moment later
comes with the effect of a reprieve. We can laugh now; we are back in
the world of the theatre; the realism to which we seemed committed, the
ugliness of an actual seduction, has been waived. But it was a near thing,
and with the relaxation of the tension the audience giggles happily in
nervous relief.

At this point a tentative definition of comedy will have to be
attempted. The agreeable reversal of an expectation that will itself be

reversed must imply two separated planes of reality which the dramatist can assume in his audience: one that of everyday commonsense, and parallel and contiguous to it the fairyland plane of Lamb's essay, 'where pleasure is duty, and the manners perfect freedom'. It is obviously in the auditor's sudden transition from the objective plane of everyday rational reality, which must always be the point of comic departure, to the subjective plane of dream-fantasy or irrational dream-fulfilment that the ridiculous is born. Its most elementary form is the top-hatted gentleman who skids on a banana-skin. In terms of the dramatic structure of a Restoration comedy it is the continuous collision of the plays' heroes (including the heroines), that is, the 'men of sense', with their grotesque opposites – Sir Fopling Flutter, the Widow Blackacre, Foresight, Lady Wishfort and their like – each of whom is imprisoned in his own fantasy. The refinements all fall within this general pattern. Thus Tattle, who is a grotesque, 'a half-witted beau', in the scenes he shares with Valentine and Scandal, is the realist in the Miss Prue episode. To her the seduction is clearly just a new game, a variant of hide-and-seek ('you shall push me down before you come in'), whereas Tattle means business ('No, I'll come in first and push you down afterwards'). And there is a similar metamorphosis of Prue's own role later in the play, when she confronts Ben, the even more fantastic sailor-fiancé.

The possibilities of serious social comment within the comic framework seem to depend upon the degree to which either or both of the opposed planes of meaning are conceptualised. The clash in that case, instead of being between casual examples of human life to which the auditor reacts realistically or fantastically, is now between *representative* examples, that is, figures or attitudes that he recognises as either typical (on the plane of common sense) or symbolic (on the plane of fantasy).

A historical approach will make it easier to appreciate the 'serious' role of sex in a Restoration comedy of manners. To the Puritans 'immorality' had virtually reduced itself to sexual irregularity, with drunkenness and blasphemy as poor seconds, a man's other sins being considered a private matter between him and God. (By the 1650 Act 'for suppressing the detestable sins of Incest, Adultery and Fornication' incest and adultery became capital crimes without benefit of clergy, as did fornication on the second offence, first offenders getting three months' imprisonment.) On the other hand, to the restored Royalists by a natural reaction sexual licence – and drunkenness and blasphemous oaths – almost became a political duty. 'Joy ruled the day and love the night', as Dryden summed up Charles II's reign in *The Secular Masque*. The two attitudes were the points of maximum social divergence between the two parties into which England remained divided. As in politics a compromise was eventually worked out, for which Addison and Steele usually get most of the credit. But the relative sexual respectability of *The Tatler* and *The Spectator* was the end-product of a long process that was closely connected with political developments. If the political problem *par excellence* in the second half of the seventeenth century was to avoid the recurrence of a second Civil War, its social parallel, essentially, was to rationalise the sex instinct. Until such a rationalisation had been achieved genuine communication between Whigs and Tories was hardly possible. Intermarriage, the final solution, was unthinkable. It is now a matter of history that a kind of sexual rationalisation was achieved, perhaps over-achieved (it is a curious fact that hardly any of the eighteenth-century poets married). From one point of view, in the mode of allegory proper to high comedy, the Restoration drama records the strains that accompanied the achievement.

The term 'Restoration comedy' is really a misnomer. The first completely successful comedy of manners, Wycherley's *The Country Wife*, was not written until 1674 – fourteen years after the Restoration itself. By that time the rationalisation of sex had already made some progress. The two extremes had come to be identified on the stage with (1) younger members of the landed gentry (Tory), who spent their winter months in London applying to the pursuit of love the methods of the chase, which was their principal occupation on their country estates, and (2) London merchants (Whig), who treated their wives as pieces of property to be even more jealously guarded than their gold. The earlier dramatists were all ex-Cavaliers and inevitably their heroes had been the gentlemanly rakes. In Wycherley's Horner, however, the rake-hero undergoes a sexual transformation, which prepared the way for Dorimant's surrender to Harriet in *The Man of Mode* and the complete rationalisation of sex by Mirabell and Millamant in the fourth act of *The Way of the World*. . . .

SOURCE: extract from article in *Essays in Criticism*, VII (1957), pp. 57–64.

Clifford Leech   'Congreve's Elegiac Strain' (1962)

. . . the quotation from Horace on [*The Double-Dealer's*] title-page – *Interdum tamen, et vocem Comoedia tollit* – . . . announced his more ambitious intention. The seriousness of purpose is seen not merely in the introduction of the villainous characters, Maskwell and Lady Touchwood, but in the manner of presentation of the two lovers, Mellefont and Cynthia. As characters they lack individuality, but they stand for a man and a woman in love yet faced with the folly which seems inevitably to attend on their married acquaintances, and faced too with the intrigues of the envious. In Act II, just after Lord and Lady Froth have given a fulsome exhibition of connubial affection, Cynthia doubts whether she and Mellefont are well-advised to proceed to marriage:

MEL. You're thoughtful, *Cynthia?*
CYN. I'm thinking, tho' Marriage makes Man and Wife one Flesh, it leaves 'em still two Fools; and they become more conspicuous by setting off one another.
MEL. That's only when two Fools meet, and their Follies are oppos'd.
CYN. Nay, I have known two Wits meet, and by the Opposition of their Wits, render themselves as ridiculous as Fools. 'Tis an odd Game we're going to Play at: What think you of drawing Stakes, and giving over in time?
MEL. No, hang't, that's not endeavouring to win, because it's possible we may lose; since we have shuffled and cut, let's e'en turn up Trump now.
CYN. Then I find it's like Cards, if either of us have a good Hand it is an Accident of Fortune.
MEL. No, Marriage is rather like a Game of Bowls, Fortune indeed makes the Match, and the two nearest, and sometimes the two farthest are together, but the Game depends entirely upon Judgement.
CYN. Still it is a Game, and consequently one of us must be a Loser.
MEL. Not at all; only a friendly Trial of Skill, and the Winnings to be shared between us.   [II i]

As so often in Congreve, the force of the passage depends on its context: it has indeed a powerful ring when the Froths have just been exhibited to us. And the presentation of the lovers' dilemma goes further than this: Cynthia is aware that her powers of perception make life a more serious concern for her than it is for the Froths and the Plyants. She reaches a point in Act III where she can envy the fools, while knowing that her own wit cannot be laid aside:

'Tis not so hard to counterfeit Joy in the Depth of Affliction, as to dissemble Mirth in Company of Fools – Why should I call 'em Fools? The World thinks better of 'em; for these have Quality and Education, Wit and fine Conversation, are receiv'd and admir'd by the World – if not, they like and admire themselves – and why is not that true Wisdom, for 'tis Happiness: And for ought I know, we have misapply'd the Name all this while, and mistaken the Thing: Since

> If Happiness in Self-content is plac'd,
> The Wise are Wretched, and Fools only Bless'd.   [III i]

There is in this something of the elegiac note that can be heard in *The Way of the World*. If, however, Mellefont and Cynthia are better for the things they say than for the impression they make on us as imagined beings, Maskwell and Lady Touchwood are wholly mechanical pieces of villainy. Congreve was not capable of fully imaging the degree of malignity that he planned for them. He was to do better with Fainall and Mrs Marwood, partly because their villainy is less and their excuse more powerful: envy and spite and the desire for revenge were of his world, but the fiercer, elemental passion was beyond its scope. . . .

. . . That [*The Way of the World*] failed to win much applause at its first performance is usually attributed to its defects in plotting, the thinness of the intrigue in the first four acts and the crowding of incidents into the fifth. But not only is bustle wanting: the appreciation of *The Way of the World* needs a sensitivity to emotional overtone that is rare in an audience seeing a new play.[1] If for us this is the play that justifies all Restoration drama, from many of its contemporaries it was simply a less entertaining comedy than Vanbrugh's *The Relapse* (1696) or Farquhar's *The Constant Couple* (1699). Steele, in commendatory verses, echoes Congreve's motto for *The Double-Dealer*:

> By your selected Scenes and handsome Choice,
> Ennobled Comedy exalts her Voice;

but that was the judgement of a more than usually sympathetic spectator. To the discerning eye, indeed, there is more variety, more planning in *The Way of the World* than in *Love for Love*. The characters are less strongly etched, but their individualities are sure and the differences between them are brought out in the juxtaposition of scenes. It is no accident that the bargaining-scene between Mirabell and Millamant follows immediately after Sir Wilfull has approached Millamant with all the rustic embarrassment of the natural man, or that Mrs Fainall, the cast-off mistress still mistress of herself, is placed side-by-side with Mrs Marwood, the victim of thwarted inclinations. But the colours are subdued. Fainall does not gloat over his villainy as Maskwell did in *The Double-Dealer*. Sir Wilfull brings the raw air of Shropshire into the drawing-room, but he does not nearly run away with the play as Ben did in *Love for Love*. Millamant is thoughtful like Cynthia, but not sententious, is in sure command of her speech but not given to pert repartee as on occasion Angelica is. Lady Wishfort is true to her name, but even her languishings and her vituperation have a smoothness and a comic elegance. Witwoud and Petulant are creatures of a summer's fancy, not earth-bound in the way of Tattle. And Mirabell, for all his association with Mrs Fainall, for all his pretended wooing of Lady Wishfort – which Congreve tactfully leaves outside the action of the play – appears not merely the wit but the thoughtful man. He is no victim of a sudden reformation, like Cibber's Loveless, but he has a plan for rational living, a plan in which Millamant constitutes a necessary part, a part to be kept in place. And for his own sake, he must see to it that she remains herself, no mere devoted complement to her husband. The bargaining-scenes that appear so frequently in seventeenth-century comedies, from the reign of Charles I right up to this year 1700, seem all anticipations of the meeting of Mirabell and Millamant in Act IV of this play: here Congreve developed the hesitations and the safeguards that he had sketched in the conversation of Mellefont and Cynthia: Restoration comedy had been principally concerned with sex-relations, and here Congreve gave to the dying age a satisfying expression of the attitude it had been fumbling for.

But the final impression the play leaves is perhaps one of suppressed melancholy. At the end of Etherege's *The Man of Mode*, the fortunate Harriet, secure of Dorimant's love, joins a little grossly in the jeering at the cast-off Mrs Loveit. When Millamant speaks to Mrs Marwood, there is an echo of this, but Congreve's raillery is altogether less pert: indeed, at the end of this encounter the mocking tone becomes subdued.

To Mrs Marwood's protest that she hates Mirabell, Millamant replies:

O Madam, why so do I – And yet the Creature loves me, ha, ha, ha. How can one forbear laughing to think of it – I am a Sybil if I am not amaz'd to think what he can see in me. I'll take my Death, I think you are handsomer – and within a Year or two as young. – If you cou'd but stay for me, I shou'd overtake you – But that cannot be – Well, that Thought makes me melancholick – Now I'll be sad.   [III i]

With Congreve we do not forget the passage of time: its ruins may amuse us, as in Lady Wishfort, but even in her presentation there is a reminder that she is not alone. Sometimes the elegiac note seems to be communicated through the cadence, as when Mirabell speaks in Act II:

An old Woman's Appetite is deprav'd like that of a Girl – 'Tis the Green-Sickness of a second Childhood; and like the faint Offer of a latter Spring, serves but to usher in the Fall; and withers in an affected Bloom.   [II i]

And in Act I, before we have met Millamant, Fainall and Mirabell are discussing her and this exchange ensues:

FAIN. For a passionate Lover, methinks you are a Man somewhat too discerning in the Failings of your Mistress.

MIRA. And for a discerning Man, somewhat too passionate a Lover; for I like her with all her Faults; nay, like her for her Faults. Her Follies are so natural, or so artful, that they become her; and those Affectations which in another Woman wou'd be odious, serve but to make her more agreeable. I'll tell thee, *Fainall*, she once us'd me with that Insolence, that in Revenge I took her to pieces; sifted her, and separated her Failings; I study'd 'em, and got 'em by Rote. The Catalogue was so large, that I was not without Hopes, one Day or other to hate her heartily: To which end I so us'd my self to think of 'em, that at length, contrary to my Design and Expectation, they gave me ev'ry Hour less and less Disturbance; 'till in a few Days it became habitual to me, to remember 'em without being displeas'd. They are now grown as familiar to me as my own Frailties; and in all probability in a little time longer I shall like 'em as well.

FAIN. Marry her, marry her; be half as well acquainted with her Charms, as you are with her Defects, and my Life on't, you are your own Man again.

MIRA. Say you so?

FAIN. Ay, ay, I have Experience: I have a Wife, and so forth.   [I i]

Mirabell lovingly considers the twists and turns of his mistress's mind and delights in his own subjection: there is wisdom in the comic presentation as well as shrewdness and good phrasing. And the last words in the scene are given to the man of experience, who has tried marriage for himself. The acid is there, the shrug that goes with Congreve's wit. Bonamy Dobrée has noted that many of Congreve's set speeches are just not metrical, that a regular iambic beat is never quite established.[3] This may be the formal analogue to that undertone of melancholy which runs through the same speeches, giving to *The Way of the World* in particular an added dimension within which the characters move as symbols: there their separateness vanishes and they become aspects of a single humanity. Congreve, bringing Restoration comedy into clear focus, brought it also, for a brief moment, into a larger world. . . .

SOURCE: extracts from 'Congreve and the Century's End', *Philological Quarterly*, XLI (1962), pp. 287–9, 291–3.

NOTES

[These have been reorganised and renumbered from the original – Ed.]

1. The point was sharply made by Bonamy Dobrée in *Restoration Comedy* (Oxford, 1924), p. 140.
2. Congreve, while keeping our sympathy with Mirabell, recognises a considerable range of conduct in him. Norman N. Holland, in an otherwise most perceptive study of the play, simplifies notably in labelling Mirabell 'a good clever man': *The First Modern Comedies: The Significance of Etherege, Wycherley and Congreve* (Cambridge, Mass., 1959), p. 160.
3. Bonamy Dobrée (ed.), *Comedies by William Congreve* (Oxford, 1925), p. xxiv. [Excerpted above – Ed.]

William Myers   Plot and Meaning (1972)

The decline of English comedy is notoriously sudden. About six great plays were written in the 1690s, but with the exception of *The Beggar's Opera* none after that for about seventy years. And then, though

Goldsmith attacked the sentimental comedies 'in which the virtues of Private Life are exhibited, rather than the Vices exposed', and in which 'Folly, instead of being ridiculed, is commended',[1] neither he nor Sheridan in fact returned to the great Jonsonian preoccupation with folly and vice. They did offer some neat reversals of Restoration comedy conventions, but finally they only require us to make minor adjustments to those attitudes to literature and life which are implied either by an undiscriminating acceptance or an undiscriminating rejection of the assumptions of seventeenth-century comedy. The movement is clearly away from the World of Jonson and Congreve and towards the lively unrealities of Wilde.

This divorce of English comedy from the World points to a radical incompatibility between modern society and classical norms of comic action. This can best be understood in terms of developing ideas about how man functions in society; and we can usefully take as the starting point of seventeenth-century thinking on this subject the notion that social and political relationships have somehow or other to accommodate man's potentiality for power and freedom. There is, for instance, the Hobbist position which presupposes first that notorious state of nature, where, as Manly puts it in *The Plain Dealer*, 'honest, downright Barbarity is profest; where men devour one another like generous hungry Lyons and Tygers',[2] and secondly a collective agreement among men restraining anarchy and restricting liberty, this agreement being supervised by a monarch who is not himself a party to it, but who simply imposes social order on others to satisfy his own appetite for power. Hence Sir Sampson Legend's remark in *Love for Love* that 'nothing under an Emperour should be born with Appetites' [II i]. At the other extreme is Dryden's world order in which God's free gift of grace to man finds its political equivalent in the prerogative of kings: politics and religion are perfected when by the free exercise of his will the sovereign performs acts of mercy.

A more private concept of freedom seems to have been Etherege's principal concern in *The Man of Mode*, but even the freedom pursued there by the man of wit has its social implications. Etherege is certainly careful to remind his audience in the first scene of the social conditions which make freedom possible, of the poverty and ugliness which support the World of the action from below. Freedom is clearly predicated on inherited status and an estate. But it is also inseparable from the supreme Hobbist talent of wit, the principal cause of which is the desire for power, that 'general inclination of all

mankind, . . . [that] perpetual and restless desire of Power'³ which is
the over-riding passion of the heroic drama. In *The Man of Mode*, more
subtly, it takes the form of Dorimant seeking mastery of emancipation
itself. But he has also, unlike the protagonists of the heroic drama, to
look outwards and downwards at the economic and psychological
weaknesses of his position. The question posed by the play is whether his
search for personal fulfilment is compromised by his ruthless preoccupation with his social position. No matter how cynical Etherege or
Dorimant's values may be, therefore, the relationship of cleverness to
fulfilment, and so of folly to vice, is an intrinsically open question in *The
Man of Mode*, a question which can only be resolved by events. In a
World in which the crucial problem is not what arrangements ought to
be made to secure good order, but what talents and circumstances are
required to secure a man's freedom, the plot – the sequence of
adequately motivated intrigues and unforeseen complications which
are resolved by the hero's talent for improvisation – constitutes the
meaning.

In the eighteenth century, however, Jonson is replaced by Hogarth as
the representative satirist, Hobbes by Locke as the representative
philosopher, and Power and Appetite by Reason and Law as the fuel of
politics. Locke declares that 'though the law of Nature be plain and
intelligible to all rational creatures', yet the need for 'an *establish'd*,
settled, known *Law*' remains if 'The great and chief end . . . of men
uniting into commonwealths . . . the preservation of their property'⁴ is
not to be frustrated. Personal freedom in this new scheme of things
becomes a wholly private matter which must be carefully quarantined
from the crass contractual relationships which govern the World.

In such a world-view there is obviously little place for an action. In so
far as intelligence and virtue have been synthesised in prudence, and
the laws of God and man made intelligible and plain, what mysteries
remain have merely to be searched out in the corners of the
commonwealth and men's minds. Typically, the eighteenth-century
satirist's viewpoint is that of the private observer moving at random
through a complicated, densely populated society, looking for striking,
but, once properly seen, not puzzling social and psychological forms.
Jonsonian comedy, concerned with a sequence of events in a single
place and time, is irrelevant to such a search. The plot of Steele's *The
Conscious Lovers*, therefore, may derive loosely from the *Andria* of
Terence, but it is not classical in the English sense of belonging to the
Jonsonian tradition. There are no important connections, for instance,

between the complications of the Fourth Act and the dénouement in the Fifth. Even the scene for which, Steele tells us, 'the whole was writ . . ., wherein Mr Bevil evades the quarrel with his friend'[5] is wholly unprepared for and is without issue in terms of the action. Not that this is a stupid play. It is just that from the start both the legal and moral relationships of the characters to each other are intelligible and plain. The only exception is the mystery of Indiana's parentage, which is thus the one knot the action has to untangle. The plot is not therefore a testing of the relation of virtue to wit, but merely an illustration of it. In Steele's rational merchants' World, 'a play has the effect of example and precept'.

Congreve is mainly important, I believe, because he stands between these two Worlds of Etherege and Steele. . . .

[Myers's enquiry is continued below in regard to *Love for Love* (page 165) and to *The Way of the World* (page 190) – Ed.]

SOURCE: extract from 'Plot and Meaning in Congreve's Comedies', in Brian Morris (ed.), *William Congreve* (Mermaid Critical Commentary series, London, 1972), pp. 75–7.

NOTES

1. Oliver Goldsmith, 'An Essay on the Theatre; or, A Comparison between Laughing and Sentimental Comedy', in Arthur Friedman (ed.), *Collected Works* (Oxford, 1966), III, p. 212.

2. *The Plain Dealer*, I i: Gerald Weales (ed.), *The Complete Plays of William Wycherley* (New York, 1966).

3. Thomas Hobbes, *Leviathan*, ed. Michael Oakeshott (Oxford, 1957), I v 64.

4. John Locke, *Two Treatises of Civil Government*, ed. Peter Laslett (Cambridge, 1960), IX 123, 124, pp. 368–9.

5. Richard Steele, *The Conscious Lovers*, ed. Shirley Strum Kenny (London, 1968), p. 5.

Peter Holland   'Text and Performance' (1979)

On 9 November 1710, Congreve wrote to his friend Keally that 'I would send you my books, which will be published in a month'.[1] *The Works* was advertised in the *London Gazette* for 5/7 December. Though Congreve made minor revisions in the second edition of 1719–20, it is *The Works* of 1710 that provides the substantial alternative to the original quartos of the plays. Certain of the plays underwent revision in second and subsequent quarto editions, prior to 1710, but the quartos and *The Works* represent the twin poles of intention, the one substantially the text as record of performance, the other an entirely new approach to the presentation of Restoration plays as reading-texts. . . .

The 1710 edition emphasises the form of the text as a 'reading edition' through a series of devices alien to the practice of the play-quarto. There is no way in which *The Works* could mediate the stage presentation because it does not represent the shared context within which that might be possible. All the 'French' styles of the edition serve to construct an ideal, imaginary and non-specific theatrical representation divorced from Drury Lane or Lincoln's Inn Fields. The whole force of the ordinary play-quarto . . . is towards a form of shorthand, providing a simple connection that the play-reader could make with his experience as play-goer. The play-quarto, as a body of conventions, could refer back to the theatre with a small gesture, as, for example, in its indications of scene-changes. A quarto is not uninformative because its devices are perfunctory. That perfunctoriness is an indication of its methods: it 'presents' the stage; it constitutes a combination of text and performance. *The Works*, as Congreve knew, was a new departure, an entirely original approach to the presentation of contemporary drama, of the text as text, a deliberate obscuring of the actual theatrical performance in search of what a non-playgoing reader might comprehend. . . .

. . . [The] status as a reading-text rather than a memory of performance, combined with the desire to be a Terentian playwright, led Congreve to divide the plays into 'French scenes'. . . . The notion of the scene as defined by entrance or exit is enshrined in Restoration critical theory, with a distinguished ancestry. All major editions of Terence and Plautus were divided up in this fashion, from the *editiones principes* of the fifteenth century. Ben Jonson started using the system in the quartos of *Cynthia's Revels* and *Poetaster* and perfected it for *Sejanus, Volpone* and *The Alchemist*. Jonson's purpose was clearly emulation of the classical model and his folio of 1616 became in turn the new model for emulation. Comparatively few play-quartos followed the plan, though it was quite common in the first few years after the Restoration, especially for those plays written in the Interregnum and unper-formed or published in a way unconnected with theatrical norms. . . . Echard's translations of Terence and Plautus use 'scene' in this way. Hence, Terence's '*Scenes* are always unbroken, so that the Stage is never perfectly clear but between the Acts'.[2] Echard uses the word in this way throughout his preface and notes.[3] He divides his text of Plautus into acts and scenes 'according to the true Rules of the Stage'.[4] But Echard does not divide his text of Terence in this way 'because they are of no such use; only the Reader may take notice that whenever any particular *Actor* enters upon the Stage, or goes off, that makes a different *Scene*; for the *Ancients* never had any other that we know of'.[5] The scene-divisions are unnecessary because the strong internal logic of the drama diminishes the necessity of pointing up the changes of tack in the action, the introduction of new business. . . . Echard's avoidance of the scene divisions maintains a fluidity and verve that give his translations the vitality of contemporary comedy. The classical authority that the scene-divisions confer does not need to be expressed in the printed text.

Certainly, as, for example, the preface to *Love for Love* shows, Congreve always thought of a scene in the classical sense. He announces there that he allowed the cutting in performance of 'one whole Scene in the Third Act' (A4a) and, as Anthony Gosse has shown, it is a 'French' scene that was omitted.[6] But a remark of Gosse reveals how the divisions can intrude and obstruct: 'The French method of scene division, however annoying to the casual reader, is of inestimable value in calling attention to a play as an acting script and in emphasising its dramatic structure'.[7] If it was 'annoying', then that was precisely what Congreve had tried to avoid, and, if it recalled the stage, the disaster was compounded. But, as we shall see, one effect of this method, when imposed on a play not originally constructed in this way, is to blur entrances and exits and to make of each scene a unit with a separable weight of meaning, rather than to accept the fluidity and over-arching structure of the act as unit. As Hédelin warned, unmotivated scene-divisions make every scene 'as it were an *Act* by it self'.[8]

The effects are particularly marked in *The Old Batchelour* where the subtlety of the connection between the Fondlewifes and the park in Act IV (marking out Vainlove's gullibility as parallel to Fondlewife's) tends to be submerged by the apparent significance of the scenic unit. In this play too, Congreve's conscious 'de-theatralisation' produces moments as inelegant as my term to describe them. In Act I, Wittoll and Bluffe are not 'seen' by the reader to 'cross the Stage' (p. 8), but instead Bellmour remarks 'I see he has turn'd the Corner, and goes another way' (*Works* I 17). In Act II, Betty is present throughout Araminta's conversation with Belinda, so that her comment 'Did your Ladyship call, Madam?' (*Works* I 34) becomes redundant. Instead of the entrances and exits of the Footman and Betty flowing across the dialogue over Belinda's indecision, highlighting her affectation, they are grouped by the ends of scenes iv, v and vi. Similarly, the Footman is irrelevantly on stage throughout II vii so that he can give the final line of that scene. In Act III, Vainlove's exit line 'Well, I'll leave you [Bellmour] with your Engineer [Setter]' (*Works* I 49), is made meaningless as he does not leave until Bellmour does, at the end of the scene. In Act IV, the servant is apparently present throughout Bellmour's soliloquy on his disguise (IV vi). The theatrically necessary delay between Bellmour's hiding in the chamber and Laetitia's opening the door to Fondlewife disappears because the direction 'Bell. goes in' is cut and is now implicit in the end of the scene (IV xv), two lines further on.

In Act V, Heartwell and Lucy are not directed to 'appear at *Sylvia's* Door' (p. 44), but instead are assumed to be there because of Bellmour's comment. Again Congreve's concern is to reduce the visual element, the re-creation of performance that the conventional play-quarto draws attention to. In V xi, Sharper's exit is uselessly delayed until the end of the scene; in V xii, the Boy is present during Heartwell's soliloquy (Congreve cut Heartwell's 'Leave me' as well as the exit); in V xiv, Sharper does not go out and bring in Bluffe and the others but summons them instead.

Almost every one of these changes is necessitated solely by the scene-divisions. None of them adds anything to the play; most detract. Theoretic demands work against Congreve's own dramaturgic skills so that if the play is visualised as read, it appears rather inept. Congreve's careful defence of soliloquy in the preface to *The Double-Dealer* is rendered nonsensical by the observed soliloquies here. Congreve's pursuit of his ideals has pushed his most 'conventional' play into a theoretic straitjacket.

In the other comedies, Congreve's change of theory had preceded practice and the changes are fewer. In *The Double-Dealer*, the exit of Froth, Brisk and the others at I v is justified by the introduction of a *liaison de vue* (Froth's 'here is Company coming', *Works* I 171), which gives classical correctness to what would otherwise be a clear stage in the middle of an act – a point that on stage would not matter at all. Minor adjustments are made in the exits at the end of II ii and III i. The pattern of hiding in Act IV now involves three ridiculously short scenes (xv, xvi and xix). At the very end of the play, the exit of Lady Touchwood is delayed until after Lord Touchwood's sentence on her ('Go, and thy own Infamy pursue thee') and is now simultaneous with the irruption of Maskwell hauled in by Mellefont. Here again the stage direction that points up the switch in the theatre audience's attention, Mellefont's entry 'from the other side of the Stage', is deleted.

In *Love for Love*, the scene-divisions leave on 'stage', characters who ought not to remain there. In II iv, the Servant, Angelica and the Nurse are present for Foresight's brief soliloquy 'Why, if I was born to be a Cuckold there's no more to be said –' (*Works* I 355).[9] Tattle no longer ends the act with a single line *before* rushing off in pursuit of Prue ('Exit after Her' 1695, p. 33); they both leave at the same point. The song in III iii is now apparently sung by Tattle as no singer is brought on stage. . . .

In *The Way of the World*, the care over scene-divisions is twice beneficial. The division after III x for the exit of Mincing links the phrase 'the Town has found it' with 'What has it found?' rather than with 'their Folly is less provoking than your Mallice' as the misplaced exit in Q1 produced (p. 40).[10] In v viii, Sir Wilfull 'Goes to the Door and Hems', instead of going out to bring in Mirabell, a pattern of exit and immediate re-entrance that, as we have seen, Congreve tries to avoid. Barnard considers that this may be 'a detail of the original staging',[11] but, even if it is, its presence is primarily for neo-classical, rather than theatrical, reasons.

But other changes are as messily untheatrical as the ones examined before. Hence Peg's exit in III iv is shifted, leaving no time for her to fetch Foible before III v. Millamant's laughter is now more contemptuous because it sounds in Sir Wilfull's presence (IV iv) and the great moment immediately after, when Mirabell, stealing in, completes Millamant's couplet, is altered because Sir Wilfull's exit is now simultaneous with Mirabell's entrance.

Very rarely does Congreve realise the effect of an alteration and change the dialogue accordingly.[12] In spite of Anthony Gosse, the 1710 text is clumsy 'as an acting script' in a way that the quartos were not. No one would guess from *The Works* that Congreve was a brilliant theatrical craftsman, a skilled man of the theatre.

In the search for what would constitute a reading edition, Congreve's need to elevate his drama led him to choose the wrong models. In refusing to offer his readers plays as plays, Congreve found that he had no useful precedent to follow. . . . 'Since all Traditions must indisputably give place to the *Drama*, and since there is no possibility of giving that life to the Writing or Repetition of a Story which it has in the Action, I resolved in another beauty to imitate *Dramatick* Writing, namely, in the Design, Contexture and Result of the Plot.'[13] Congreve's statement in the preface to [his novel] *Incognita* indicates that from the beginning he recognised the primacy of theatrical representation over all forms of literature. There seems to be an increasingly common view that Congreve begins as a man who 'had read more plays than he had seen',[14] and by 1700 abandons the stage, contemptuous of the audience.

But there is another side to the case. In that preface to his only novel, Congreve is describing the transposition of dramatic techniques into another mode (precisely the endeavour of Richardson). Between the first drafts of *The Old Batchelour* and its eventual performance came a long period of revision with help from Dryden and Southerne; Congreve was given author's privileges of free entry at the playhouse six months before the first performance. Even after the relative failure of *The Way of the World*, Congreve wrote *The Judgement of Paris* and a part of *Squire Trelooby*, as well as taking a brief share in theatre management with Vanbrugh. For all the frustrations caused by imperceptive audiences, Congreve is, for at least as long as he was writing comedy, first and foremost concerned with the possibilities of the theatre.

Congreve's plays pose particular problems for the audience in performance, problems that cannot be reconciled with a view of the plays as moving away from the stage. The audience is deliberately confused, refused the security of expectation of what a play ought to do. The result is that the audience has to follow the chain of the play extraordinarily closely; they must pursue the syntagmatic sequence of juxtaposition and substitution. That sequence often refuses to obey traditional dramatic laws of procedure, denying rational motivation. Its movement is frequently metonymic rather than causative. Bewildered, the audience – so Congreve hoped – followed the play towards 'the artful Solution of the *Fable*'.[15] This kind of confusion, though strongly rooted in the experience of the plays in the theatre, is totally alien to Hédelin. Hédelin's view of all dramatic devices is that they should be clear. We can compare Hédelin's authoritative statement on disguise directly with Congreve. Hédelin states:

> But if it be necessary that an Actor should be *incognito* both as to his Name and Quality, in order to his being known with more pleasure towards the end of the Play, then the Spectators must at least know that he is *incognito*; and in a word all confusion must be avoided . . .[16]

Congreve wrote to Catharine Trotter, commenting on her tragedy *The Revolution in Sweden*,

> One thing would have a very beautiful effect in the catastrophe, if it were possible to manage it thro' the play; and that is to have the audience kept in ignorance, as long as the husband (which sure they may as well be) who *Fredage* really is, till her death.[17]

The greater the audience's ignorance the more it is affected. In Congreve's comedies, actions that the audience had followed with rapt attention are proved to have been made totally redundant, their purpose already circumvented. Plots and plotting fail, while the plot, the design of the play, is carried forward. Congreve's best description of his method places the emphasis on the plot as the expression of the moral and didactic purpose of his play,

> I design'd the Moral first, and to that Moral I invented the Fable, and do not know that I have borrow'd one hint of it any where. I made the Plot as strong as I could, because it was single, and I made it single, because I would avoid confusion. . . .[18]

'Confusion' here means a confusion of purpose by dividing the audience's attention between various plots. The audience is still confused by the conflict between prediction and result in the events of the play.

The consequence of overvaluing Congreve's dependence on Hédelin has been to allow critics to ignore the 'how' of the plays' methods, the distinctiveness of Congreve's approach to comedy, in pursuit of more and more refined and discriminating concepts of 'what' he was trying to say. The plays are increasingly described as if they were indistinguishable from novels. The failure of the contemporary audiences to comprehend becomes the symbol of the non-theatricality of Congreve's method. As I have already shown, reading weakens the linearity of the plot, reducing its dependence on its sequential presentation in time. But this sense of sequence, of theatrical process, is fundamental to Congreve. . . .

[Peter Holland's examination of these arguments in relation specifically to *Love for Love* are given below, in section 3 of Part Three. – Ed.]

SOURCE: extracts from *The Ornament of Action* (Cambridge, 1979), pp. 125, 126, 132, 133, 133–4, 134, 134–7, 204, 229–30.

NOTES

[Reorganised and renumbered from the original. Unless otherwise stated, references to Congreve's plays are to the first published edition – Ed.]

1. J. C. Hodges (ed.), *William Congreve: Letters and Documents* (1964), p. 60.

2. L. Echard *et al.*, *Terence's Comedies* (1694), p. vi.

3. Ibid. e.g. pp. 306, 307, 319.

4. L. Echard, *Plautus's Comedies* (1694), b2b.

5. *Terence*, p. xxii.

6. A. Gosse, 'The Omitted Scene in Congreve's *Love for Love*', *Modern Philology*, 61 (1963), pp. 40–42.

7. Ibid. p. 40.

8. F Hédelin, *The Whole Art of the Stage* (1684), III, p. 88.

9. Congreve again provides a correct *liaison* for this scene: Foresight now announces 'he's here already'.

10. The correction was made in Q2 (1706).

11. W. Congreve, *The Way of the World*, ed. J. Barnard (Edinburgh, 1972), p. 106.

12. Almost the only example is in *The Double-Dealer* where Sir Paul's 'She's a passionate Woman' (p. 60) becomes 'You're a passionate Woman' (*Works*, I 277) since Lady Touchwood has not left the stage.

13. W. Congreve, *Incognita* (1692) A6b.

14. M. Novak, *William Congreve* (New York, 1971), p. 24.

15. Dedication, *The Way of the World*.
16. F. Hédelin, op. cit., III, p. 6.
17. J. C. Hodges, op. cit., pp. 212–13.
18. Dedication, *The Double-Dealer*.

2. *THE OLD BACHELOR* AND *THE DOUBLE-DEALER*

Norman N. Holland   '*The Old Bachelor* and the Intellectual Matrix of Restoration Comedy' (1959)

. . . His first comedy, *The Old Bachelor*, proved a brilliant success when it was first produced at Drury Lane in March of 1693. There are several plots, each complex and each a comment on the others. The three principal characters are: Bellmour, a conventional Restoration gallant; Vainlove, a gallant whose humour it is to woo ladies, but if they consent, to abandon the actual 'Drudgery in the Mine' to Bellmour; and Heartwell, the title character, a surly old misanthropic bachelor who has fallen in love with Silvia. He supposes her innocent, but she has in fact been through the Vainlove-Bellmour double play. All of the plots in *The Old Bachelor*, in one way or another, are concerned with the problem of marrying an unchaste woman. Congreve dramatises in this form the constant Restoration theme of inconsistency between nature (the hidden fact of infidelity and the state of mind that accompanied it) and outward appearances (the lady's pretense of chastity). The play treats different ways of coping with this inconsistency.

Like earlier playwrights, Congreve makes his fools people who consist only of appearances and who are aware only of appearances. There are two fools in *The Old Bachelor*, Sir Joseph Wittoll and the *miles gloriosus* Captain Bluffe. They drift somewhat inconclusively through the plot, cheated by the confidence man Sharper, and in the finale they marry the leftover mistresses of the gallants. Sir Joseph Wittoll is described as a suit of clothes, 'a tawdry Outside' 'and a very beggarly Lining' (35),[1] and Captain Bluffe, 'the Image of Valour' (36), 'that Sign of a Man', 'that Pot-Gun charged with Wind' (61) who is, like a drum, 'full of blustring Noise and Emptiness' (36). These people are nothing but appearances and they believe anything anyone tells them. Sir Joseph, for example, believes Sharper when he says he was the one that saved the knight from marauders and lost £100 [11 i]; Bluffe, after Sharper has abused, cuffed, and kicked him, simply denies that these blows ever took place: ' 'Tis false – he sucks not vital Air who dares affirm it to this Face.' Sir Joseph recognises the importance of the face: 'To that Face I grant you Captain – No, no, I grant you – Not to that Face by the Lord *Harry* – If you had put on your fighting Face before, you had done his Business' (62). Both fools believe Setter (a pimp) when he says one of the high plot ladies loves them; they have no idea of the real nature of the lady or of themselves. Similarly, they marry masked women on Setter's say-so (106). Appropriately, they are punished in the dénouement by having their wives' real nature carefully pointed out to them (107). Their answer, in short, to the Restoration problem of perception is that of all the fools in the comedies: 'Ignore it; concentrate your attention on appearances alone.'

The comedy concerned with Fondlewife presents a more sophisticated answer to the problem of appearance and nature involved in marrying an unchaste woman. Fondlewife, an elderly hypocritical Puritan, has a young and beautiful wife Laetitia, who is no fonder of him than one would expect. At a party, Vainlove has made an assignation with her, but in his usual way he turns the lady over to Bellmour. Bellmour disguises himself as a parson and makes his entrance; Fondlewife returns, is assured his wife mistook Bellmour for a real parson, and, more or less consciously, allows himself to be deceived.

Fondlewife is aware (as the fools are not) of the difference between appearance and nature: 'But does not thy Wife love thee, nay doat upon thee? – Yes – Why then! – Ay, but to say truth, she's fonder of me, than she has reason to be; and in the way of Trade, we still suspect the smoothest Dealers of the deepest Designs' (69). He adds, furthermore, a new coloration to the problem: what a man wants he sees as the appearance (a loving, doting wife) but what he gets is hidden nature (infidelity). Like Heartwell, Fondlewife goes through a laughable reason-passion soliloquy, trying to resolve the difference. He tries to reason his wife into living up to his expectations (68–9). Reason, however, is not enough to overcome either his own passionate desire for his wife, or hers for satisfaction. Reason, though it tells him to avoid the trap of reality with its basic inconsistency, cannot keep him free of its appearances. When he returns and is confronted with a highly suspicious situation and a doubtful explanation, Fondlewife accepts the choice of self-deception. Belief has the power to persuade him of the existence of a nature that lives up to his desires ('As long as I believe it, 'tis well enough'), even though his belief is inconsistent with even the appearances of the situation, let alone the hidden reality: 'I won't believe my own Eyes', he finally says (90). Bellmour commends him ironically: 'See the great Blessing of an easie Faith; Opinion cannot err' (and, of course, Fondlewife as a Puritan fanatic is the ideal choice to develop this aspect of the theme):

> No Husband, by his Wife, can be deceiv'd:
> She still is vertuous, if she's so believ'd. (90)

We recognise the coldly epistemological comfort allotted to the cuckolds in *The Country Wife*.

Heartwell, like Fondlewife, knows the general inconsistency between appearance and nature, and hates and fears it. Unlike Fondlewife, however, he cannot accept the solution of a self-deception; instead, he rails at the dilemma: 'My Talent is chiefly that of speaking Truth, which I don't expect should ever recommend me to People of Quality' (34). His highest social ideal is not the hope that people will improve, but that the inconsistency will be resolved: 'I am for having every body be what they pretend to be; a Whoremaster be a Whoremaster' (33). Because he sees the trap, he does not rush into temptation, but tries to remain aloof: ' 'Tis true indeed, I don't force Appetite, but wait the natural Call of my Lust' (32).

Heartwell, though both misanthrope and misogynist, has fallen in love with Silvia, formerly Bellmour's mistress, who pretends chastity to induce Heartwell to marry her. In a soliloquy he debates with his reason against his passion, trying to escape Silvia (54), but cannot resist, and almost takes Fondlewife's way out: 'I'll run into the Danger to lose the Apprehension.' Heartwell is tempted and deluded, both by Silvia's 'dissembl[ing] the very want of Dissimulation' (53) and by his own tendency to see what he wants to see, her supposed innocence that at once torments and pleases him (65). Silvia very cleverly pretends to be the one thing dearest to the old bachelor's heart, a girl whose outward appearance and nature are the same, both 'honest'. Yet even so, Heartwell fears that she must have the same double aspect as the rest of reality: 'dear Angel, Devil, Saint, Witch', 'thou beauteous Changeling' (64). He tries to buy her, but she refuses. Then, he cannot resist and consciously asks for 'One Kiss more to confirm me mad', willingly deluding himself as Fondlewife does, but only so long as he believes she is true to his ideal.

Finally, of course, the gallants teach him again what he has known all along, that Silvia is, as all reality is, an illusion, a wish-fulfillment – that her appearance was his hope; her nature, his disappointment. He learns, in short, that

> We hope to find
> That Help which Nature meant in Woman-kind,
> To Man that Supplemental Self design'd;
> But proves a burning Caustick when apply'd. (103)

Like Manly [in Wycherley's *The Plain Dealer*], Heartwell is saved from the trap of reality by an improbable *deus ex machina*. Once he has decided to marry, he luckily fails to find his brother's chaplain. Instead, he happens to pick a Puritan fanatic to perform the ceremony. But the fanatic, *mirabile dictu*, is actually Bellmour disguised as a parson, returning from the seduction of Laetitia Fondlewife. The gallant decides to release the old bachelor from his predicament and persuades Silvia and her maid to go along with the joke. The three factors that make up Heartwell's improbable rescue are luck, the friendship of a gallant he contemns for his fawning on the ladies, and disguise, the very division between appearance and nature he despises. Heartwell's rescue is, like Manly's, improbable, but Manly's was so idealised and so unlikely that it made us think him a man with one foot in eternity. Heartwell's is less so and hence we do not feel as with Manly that there is no escape from the deception of reality but the supernatural. Instead, we feel that Heartwell trapped himself but was saved by the charity that a pretending person like Bellmour may actually have. (The gallant's disguise as a minister, while a common device, is in this case meaningful.)

The chief weakness of the play, of course, is the improbability of this episode, Heartwell's rescue. It is this incident that makes the play look like 'a hodge-podge of characters and incidents',[2] as though it were trying to suggest the amount of sheer improvisation required simply to get along in the London Heartwell faces. Heartwell himself is unwilling to improvise, and his solution – or lack of one – to the problem of appearance and nature embodied in marrying an unchaste woman is a fruitless railing at it.

Bellmour offers as a solution the same kind of tolerant acceptance of the dilemma that Freeman offered Manly. Bellmour, moreover, is the only one in the play who in the finale enters into a real marriage (with the witty and charming Belinda). He accepts with a vengeance the contradictions of existence: 'What else [but pleasure] has meaning' (25). 'Then I must be disguised – With all my Heart – It adds a Gusto to an Amour' (27). A Socratic in believing that wisdom is the ability to distinguish accidents from substance, Bellmour is hedonistic and sceptical in his doubt that such knowledge is possible or even necessary if one devotes oneself to pleasure. 'Ay, ay, Wisdom's nothing but a pretending to know and believe more than we really do. You read of but one wise Man, and all that he knew was, that he knew nothing. Come, come, leave Business to Idlers, and Wisdom to Fools: they have need of 'em: Wit, be my Faculty; and Pleasure, my Occupation; and let Father Time shake his Glass' (25–6). Bellmour accepts disguise, infidelity, and self-contradiction, and is even willing – up to a point – to be a victim: 'Why faith I think it will do well enough – If the Husband be out of the way, for the Wife to shew her Fondness and Impatience of his Absence, by chusing a Lover as like him as she can, and what is unlike, she may help out with her own Fancy. . . . The Abuse is to the Lover, not the Husband: For 'tis an Argument of her great Zeal towards him, that she will enjoy him in Effigie' (26–7). The fact that Bellmour is willing to carry on affairs with women who love Vainlove shows he is concerned with externals as the fools in the play are; it stresses again the kinship of rake and dupe in this respect (like Olivia and the Widow Blackacre or Dorimant and Sir Fopling).

Dissembling comes as naturally to Bellmour as to Silvia and the other women of the play: 'I confess, I could be well enough pleas'd to drive on a Love-Bargain in [silence] – 'twould save a Man a world of Lying and Swearing at the Years end' (51). Belinda describes their marriage as a banquet that 'when we come to feed, 'tis all Froth, and poor, but in show'; he describes it as a play, i.e., a continued pretense or disguise (102); finally, they both describe it as a prison, a 'lasting Durance' to that reality which Heartwell calls a 'Snare' (108, 107). Only Bellmour and the fools are married at the end. If he is the hero, it is with a qualification.

Vainlove offers the opposite solution, the possibility that qualifies Bellmour's answer. Like his peers Bellmour and Sharper and his servant Setter, Vainlove is a master of the arts of conversation and social pretence. Confronted with the problem of a note of assignation supposedly from his beloved Araminta, he comments, 'Now must I pretend Ignorance equal to hers, of what she knows as well as I' (80).

Very quickly he and Araminta unravel Silvia's simple forgery.

Unlike his friend Bellmour, however, Vainlove voyages on and on, refusing to come to rest and accept a lesser aim, a permanent compromise, such as marriage, wenching, or money. He refuses to marry his sweetheart Araminta at the end, just as, in his random gallantries, he enjoys the courtship but leaves the consummation to Bellmour. He insists on 'the Pleasure of a Chase'. By being always in pursuit, he sees only the idealised appearance; as soon as a woman consents, he becomes aware of the inferior inner self, becomes disgusted, and turns away. He pursues Araminta because she continually eludes his success, 'is a kind of floating Island; sometimes seems in reach, then vanishes and keeps him busied in the search' (31). 'Could'st thou be content to marry *Araminta*?' asks Bellmour. 'Could you be content to go to Heav'n?' he replies (55). He flirts with the trap of reality, but refuses to commit himself, holding off for an ideal. In Heartwell's terms, '*Vainlove* plays the Fool with Discretion' (31).

The comedy, then, leaves us with a dilemma represented by Vainlove and Heartwell on one side and Bellmour on the other. As Shaw says: 'There are two tragedies in life. One is not to get your heart's desire. The other is to get it.' Bellmour gets his heart's desire; Vainlove refuses to. In the finale, Bellmour calls his impending marriage imprisonment, while Vainlove can still speak of 'hope'. The trick of reality is, as the epilogue applies it to the way an audience treats a play:

> Just as the Devil does a Sinner . . .
> You gain your End, and damn 'em when you've done.

Coming to rest means the acceptance of something less than ideal, a thing that Heartwell and Vainlove refuse to do. Reason tells you to avoid the trap. Passion draws you into it. Only a discretion like Bellmour's can make the best bargain the limitations of the world permit; only in Vainlove's 'Heaven' is what men hope for, what they get, or appearance nature. The play does not resolve the question it raises: Which is better, Bellmour's reality or Vainlove's unrealised ideal?

The women of the play are differentiated along much the same lines, although Congreve drew them in less detailed strokes. They, too, are grouped about the basic problem of appearance and nature. Whereas the men are ranked by their ability to deal with the problem, the women rate according to their ability to create it. As Silvia puts it: 'I find dissembling to our Sex is as natural as swimming to a *Negro*' (66). It is 'natural' because sexual desire is part of their nature, but must not openly appear. Error and absurdity lie (as in earlier plays like *She wou'd if she cou'd*) in wrongful satisfaction of that desire, in letting that satisfaction appear openly, or in letting dissimulation creep in where it does not belong. Silvia is the worst offender. She does not conceal her desires, nor can she maintain for long the reputation of not satisfying them. Her deceptions are not clever. The trick of forging a note from Araminta had become very stale indeed by 1693. Appropriately, Silvia at the end is reduced to the level of her maid, who marries Captain Bluffe; Silvia marries the other fool, Sir Joseph Wittoll. Laetitia, with Bellmour's help, manages to hide her *faux pas*, though she erred earlier and lost Vainlove by letting him know he could have her. Her future, moreover, bodes no good for her: her estimable husband will probably be even more reluctant to leave her alone. As tokens of their lesser stature, both she and Silvia are forced to accept the disguised Bellmour in lieu of Vainlove.

Araminta and Belinda are in another class entirely, at the top of the scale. Belinda, however, carries her dissimulation too far in pretending to her friend that she does not love. 'Fie, this is gross Affectation', says Araminta (45), and the *dramatis personae* so describes Belinda: an 'affected Lady'. Araminta is the mistress of this delicate sort of dissimulation, as indeed she has to be to please Vainlove. She keeps an equilibrium between desire and admitting to it that corresponds to his discretion in refusing to commit himself to what might be a disappointment.

Dr Johnson calls this play 'one of those comedies which may be made by a mind vigorous and acute, and furnished with comick characters by the perusal of other poets, without much actual commerce with mankind. . . . The characters, both of men and women, are either fictitious and artificial . . . or easy and common.'[3] He is right – the characters are artificially created, but for once, I think Steele is correct when he says, 'In [this] comedy there is a necessary circumstance observed by the author, which most other poets either overlook or do not understand, that is to say, the distinction of characters. . . . This writer knows men; which makes his plays reasonable entertainments, while the scenes of most others are like the tunes between the acts.'[4] Each character is created from a single factor, his reaction to the central problem of appearance contradicting nature. While this method does not make for very lifelike characters, it does give the play a beautiful unity: every detail of character, action, and language becomes linked to the focal concept of disguise.

'The dialogue', says Johnson, 'is one constant reciprocation of conceits, or clash of wit, in which nothing flows necessarily from the occasion, or is dictated by nature,[5] and there he was right. The 'polish' of Congreve's prose is proverbial, but there seems to be no very clear idea of what that 'polish' consists. Professor Dobrée has analysed Congreve's prose rhythms in some detail and shows that he closed satiric passages with a spondee or iambic, strong endings, but used a trochee for the close of delicate passages requiring sympathy, a 'dying fall' like Fletcher's feminine double ending. Congreve used contrasts in vocal sounds to set off the antithetical parts of a sentence, and in a succession of repetitions varied the last one to stress it.[6]

Sentence structure, of course, plays an important part in creating this impression of polish. Constructed always with an element of paradox and antithesis, Congreve's sentences suggest a dialectic between general principles of human behaviour and the particular occasion of speech – Vainlove's description of Fondlewife, for instance:

> *Vainlove.* A kind of Mongrel Zealot,
> [1]   sometimes very precise and peevish:
>   But I have seen him pleasant enough in his way;
> [2]   much addicted to Jealousie,
>   but more to Fondness:
> [3]   So that as he is often Jealous without a Cause,
>   he's as often satisfied without Reason.
> [3a] *Bellmour.* A very even Temper,
> [3b]   and fit for my purpose.   (28)

Vainlove announces his topic, Fondlewife, then [1] finds a contradiction in it, [2] explores the contradiction, and [3] resolves it in a general rule about Fondlewife's behaviour. Bellmour indicates [3a] his awareness of the principle (that Fondlewife believes what he wants to believe) and [3b] relates that general principle to the particular occasion of the speech. Despite the prodigious number of subordinate clauses, Congreve keeps his prose moving by this dialectic between particular case and general rule, which is the matter as well as the style of his discourse. So too, leaving an antithesis open or unresolved tends to push the dialogue forward; closing it suggests a half-stop or full stop depending on the degree of epigrammatic or paradoxial quality in the final clause.

Even more important is the sheer number of figures of speech. Judging simply from a count of the slips on which I note such things, I would guess that there are 30 per cent more figures of speech in *The Old Bachelor* than in *The Man of Mode*. There are approximately the same number in *The Country Wife* as in this play, but *The Country Wife* is between 35 and 40 per cent longer than *The Old Bachelor*. The metaphorical density of Congreve's prose is enough greater than any we have encountered so far as to create a distinctly new impression. Like a jewel with more facets, his prose sparkles more. One would expect, however, from this density not the 'polish' we do find, but the busyness and energy we associate with Jacobean writing. The key to Congreve's style is not so much the number of metaphors but the way he handles them. While Wycherley and Etherege most often make use of what we have called the right-way-wrong-way simile, Congreve is the master of 'the language of split-man observation', which sets up the question of the extent of the speaker's involvement with the action described. Because the speaker comments dispassionately on his own actions, the 'split-man observation' divides him into actor and observer and hides in the apparent indifference created by this separation the metaphorical energy of the play. The language does not add to the intensity of the action; rather action and language each cast a comic perspective on the other. The language covers over the action much the way appearance covers nature.

The speech of Bellmour's which opens the play is a good example: '*Vainlove*, and abroad so early! good Morrow; I thought a Contemplative Lover could no more have parted with his Bed in a Morning, than he could have slept in't.' The action involved in the speech is simply one young man's greeting another and expressing interest in his current love affair. The exposition carries the information that Vainlove is in love and is a 'Contemplative Lover'. Bellmour shows his interest and involvement in Vainlove's love affair by his opening exclamation. He establishes a perspective on his interest in the second sentence by assuming the role of an observer trying rather dispassionately to relate Vainlove's appearance on the street to a general principle of human nature: that lovers sleep poorly. The metaphorical energy of Bellmour's speech is all concentrated in the general principle – the faint paradox of 'Contemplative Lover'; the implicit comparison of the bed to the person contemplated through the use of the verb 'parted' with its association of two persons parting; the contrast between thinking in bed and sleeping in bed; the image of the lover confined to his bed, yet unable to sleep in it. The language applies its force to the general principle, not the action. The forces of language and action subtract, rather than add. They pull apart, creating an outward appearance of lassitude that masks a hidden internal tension between involvement and noninvolvement. This, of course, is Congreve's sense of the comic: the felt conflict between a decorous appearance and a passionate nature. Johnson was right: practically none of Congreve's figures of speech 'flows necessarily from the occasion, or is dictated by nature', but that is Congreve's joke, and, in that sense, they do flow from the occasion.

Within the larger scheme of split-man observation, Congreve uses the tropes his predecessors prepared for him; for example, the conversion downward of abstractions or emotions to things, as when Belinda says of love: ' 'Tis in the Head, the Heart, the Blood, the – All over' (45). For the most part, however, this figure is confined to the low characters and to Heartwell, who says, 'chinking' his purse after an entertainment at Silvia's:

Why 'twas I sung and danc'd; I gave Musick to the Voice, and Life to their Measures – Look you here *Silvia*, here are Songs and Dances, Poetry and Musick – hark! how sweetly one Guinea rhymes to another – and how they dance to the Musick of their own Chink. This buys all the t'other.   (63)

Of his affections he says: 'No reflux of vigorous Blood: But milky Love, supplies the empty Channels; and prompts me to the Softness of a Child – A meer Infant and would suck' (63). It is not surprising, then, that for the most certain sign of his love for Silvia, he gives her his money (64). Fondlewife, in a similar comparison, speaks of his wife's body as 'her separate Maintenance', i.e., her trust fund, that 'she'll carry . . . about her' (89). Captain Bluffe, in one of Congreve's rare puns, converts 'mettle' down to 'metal' (41); he substitutes his sword for wit or logic: 'This Sword I'll maintain to be the best Divine, Anatomist, Lawyer or Casuist in *Europe;* it shall decide a Controversie or split a Cause –' (43–4). 'I'll pink his Soul,' he threatens Sharper (59). The gentle Sir Joseph can say to Sharper, 'I'm very sorry . . . with all my Heart, Blood, and Guts, Sir' (38). Lucy, Silvia's maid, exemplifies the figure, by thinking of her mistress's reputation as a physical thing that Vainlove and Bellmour have made a 'gap' in, 'And can you blame her if she make it up with a Husband?' (92). Setter gives the clue to the anti-heroic basis of this kind of metaphor when he, the servant, uses heroic language: 'Why, how now! prithee who art? . . . Thou art some forsaken Abigail, we have dallied with heretofore' (57).

This conversion downward of love is paralleled in physical terms by images of weight, such as Fondlewife's amusing description of adultery as 'a very weighty Sin; and although it may lie heavy upon thee, yet thy Husband must also bear his Part' (69), i.e., his horns. Bellmour, with mock sorrow, describes his promiscuity as 'too heavy' a load: 'I must take up, or I shall never hold out; Flesh and Blood cannot bear it always' (29). Thus Heartwell describes the gallants as 'Womens Asses bear[ing] greater Burdens; Are forc'd to undergo Dressing, Dancing, Singing, Sighing, Whining, Rhyming, Flattering, Lying, Grinning, Cringing, and the drudgery of Loving to boot' (33). He feels the 'Load of Life' (103) and finds women no help in carrying it; rather man becomes a beast 'and with what anxious Strife,/What Pain we tug that galling Load, a Wife' (108).

Balancing these conversions downward are comparisons that tend to point the action up toward a supernatural level; for example, Vainlove's statement that to marry Araminta would be like going to Heaven (55). Bellmour puts himself at a more earthy level when he replies that he would rather not go immediately: 'I'd do a little more good in my generation first, in order to deserve it.' Vainlove, as the highest character in the scale, is the one most given to this kind of neo-platonic imagery: the favours of a much-petitioned lady are 'due Rewards to indefatigable Devotion – For as Love is a Deity, he must be serv'd by Prayer' (48–9). Belinda, too, can talk this way: 'A Lover in the State of Separation from his Mistress, is like a Body without a Soul' (79–80); more often she laughs at a lover with 'Darts, and Flames, and Altars, and all that in his Breast' (45). Rather, she says, 'I would be ador'd in Silence' (50).

Most often these images appear ironically, as when Bellmour assures his helper he will 'confess' Laetitia (55), when he tells her eternity was in the moment of her kiss (75), or when he speaks of adultery as 'Zeal' (27). Sharper kindly explains to Heartwell, who thinks he is married to Vainlove's ex-mistress, 'Few Women, but have their Year of Probation, before they are cloister'd in the narrow Joys of Wedlock' (99–100). Setter, Vainlove's servant, describes Bellmour's plan to seduce Laetitia as going well, 'As all lewd projects do, Sir, where the Devil prevents our Endeavours with Success' (55). Even Bluffe and Wittoll come in for a bit of religion: Bluffe 'is ador'd by that Biggot Sir *Joseph Wittoll*, as the Image of Valour' (36).

Araminta sums up the tension expressed by these faintly supernatural conversions upward and bestial conversions downward when she replies to Belinda's raillery: 'Love a Man! yes, you would not love a Beast' (45). Naturally, most human relations take place neither at the exalted level of neo-platonic love imagery nor at some subhuman depth, but on a realistic plane. At this level, love is an adversary proceeding, a lawsuit to Vainlove's servant (58) or, to Sir Joseph, a military attack (78). For his major characters, however, Congreve sets up a more subtle kind of adversary relationship.

To the men, love is something that affects the inner man. From the neo-platonic convention comes the notion that love is a wound: 'By those Eyes, those killing Eyes; by those healing Lips' (75). To Heartwell, love is a disease, a folly, a madness (64) for which 'if whoring be purging (as you call it) then . . . Marriage, is entering into a Course of Physick' (34). In another sense love is something one puts inside oneself, for Laetitia is a 'delicious Morsel' (27) and even Araminta, after Vainlove received her supposed note, is 'a delicious Mellon pure and consenting ripe, and only waits thy cutting up' (72). Bellmour, when he and Belinda have resolved to marry, says to the equilibrists, 'May be it may get you an Appetite to see us fall to before ye' (108). Thus a man (as in Etherege's plays) is a hunter. Vainlove is 'continually starting of Hares for [Bellmour] to course' (27). It is not true that Vainlove cannot digest love; he can,

But I hate to be cramm'd – By Heav'n there's not a Woman, will give a Man the Pleasure of a Chase: My Sport is always balkt or cut short – I stumble over the Game I would pursue – 'Tis dull and unnatural to have a Hare run full in the Hounds Mouth; and would distaste the keenest Hunter – I would have overtaken, not have met my Game. (72)

Man's appetite for love means that he can be baited and trapped. Thus, Silvia's maid encourages her to 'Strike *Heartwell* home, before the Bait's worn off the Hook. Age will come. He nibbled fairly yesterday, and no doubt will be eager enough to Day, to swallow the Temptation' (52), for a man's passion is 'that very Hook your selves have baited' (32).

While man engulfs woman, woman engulfs man, consuming him almost as Thurber's famous cartoon suggests. Over and over again, woman is (à la Freud) a house, to Fondlewife a 'Tabernacle' (68), and to Vainlove 'the Temples of Love' (49). Heartwell thinks of his supposed wife as 'that Corner-house – that hot Brothel' (100). For a man to have a handsome wife, says Fondlewife's servant, '[if] the Man is an insufficient Husband. 'Tis then indeed, like the Vanity of taking a fine House, and yet be forced to let Lodgings, to help pay the Rent' (68). Setter calls Silvia's maid 'the Wicket to thy Mistresses Gate, to be opened for all Comers' (57), and even Belinda finds a country girl she meets 'like the Front of her Father's Hall; her Eyes were the two Jut-Windows, and her Mouth the great Door, most hospitably kept open for the Entertainment of travelling Flies' (77). A house can easily become a prison. Vainlove thus can consider himself an 'Offender' who 'must plead to his Araignment, though he has his Pardon in his Pocket' (80), and Bellmour says, when he and Belinda decide to get married, he has become a 'Prisoner', committed 'to a lasting Durance' and 'Fetters' (108). Quite literally thinking of woman as surrounding man, Heartwell calls falling in love 'to put on the envenom'd Shirt, to run into the Embraces of a Fever, and in some raving Fit, be led to plunge my self into that more consuming Fire, a Womans Arms' (54). He hesitates, but 'her Kiss is sweeter than Liberty' (66), and he suffers the 'Execution' of marriage (91, 105). His wife becomes absorbed into him so that he would have to be maimed to be divorced (105).

The paradox of man ingesting love and woman surrounding man matches on a human, realistic plane the tension between upward conversions toward Heaven, and downward conversions toward physical animality. It matches, too, the central paradox of the play: the contradiction between appearance and nature. Just as men and women consume each other, so they deceive each other. As Heartwell with great solemnity counsels the supposedly innocent Silvia: 'Lying, Child, is indeed the Art of Love; and Men are generally Masters in it: But I'm so newly entred, you cannot distrust me of any Skill in the treacherous Mystery' (64). The women are the real experts, however, for as Lucy says, 'Man, was by Nature Womans Cully made' (53). Setter, Vainlove's servant, when he sees Lucy in a mask tells her: 'Lay by that worldly Face and produce your natural Vizor', while she accuses him of being 'made up of the Shreds and Pairing of [thy Master's] superfluous Fopperies' (57).

Just as one is composed of appearances and a nature underneath them, so one is moved by these tensions but at the same time is a spectator of one's own motion. Thus, the crotchety Heartwell debates with himself before Silvia's house:

Why whither in the Devil's Name am I a going now? Hum – let me think – Is not this *Silvia*'s House? . . . Ha! well recollected, I will recover my Reason, and be gone. . . . Well, why do you not move? Feet do your Office – not one Inch; no, foregad I'm caught – There stands my North, and thither my Needle points – Now could I curse my self, yet cannot repent. . . . Death, I can't think on't – I'll run into the danger to lose the Apprehension.   (53-4)

So, too, Belinda warns Araminta: 'But you play the Game, and consequently can't see the Miscarriages obvious to every stander by' (45). Bellmour tries to persuade his beloved that 'Courtship to Marriage, is but as the Musick in the Play-House, 'till the Curtain's drawn; but that once up, then opens the Scene of Pleasure', though she insists, 'Rather Courtship to Marriage, as a very witty Prologue to a very dull Play' (102). To Congreve, each of us plays both actor and spectator and our two roles interact. In a sense, watching can change actuality, as Bellmour says, '[A Wife] still is vertuous, if she's so believ'd' (90). Understandably, this further paradox leads one quite naturally to Bellmour's hedonistic scepticism, where only pleasure has meaning and wisdom is only a pretending to know. The conflict between actor and spectator represents still another tension. . . .

SOURCE: extract from *The First Modern Comedies: The Significance of Etherege, Wycherley and Congreve* (Cambridge, Mass., 1959), pp. 132–44.

NOTES

[Reorganised and renumbered from the original – Ed.]

1. The edition to which I refer is: *Comedies by William Congreve*, ed. Bonamy Dobrée, The World's Classics (Oxford, 1925), pp. 13–109. The numbers in the text refer to pages in this edition, but they may be related to other editions by the following table:

Act I: 25–36.   Act III: 51–67.   Act V: 90–108.

Act II: 37–51.   Act IV: 67–90.

I have not listed scenes in Congreve's plays because they vary widely in the several current editions of the plays. Congreve himself dropped the sensible

English style of scene division (the scenes changing with the acts or with a change of locality), which he had used in the early quartos, and in the definitive *Works of Mr William Congreve* (1710) he adopted the French style (in which the scenes change with the entrance and exit of each character). Thus, for example, in *The Old Bachelor*, in Act IV alone, there are twenty-two scenes in Dobrée's edition, which follows the *Works* of 1710, four in Bateson's and Summers's editions, which follow the quarto, and six in the Mermaid edition.

    2. Henry Ten Eyck Perry, *The Comic Spirit in Restoration Drama* (New Haven, Conn., 1925), p. 61.

    3. Samuel Johnson, 'William Congreve', *Lives of the English Poets*, ed. George B. Hill, 3 vols. (Oxford, 1905), II, p. 216.

    4. Richard Steele, *The Tatler*, no. 193 (4 July 1710).

    5. Johnson, op. cit., p. 216.

    6. Bonamy Dobrée, 'Congreve's Life', in *Variety of Ways* (Oxford, 1932), pp. 82–3.

Anthony Gosse   Plot and Character in *The Double-Dealer* (1968)

Critical estimates of Congreve are based almost exclusively on *Love for Love* and *The Way of the World*. His two earlier comedies, *The Old Bachelor* and *The Double-Dealer*, are generally written off as apprentice works, significant only of his future development. *The Double-Dealer*, in particular, suffers an unjustifiable eclipse. Its first performance in the autumn of 1693 is usually labelled a failure by modern critics, and the comedy is judged accordingly. Though it had nothing like the popularity of *The Old Bachelor*, it was apparently a genuine *succès d'estime*. At the time of its initial production, Dryden wrote to a literary friend: '[*The Double-Dealer*] is much censured by the greater part of the Town: and is defended onely by the best Judges, who, you know, are commonly the fewest. Yet it gets ground daily, and has already been acted Eight times.'[1]

    Nevertheless, the best judges of the past two centuries have regularly levelled the same charge at the comedy to account for its 'failure'. As John Wain puts it: 'The whole play is full of disastrous and jarring changes of mood, owing to the presence of irreconcilable elements.'[2] Practically speaking, such irreconcilability is created by Maskwell, the double-dealer, and the passionate Lady Touchwood ('too near to the tragedy-queen', according to Hazlitt).[3] This critical commonplace, however, is entirely erroneous. Maskwell is no skulking villain, nor is Lady Touchwood Clytemnestra. That Betterton and Mrs Barry, for whom the roles were written, were great tragedians is true, but they were equally great in comedy and appeared in it frequently. In fact, Betterton played Heartwell in *The Old Bachelor* and Valentine in *Love for Love*, and Mrs Barry appeared as Laetitia in the former comedy and as Mrs Frail in the latter. Downes, moreover, lists *The Double-Dealer* as one of the plays that were particularly well acted during the season of 1693–94.[4] It is noteworthy that none of Congreve's immediate contemporaries objected to anything smacking of melodrama in *The Double-Dealer*. Dryden ascribes its limited appeal to its satirical exposure of female 'Bitchery' and masculine folly and deceit.[5] The impulse to shudder over its 'tragic venom' and 'monstrous vices'[6] first arose among the moralists of the 1730s, when the comedy began a period of some popularity, and is perhaps attributable to the 'solemn declamatory Way' of the actor Quin who played Maskwell.[7]

This is not to deny that Maskwell and Lady Touchwood are villainous, but to insist that they are also comical characters. Two twentieth-century revivals of *The Double-Dealer* support this view. The more important of these was the Old Vic production in 1959, a hit at both the Edinburgh Festival and in London. As might be expected, critical reaction to the acting of Maskwell and Lady Touchwood and to the general tone of the piece varied. The critics agreed, however, in praising the characterisation of Maskwell as 'bluff and honest to outward view' and in noting that 'the emotional volcano' created by Lady Touchwood did not disrupt the play.[8] As for the tone of the piece, Eric Keown remarked: 'In the extravagances of *The Double-Dealer* a good company from the Old Vic was riotously at home.'[9] The reviewer for *Theatre World* noted that 'one hardly expects to see artificial period comedy so well presented in these days'. J. C. Trewin was all but carried away by the production. Admitting that he had gone to the Old Vic expecting little, Trewin said: 'The comedy was more genuinely comic than any Restoration play I recalled . . . it has a crazy joy in life that I find infinitely and unexpectedly attractive.'[10] *The Double-Dealer* is clearly no failure as a stage comedy. For most of the reviewers it was extraordinarily funny.

But is *The Double-Dealer* really intended only to be funny? Not so, according to literary critics – some of whom find it depressing – and not according to Congreve either, who indicates his intentions both in his

'Dedication' and in the epigraphs prefixed to the title page. He says in
the 'Dedication': 'I confess I design'd (whatever Vanity or Ambition
occasion'd that Design) to have written a true and regular Comedy.'[11]
The quotations from Horace and Terence on his title page indicate the
kind of 'true' comedy he was attempting and something of his theme
and method. The former, a line from the *Ars Poetica*, suggests a more
serious concern than is usual in contemporary examples of the genre:
'Yet even Comedy at times assumes a higher tone.' The other
quotation, from Terence's serious comedy, *The Self-Tormentor*, points
out Maskwell's method of deception – an essentially comical one – and
also the nature of his villainy. The clever slave Syrus congratulates
himself: 'I give the palm to this plan; I am proud of having such force in
myself, and the mastery of such cunning as to deceive them both by
telling the truth.' Thus hypocrisy, one of the traditional themes of
Restoration comedy, is given a new twist. To deceive by telling the
truth is not only a cleverer method than lying; it is a disturbing
reflection on human nature.

In his prefatory verses to *The Double-Dealer*, Dryden also suggests
something of the serious quality of the comedy. It is important to note
that Dryden particularly commends Congreve for his 'strength': he uses
this term and its various cognates (force, judgement) nine times in the
first thirty lines of the poem. Nor by 'strength' does Dryden simply
mean that *The Double-Dealer* is a well-made play, for, as he carefully
points out, 'So bold, yet so judiciously you dare,/That your least Praise,
is to be Regular' (lines 57–8). And in this boldness lies the crux of the
problem of interpreting *The Double-Dealer*, which was not designed
simply to please the popular taste, as was *The Old Bachelor*, with obvious
targets of ridicule and conventional character types.

Though the characters of *The Double-Dealer* are ostensibly the
familiar ones of Restoration comedy, each type is treated with a
difference. The truewit libertine hero (e.g., Bellmour of *The Old
Bachelor*) becomes a villainous Maskwell, the apotheosis of Hobbesian
egotism. On the other hand, the nominal hero, Mellefont, often speaks
like a truewit, but he is too imperceptive and good-natured to act like
one. Indeed, Congreve in his 'Dedication' refers to him as 'The Hero of
the Play, as they are pleas'd to call him, (meaning *Mellefont*)' (p. 115)
and thus suggests that we are to regard him with something less than
admiration. The comical cuckold appears not only as the silly, old Sir
Paul Plyant, but also as the fatuous, youthful Lord Froth and again as
the dignified, elderly Lord Touchwood. The truewit confidant,

Careless, accomplishes a conventional seduction (that of Lady Plyant), but the witwoud Brisk ('A pert Coxcomb') also succeeds in seduction (with Lady Froth). The female dupe, traditionally an unmarried woman, becomes in Lady Touchwood the third adulteress of the cast.

Yet the action and characterisation of *The Double-Dealer* remain within an essentially comic focus. Adultery, treated as a vice in Lady Touchwood, appears so absurd in Lady Plyant and so trivial in Lady Froth that even moralists like Aaron Hill were unoffended by it: 'Their Characters are so drawn, that their *Adultery* seems less than *Simple Fornication* in another, not being of Weight enough to give any of the Actions the Stamps of *Virtue* or *Vice*.'[12] All of the characters, in fact, are so drawn as to discourage any simple siding with the good against the bad, for *The Double-Dealer* is not a comical melodrama but a 'true' comedy. It derives its 'strength' from its insistently ironic tone. Conventional responses to the conventionally good and bad figures of Restoration comedy are continually being short-circuited by its action, so that we are led to look with more censure than sympathy upon the complacent Mellefont, caught in a net partly of his own weaving; with some admiration for the daring and high spirits of Maskwell's villainy; with amusement at Lady Touchwood's furious appetites; and with a slight edge of contempt for Lord Touchwood's gullibility.

As a result, the themes of the play do not spring solely from the conventional confrontation of wisdom and folly (in Restoration terms, truewit and witwoud). Here I will distinguish between the traditional view of this conflict, so ably expressed by Norman Holland,[13] and my own. From his point of view, the play is a 'hodge-podge of tragedy and comedy' (p. 158); from mine, it is unified in tone, an ironic dark comedy. He sees Mellefont as a good man whose 'noble impulses' (p. 160) are obscured by the social context. I believe that Mellefont is only a good-natured man, the familiar *honnête homme*, like Young Bellair in *The Man of Mode*, who is described by Dorimant and Medley as 'A very pretty Fellow . . . Handsome, well bred, and by much the most tolerable of all the young men that do not abound in wit.'[14] Finally Holland says that 'the comic axis is no longer wisdom and folly, but good and evil' (p. 160). I believe, however, that the comedy is not about right and wrong *per se*, but is concerned with the interplay between a credulous goodness, presented unsympathetically as a form of folly, and an evil which expresses itself, not diabolically as in tragedy, but in the perceptive and daring pursuit of self-interest, a debased type of comic wisdom. Maskwell does not wish to destroy Mellefont but to supplant him as heir to Lord Touchwood and husband of Cynthia. Consequently, the focus of *The Double-Dealer* is on the subtle, ironic action – a disquieting analysis of one way of the world – rather than on the fortunes of the hero or on those of the double-dealer; both Mellefont's folly, signified by his complacency and inefficiency, and Maskwell's treachery prevent the spectator from sympathetic identification with either.

This is an obvious point in the case of Maskwell, or indeed of any antagonist, but in respect to Mellefont it requires justification, since our common tendency is to accept the nominal hero of a comedy as representing its ethos, especially if he is initially shown to be amiable and virtuous, as Mellefont is in Act I. Thereafter, however, Congreve carefully undermines Mellefont's heroic status, for the major intrigue of *The Double-Dealer* is made up of a series of outwitting situations in which, until the very end, the villains always triumph over the serious characters. Their triumphs, moreover, are paralleled by those of Careless and Brisk, the successful seducers in the two comic plot strands.

On the other hand, Mellefont's inefficiency – particularly signified by his credulousness – is continuously emphasised. He fails to cope not only with villainy (which culminates in Lady Touchwood's turning the tables on him at the end of Act IV, when he has her in his power), but also with folly, since the match between Cynthia and himself is broken off in Act II by his inability to convince Cynthia's stepmother, Lady Plyant, that he has no intention of seducing her. Mellefont's credulity is emphatically shown at his last appearance before the dénouement. A sudden flash of insight would by no means be inconsistent with his good nature, yet even when warned of Maskwell's suspicious behaviour by Careless and Cynthia, he replies: 'I cannot think him false' [v xv].

Mellefont's complacency is similarly emphasised. This is a key point in his characterisation, for it is Mellefont's complacency, rather than his credulity, that makes him a gull. Otherwise, he would garner the sympathy paid to virtue in distress. Thus, at the outset he is shown discarding Careless's warning about Maskwell [I iii]. At his first meeting with Cynthia, she refers to their coming marriage as a game of cards in which 'if either of us have a good Hand it is an Accident of Fortune'. The confident Mellefont compares it to a game of bowls which 'depends intirely upon Judgement' [II iii]. In the very next scene, however, he loses Cynthia and is reduced to helpless protestation by Lady Plyant's voluble appeal to him to spare her 'uncomatible' honour ('For Heav'ns sake, Madam, – '; 'Death and Amazement, – Madam, upon my Knees – '). At her exit, he sums up his situation thus: 'So then, – spight of my Care and Foresight, I am caught, caught in my Security' [II vi]. Mellefont's 'Security' is shown again in the next scene of this act and in two scenes of the following act [III ii & iv].

Act IV begins with an encounter between the serious couple in which Cynthia issues the traditional challenge of the Restoration heroine to the hero to win her with his wit. Significantly, she refuses to elope with Mellefont on the following grounds:

If you had not been so assured of your own Conduct I would not [refuse to elope] – But 'tis but reasonable that since I consent to like a Man without the vile Consideration of Mony, he should give me a very evident Demonstration of his Wit: Therefore let me see you undermine my Lady *Touchwood*, as you boasted, and force her to give her Consent. . . . [IV i]

When Mellefont goes off to undermine Lady Touchwood, he exclaims: 'Now Fortune I defie thee'–a remark that elicits Maskwell's dry comment: 'I confess you may be allow'd to be secure in your own Opinion' [IV xii & xiii].

Cynthia and Lord Touchwood, the other good characters, also share Mellefont's credulity. Lord Touchwood, easily persuaded by his wife to disinherit Mellefont [III i] before the table-turning incident at the end of Act IV, is Maskwell's cuckold and dupe. Cynthia, too, trusts Maskwell, who persuades her (off stage) to elope with Mellefont, despite his failure to meet her challenge, a condition of their marriage. Her explanation of her change of heart is at odds with her behaviour: 'I find I have Obstinacy enough to pursue whatever I have once resolv'd; and a true Female Courage to oppose any thing that resists my Will, tho' 'twere Reason it self' [v ix].

Though Cynthia speaks of obstinacy, she allows Maskwell to talk her into doing exactly what she had refused Mellefont earlier. With her, as with Mellefont and Lord Touchwood, word and deed tend to pull apart. Norman Holland points out instances of this tendency in the comic plots of *The Double-Dealer* where 'figures of speech enlarge the most trivial actions to epic proportions' (p. 152). These verbal ploys in the comic plots, however, are only reflectors of the fundamental discrepancy between word and action in the serious as well as in the villain plots. Maskwell's double-dealing by means of truth-telling lies is not simply a comic gimmick, but denotes the basic metaphor of the action. His deliberate deception is paralleled by the self-deception of both serious and comic characters who, ironically, are constantly demanding 'Mathemacular Proof' and 'Demonstration'. Moreover, to underline his ironic treatment of the good, Congreve draws his serious characters with traces of mediocrity in their persons, a term applied to Mellefont by Lady Froth [II i]: Cynthia's priggishness, for instance, at her first appearance [II i] and Lord Touchwood's offer to 'purchase' her for Maskwell [v iii] and to cover up Maskwell's betrayal of his friend Mellefont [IV xiv].[15]

The point of Mellefont's – and of the good characters' – inability to recognise, let alone deal with, evil is finally made by Maskwell in a soliloquy in the middle of the last act, which serves more accurately than the official concluding moral to summarise the ethos of the comedy: 'Why, *qui vult decipi decipiatur.* – 'Tis no Fault of mine, I have told 'em in plain Terms, how easie 'tis for me to cheat 'em; and if they will not hear the Serpent's Hiss, they must be stung into Experience, and future Caution' [v xi].

The actual moral of *The Double-Dealer* serves mainly to emphasise its ironic action. The comforting notion that secret villainy is self-defeating is enunciated by the principal victim of the comedy, Lord Touchwood, whose cuckoldry has become a public scandal. In contrast, the secret villainy of Brisk and Careless in cuckolding Lord Froth and Sir Paul Plyant shows every sign of continuing success, perhaps even to the benefit of its trusting victims. Sir Paul, at least, may get the heir he desires. Most importantly, the moral points back to the crowning irony of the action, the fact that the 'hero', Mellefont, succeeds only by chance, as a result of Cynthia and Lord Touchwood overhearing a violent quarrel between the two villains. Congreve, in fact, emphasises this fortuity. Ignorant of his real enemy, Maskwell, and unable to outwit his overt enemy, Lady Touchwood, Mellefont is actually running away with Cynthia (and into a trap prepared by Maskwell) when the happy accident of the overheard quarrel occurs [v xvii]. This incident, moreover, is heralded in an earlier scene: Careless – by chance – overhears one of Lady Touchwood's outbursts to her husband, and is confirmed in his suspicion of Maskwell [v xiv].

In his plotting of *The Double-Dealer*, Congreve achieves his general goal of subordinating villainy to a comic action by creating five plot strands from his three types of characters (serious, comic and villain), by separating his villain plots from his comic, and by de-emphasising the basically villainous characterisation of Maskwell and of Lady Touchwood – that is, he avoids making them heavies.

The first act offers a good example of Congreve's way of handling villainy. The three major groups of characters are introduced successively in three blocks of scenes: serious (i–iii), comic (iv–v), and villain (vi). Mellefont, on stage in the first two blocks, has the longest part in this act and dominates the serious group. Congreve emphasises his status as 'hero' in a number of other ways as well. His opening speeches with Careless show that both are truewits, as indicated by the quality of their diction, their references to 'reason' and 'sense', and the distinctions they draw between themselves and the fools of the cast. Their status is reinforced in the second scene by their contrast with one of the fools, Brisk, and by Brisk's open admiration for Mellefont. The third scene continues to build up Mellefont, for he is shown confidently setting up his defences against Lady Touchwood. For well over a third of the opening act, Mellefont is presented not only as the conventional comic hero dominating the action, but also, and unconventionally, in a morally commendable light. He is neither cynic nor rake in respect to his uncle, Lord Touchwood, and his uncle's wife.

The second group of scenes (iv–v) introduces the comic action. The mood of these scenes is literally festive; three families are gathered to celebrate a marriage. Mellefont, with but two lines of dialogue in Scene iv, fades into the background, especially since the comical characters are all tipsy. The silent contrast not only emphasises his well-bred composure, but also foreshadows his essentially passive role in the coming action.

The concluding, and longest, scene of Act I, introducing Maskwell and Lady Touchwood, is dramatically the most powerful and illustrates Congreve's principal aesthetic problem: how to prevent the forceful note of villainy from destroying the comic tone. To do so, he exploits all of the potentially ridiculous aspects of character and situation, while at the same time keeping audience sympathy on the side of Mellefont. Both Maskwell and Lady Touchwood are depicted, not as truewit opponents of a gullible Mellefont, but as clear-cut villains. Mellefont's credit as hero remains intact in order to focus the scene on Maskwell's treachery.

Essentially, the action is one of quarrelling followed by gulling. It is based on a traditional comic situation, a virago of a mistress berating an insolent servant, who alternately fans and cools her temper for his own amusement. Comical elements in the characterisation of both villains are also clearly delineated in this scene. Maskwell is more obviously comical than Lady Touchwood, but to see her as a member of the 'house of Laius', as Macaulay does,[16] is a serious misunderstanding of her characterisation. True, she is lustful, malicious, unscrupulous, and dangerous; but she is also ridiculous. Her tirades are undercut by their excessiveness, by the mechanical nature of her emotional responses, and by her hypocrisy. This is particularly evident in the first half of the scene in her quarrel with Maskwell, where she is abusive and sanctimonious by turns. Only one of her outbursts appears to strike a tragic note:

O, *Maskwell*, in vain I do disguise me from thee, thou know'st me, knowest the very inmost Windings and Recesses of my Soul. – Oh *Mellefont!* I burn; married to Morrow! Despair strikes me. Yet my Soul knows I hate him too: Let him but once be mine, and next immediate Ruin seize him.

The rhythm, the Medean suggestion of labyrinth and burning, and the confession of helplessness in these lines may suggest – out of context – the painful self-knowledge that evokes sympathy, but not in the scene itself where they clash with the facts of her situation (she wants her current lover, Maskwell, to help her seduce Mellefont). Moreover, as Lady Touchwood's mood modulates from her desire to possess Mellefont to her intention to destroy him, the imagery of her lines follows a progressively reductive, hence comic, course – from the climactic intensity of 'Despair strikes me' to the comparative flabbiness of 'and next immediate Ruin seize him'. In Lady Touchwood, Congreve is parodying the rhetoric of Restoration tragedy. The critical failure to distinguish between her rant and the real thing is similar – as in the case of Congreve's comic dialogue – to the insensitivity of some of his contemporaries to the difference 'betwixt the Character of a *Witwoud* and a *Truewit*,' which he complains of in the 'Dedication' of *The Way of the World*.

Emphasising comical potentialities in the character of Maskwell and Lady Touchwood is not the only method Congreve employs to subordinate villainy to comedy. He also separates his plot into five different strands. The serious lovers, Mellefont and Cynthia, make up one of these strands. Two are created by the comical characters: Careless's seduction of Lady Plyant, and Brisk's of Lady Froth. The two villain plots grow out of the efforts of Lady Touchwood and Maskwell to prevent the marriage of Mellefont to Cynthia. Lady Touchwood's motive is to ensnare Mellefont for a lover; Maskwell's to betray Lady Touchwood as well as Mellefont by disinheriting him and marrying Cynthia.

Congreve arranges these strands in his general plot in order to maintain a predominantly comic tone and, at the same time, to exploit the relationship between Mellefont and Maskwell for sensational effects. Throughout the first four acts of *The Double-Dealer,* he subordinates the villain plots to the others. The two comic plots take up over half of the number of lines in these acts, and the serious plot, a quarter of them. Having established his tone, Congreve reverses the relationship among the plots in the fifth act, given over to the turns and surprises created by the villains. Half of its lines belong to Maskwell and Lady Touchwood, one-third to Mellefont, Cynthia, and Lord Touchwood, and a handful apiece to the six characters in the comic plots. Despite this apparently daring reversal of emphasis, the plot of *The Double-Dealer* is, in fact, quite orthodox in the manner in which it conforms to neoclassical 'rules' governing comic tempo, which prescribe four acts of gaiety and mounting suspense followed by a rapidly accelerating conclusion.

Each of the three types of plot is distributed in the acts according to a different pattern. All of the scenes of the villain plots within an act are grouped and placed either at the beginning or end of it. In the over-all structure, there are only three such groups: at the end of Act I; at the end of Act II and beginning of Act III; at the end of Act IV and beginning of Act V. As a result, the three groups of scenes dominated by villains are isolated in the action. Moreover, the stretches of comic and serious action before each villain group are considerable: the first takes up 327 lines; the second, 413; and the third, extending from the early part of Act III to the latter part of Act IV, 959 lines.

The isolation of the villains is further emphasised in their relationships with the other characters. Throughout the first four acts, they appear only with Mellefont or Lord Touchwood of the serious plot. It is well along in the final act before a comic character, Sir Paul Plyant, meets a villainous character, his sister, Lady Touchwood [v viii]. In two brief following scenes, the serious Cynthia encounters Maskwell for the first time in the action.

Congreve's method of handling his comic, serious, and villain plots is essentially one of contrast, as in the tragicomedy of the period. In attempting to achieve a unity of tone in his comedy, Congreve could have blended characters and scenes of villainy with those of comedy. The confrontation of Brisk and Lady Touchwood, for example, or Maskwell and Lady Froth, is potentially comic. But since the preparation of the villains' elaborate intrigues requires a large number of scenes, few could be spared for merely episodic encounters. Thus, in order to harmonise the villainous, serious and comic actions, Congreve insulates his villain plots within long blocks of predominantly comic intrigue so that the clash of opposing tones will result in a heightening of both rather than in a reduction of one by the other, or in a standoff. Such isolation may also be thematic as well as tonal, suggesting not so much an inherent quality of evil itself – a subject fitter for tragedy – but rather, through the concentrated impact of the villains' occasional appearances, the havoc that even small doses of clear-sighted cunning can create in a society grown soft.

Unlike the grouping of scenes in the villain plots, those in which the serious lovers appear are distributed evenly in the five acts. Although in the first four acts the number of lines of dialogue given to Mellefont and Cynthia is roughly the same as that given to the two villains, the scenes in which one or both appear take up more than twice as much of the action.

The characters in the two comic plots are given more than half the lines of dialogue in the first four acts, and the scenes in which they appear take up nearly two-thirds of the action. Their purpose is principally tonal, though the Plyant plot motivates a minor strand of the main intrigue. Careless's seduction of Lady Plyant is the more important of the two comic plots, especially in the third and fourth acts, in which it is given twice as many lines of dialogue as the Brisk-Froth plot. Its stronger comic effect is Congreve's principal reason for emphasising the Plyant rather than the Froth plot. Sir Paul's farcical humours and the conflict within Lady Plyant of 'preciseness' and carnality are better able to offset the force of Maskwell's malicious glee and Lady Touchwood's ravings than the airy figures of affectation – Brisk, 'A pert Coxcomb', and Lady Froth, 'A great Coquet'.

In addition to his careful grouping of characters and manipulating of plot strands, Congreve achieves a 'true' comic tone through the use of innumerable parallelisms in both language and incident. The successful double-dealing of Careless and Brisk is, of course, the major parallelism of action. Chance discoveries by their victims occur, as in the main plot, as well as the farcical device of the soliloquy contrived to be overheard. The use of the latter in the comic plot, prior to its use in the serious action, modifies our reaction to Lord Touchwood when he is thus deceived by Maskwell.

Linguistically, the most significant parallelism lies in the employ-ment of similar cant in all of the plot strands. Lady Froth's 'heroic' poem, *The Sillabub*, is an inane counterpart to the tragic 'venting' of

Lady Plyant in defence of her 'Honour'. Careless, in fact, twice uses the term 'cant' in describing his role as her whining lover [III v; IV ii]. In the serious plot, both Mellefont and Lord Touchwood fall into the type of tragic cant that Lady Touchwood and Lady Plyant indulge in. Aside from their triteness, such outbursts are either qualified by context (Mellefont blaming others or fate for his own ineptness) or rhetorically reductive. 'Incest', for example, is first raised in regard to Mellefont's actions by the comical Lady Plyant, Cynthia's stepmother, when she accuses him of planning to seduce her [II v]. It is subsequently applied to him ('incestuous Brute!') by Lord Touchwood when his wife hints that he has been making advances to her [II i]. The term receives its final charge of comical meaning in the table-turning scene with Lady Touchwood ('–so damn'd a Sin as Incest! unnatural Incest!') where the adjective emphasises its ridiculousness [IV xx].

There is little reason to doubt that Congreve wrote *The Double-Dealer* with its original cast in mind. With but one acting company in London playing a stock repertory, many of the character types of *The Old Bachelor* reappear in *The Double-Dealer*. Verbruggen, Williams, Dogget, Mrs Bracegirdle, and Mrs Mountfort repeat their earlier roles. Betterton, the leading actor of the company, would, as a matter of course, play Maskwell. However, though Lady Touchwood belongs to the same general type of character as Silvia in *The Old Bachelor*, the role is given not to the youthful and relatively inexperienced Mrs Bowman, the original Silvia, but to the famous Mrs Barry. The casting of Powell, rather than Bowen, in the role of Brisk is also surprising. Powell usually played the rakish truewit, as he did in the part of Bellmour in *The Old Bachelor*. Brisk, on the other hand, is the forerunner of Witwoud, Bowen's part in *The Way of the World*. One might have expected Congreve to give Careless either to Powell or Verbruggen, and Brisk to Bowen. Wanting as strong a cast as possible, he decided to use both Powell and Verbruggen. Their parts are of almost equal length. Moreover, Brisk, unlike the typical pert coxcomb, is not an unsuccessful suitor of the heroine, but the seducer of Lady Froth.

Congreve's cast for *The Double-Dealer* indicates the importance of his comic plots. The third largest part in the play is that of Sir Paul Plyant, played by Dogget, whose Fondlewife in *The Old Bachelor* had been a sensational success at the end of the previous season. Lady Plyant, the fourth largest part, was taken by Mrs Leigh with twenty years' experience playing comic maids and lecherous middle-aged women (seven years later she appeared as Lady Wishfort in *The Way of the World*).[17] Verbruggen, who played Careless, was at that time a contender for the role of *jeune premier* in the company. Powell, the other contender, and Mrs Mountfort – the Bellmour and Belinda of *The Old Bachelor* – played Brisk and Lady Froth. This particular combination, as well as Brisk's successful seduction, obviously gives more weight to the comic action than if the parts had been played by Mrs Bowman and Bowen. Indeed, in the revivals of the play in the early decades of the eighteenth century, Lady Froth's Part, rather than Cynthia's, was usually taken by the leading young actress of the company.[18] Mrs Bracegirdle's subsequent career, especially in the roles written for her by Congreve and Rowe, obscures the fact that in 1693 Mrs Mountfort, a veteran actress at the age of twenty-six, was her equal, if not superior, in comedy.

With a cast as strong as this, *The Double-Dealer* is not likely to have suffered in the acting. Its modest reception in 1693 is attributable, in the main, to the stiff demands it made on its spectators, for its ultimate aim was at its own audience, not at some safe outside target, such as the cuckolded cit or booby country squire.[19] In the person of Mellefont, the virtues of the gentry were satirised as complacency and gullibility, and their vices exposed in the naked egoism of Maskwell. The plot itself with its constant teasing of expectation would have doubly irritated those who found it impossible to side wholly with or against either man.

It is clear from his subsequent playwriting career that Congreve did not regard *The Double-Dealer* as faulty in principle. His next comedy, *Love for Love*, is only superficially a rambling humours comedy harking back to the form of his popular *Old Bachelor*. Its mocking, enigmatic treatment of romantic love is not far removed from the portrayal of credulous goodness in *The Double-Dealer*. *The Double-Dealer*, moreover, is essentially the same kind of serious comedy that Congreve chose as his valedictory – and the fate of *The Way of the World* is well known. Like *The Double-Dealer* it struggled for some decades to achieve any real measure of popular success, and even today its theatrical qualities are commonly underrated.

SOURCE: essay in *Modern Language Quarterly*, XXIX (1968), pp. 274–88.

NOTES

1. Charles E. Ward (ed.), *Letters of John Dryden* (Durham, N. C., 1942), p. 63. *The Double-Dealer* also had a command performance attended by Queen Mary

and her maids of honour in January 1694. Swift wrote a lengthy poem in praise of it: 'To Mr Congreve', in J. Horrell (ed.), *Collected Poems of Jonathan Swift* (London, 1958), I, pp. 36–43. An anonymous London correspondent wrote in March 1694: 'The Double Dealer is artfully writt, but the action being but single, and confined within the rules of true comedy, it could not please the generality of our audience, who relish nothing but variety, and think any thing dull and heavy which does not border upon farce' – cited in 'An Historical Account of the English Stage', in Edmond Malone (ed.), *Plays and Poems of William Shakespeare* (London, 1821), III, pp. 162–3.

2. John Wain, 'Restoration Comedy and its Modern Critics', *Preliminary Essays* (London, 1957), p. 9.

3. 'On Wycherley, Congreve, Vanbrugh and Farquhar', *Lectures on the English Comic Writers*, in P. P. Howe (ed.), *Complete Works of William Hazlitt* (London, 1931), VI, p. 72. [See Part Two, above, for excerpts from this lecture – Ed.]

4. John Downes, *Roscius Anglicanus*, ed. Montague Summers (London, n.d.), p. 42.

5. Dryden: 'The women thinke he has exposd their Bitchery too much; & the Gentlemen, are offended with him; for the discovery of their follyes: & the way of their Intrigues, under the notion of Friendship to their Ladyes Husbands' – *Letters*, op. cit., p. 63.

6. Leigh Hunt (ed.), *Dramatic Works of Wycherley, Congreve, Vanbrugh, and Farquhar* (London, 1840), p. lxxix.

7. Emmett L. Avery, *Congreve's Plays on the Eighteenth-Century Stage* (New York, 1951), pp. 72, 89.

8. H. G. M., 'The Double-Dealer', *Theatre World*, LV (Oct. 1959); Anon., 'Restoration Comedy Restored', *The Times* (8 Sept. 1959).

9. E. Keown, 'At the Festival', *Punch* (9 Sept. 1959), p. 151.

10. J. C. Trewin, 'Promise', *Illustrated London News* (12 Sept. 1959), p. 246.

11. *The Double-Dealer*, in Bonamy Dobrée (ed.), *Comedies by William Congreve* (Oxford, 1925), p. 113. This edition, based on the *Works* (1710), preserves Congreve's division of the acts into French scenes: a means of calling attention to the play as an acting script and of emphasising its dramatic structure. [Texts based on the Quarto edition follow the same Act numbering. For a contrary view on the 'performance utility' of the 1710 revision of scene-divisions, see Peter Holland's piece, above – Ed.]

12. Aaron Hill, in *The Prompter* (11 Nov. 1735).

13. N. N. Holland, *The First Modern Comedies* (Cambridge, Mass., 1959), pp. 149–60.

14. H. F. B. Brett-Smith (ed.), *Dramatic Works of Sir George Etherege* (Oxford, 1927), II, p. 201 [I i 422–6].

15. For a view of *The Double-Dealer* as an attack on the aristocracy, see W. H. Van Voris, *The Cultivated Stance: The Designs of Congreve's Plays* (Dublin, 1963), pp. 57–61, 75–6.

16. T. B. Macaulay, *Edinburgh Review*, LXXII, No. 146 (Jan. 1841), p. 515. [See Part Two, above, for excerpts from this essay – Ed.]

17. John H. Wilson, *All the King's Ladies: Actresses of the Restoration* (Chicago, 1958), pp. 162–5.

18. Avery, op. cit., pp. 182–7.

19. In his vituperative 'Dedication' to the first quarto, Congreve concludes his defence of *The Double-Dealer* with this remark: 'I hear a great many of the Fools are angry at me, and I am glad of it; for I Writ at them, not to 'em.' This and a number of similar comments do not appear in the *Works* (1710) or in subsequent editions, but appear in Montague Summers (ed.), *Complete Works of William Congreve* (London, 1923), II, pp. 9–12.

Anne Barton   'Uneasy But Brilliant Poise: *The Double-Dealer*' (1973)

. . . In many ways, *The Double-Dealer* marks a turning point, not only in Congreve's own development as a dramatist, but in the history of Restoration comedy as a form. *The Old Bachelor*, although it was written well after the death of Charles II, is like Etherege's *She Wou'd If She Cou'd* (1668) or *The Man of Mode* (1676) in its attitudes, character types and basic structure. *The Double-Dealer* is not a sentimental comedy, but it does reflect Congreve's awareness of the changed temper of the 1690s. Even before Collier launched his attack, many comic dramatists had begun to rehabilitate traditional moral values in their plays, to look askance at the Restoration idol of wit for wit's sake, to introduce tragic elements into their comedies, and to regard uncontrolled displays of emotion, however untidy, with respect. Some went so far as to recommend rural life and suggest that parental authority ought to be respected. In *The Double-Dealer*, Congreve accommodated himself to some of these revised attitudes, while insisting upon remaining faithful – as his contemporaries, on the whole, did not – to the honesty and intellectual toughness of the Restoration and to all that was best in the comedy of Etherege.

The epigraph from Horace's *Ars Poetica* with which Congreve introduced the 1694 quarto (*Interdum tamen, vocem Comoedia tollit:* Yet, sometimes, Comedy raises her voice) was obviously meant to prepare readers for Lady Touchwood's passion and violence, the dark strain in the play which the Theatre Royal audience had found perplexing, and to claim classical sanction for its stridence. In the dedication, Congreve made a further appeal to classical authority by stressing the 'true and regular' nature of his comedy and, in particular, his strict observance of the three unities. In fact, this was special pleading. Neo-classical critics were agreed that the main function of the unities was to ensure *verisimilitude*. An audience which did not have to indulge in 'make-believe' about stage time and place was, supposedly, better able to credit the fiction of the play. Congreve, however, although he does not admit to such a strategy in the dedication, employed the unities as perversely as Shakespeare had in *The Tempest*: not to increase the realism of his plot, but to make it more strange, indeed dreamlike in its effect.

All the action of *The Double-Dealer* takes place in the gallery, and one adjoining room discovered when the *Scene* opens briefly in Act IV, of Lord Touchwood's country house near St Albans. Characters are drawn into this circumscribed space in ways that seem increasingly unreal: combining in small groups, drifting apart on individual errands, re-entering to form different groups. Only the gallery and Lady Touchwood's closet are actually visible, yet the audience is constantly being asked to imagine the whole of the great house and its surroundings: the various other rooms downstairs and on the same level into which characters vanish, or from which they have just come, the autumn gardens into which Mr Brisk retires with Lady Froth on the pretext of an interest in astronomy. There is nothing in Restoration comedy before Congreve like *The Double-Dealer*'s atmospheric and almost eerie treatment of place.

The unity of time is equally idiosyncratic. Congreve compressed the entire action of his comedy into three hours. The amount of plot handled in this short span is unrealistically great but, instead of glossing over this fact, Congreve went out of his way to emphasise it. Some fourteen references scattered throughout the play establish the precise hour at almost any point. It is impossible, as a result, not to realise that the little intrigues of Lady Froth and Lady Plyant blossom with unnatural swiftness, that Maskwell's schemes are far too intricate for the three hour space in which they unfold. The action acquires an hallucinatory quality, to which the diabolic imagery surrounding Maskwell, and the senseless, hysterical laughter indulged in continually by most of Lord Touchwood's guests, also contribute. Certainly, the clock which rules the comedy is not that of a normal, or waking, world.

Unity of action was a more common feature of Restoration comedy. In *The Double-Dealer*, Cynthia and Mellefont stand at the centre of the play. All the events, all the other characters, relate and are subservient to them. A thematic preoccupation with marriage radiates naturally from the desire and yet the hesitation of these lovers on the night before their wedding, working itself out at a comic extreme in the adulteries and strained loyalties of the Froths and Plyants, impinging upon tragedy in the disintegration of the Touchwood marriage. Cynthia and Mellefont are like many earlier Restoration couples in that their psychological doubts about matrimony represent almost as great a stumbling block to their union as do the machinations of their enemies. What puzzled the original Theatre Royal audience was not this, but their credulity and essential passivity. As nightmare waves of action, the result of Maskwell's and Lady Touchwood's plot to prevent their marriage, break over them, Cynthia retreats more and more into introspection, while Mellefont helplessly allows himself to be manipulated by an enemy he has mistaken for a friend.

Ultimately, Cynthia and Mellefont control the play, but not through intelligence or any effort of will. It seems to be a dramatic law in *The Double-Dealer* that any character who seriously threatens the happiness of the lovers at the centre invites his or her own destruction. Maskwell and his mistress Lady Touchwood are both condemned according to a strict moral code. Both are punished severely at the end for actions which Congreve nowhere treats as funny. Yet the comedy also contains a number of characters among whom the same sins of hypocrisy, affectation, adultery and deceit are not only hilarious: they flourish securely at the end of the play, even as they did at the beginning. Although it is true that the gyrations of the Froths, the Plyants and Mr Brisk present Cynthia and Mellefont with a disturbing picture of marriage, and so confirm them in their fears, these characters are not tangibly dangerous. Congreve allows them to retain their joyous self-absorption throughout the final scene, balancing it deliberately against the anguish of Lord Touchwood – a cuckold who is emphatically not ridiculous, as Sir Paul Plyant is – the violence of Maskwell's and Lady Touchwood's ruin, Mellefont's bitter awakening. Thanks to what feels almost like the shift in atmosphere of a dream, the simultaneous rise of suspicion in three different people, the wolf's face has suddenly become visible beneath the jovial mask of Mellefont's friend. All is revealed: the two serious adulterers are condemned, the union of the young lovers confirmed. The fools, however, remain themselves, their reaction to it all typified by the languid comment of Lady Froth, who has just been seduced under the stars by Mr Brisk: 'You know I told you Saturn look'd a little more angry than usual'. Congreve claimed in his dedication to Montague that he had designed the Moral of the comedy first, and then invented a Fable to embody it. In fact, moral rigour is combined throughout the play with a large measure of tolerance. In this respect, as in its intensely individual treatment of time, place, action and character, *The Double-Dealer* maintains an uneasy but brilliant poise between the comedy of the Restoration itself and that of the century to come.

Source: Introductory Note to the Scolar Press facsimile reproduction (London, 1973) of the 1694 Quarto edition of *The Double-Dealer*.

3. *LOVE FOR LOVE*

Malcolm M. Kelsall   'Flirting with
Experience' (1969)

. . . Whatever refinements of interpretation one may place on it, *Love for Love* is primarily a stage comedy and it is upon the theatrical effectiveness of action and style that it must mainly be judged. One instance may initially suffice [Miss Prue is speaking]:

Look you here, madam, then, what Mr Tattle has given me. Look you here, cousin, here's a snuff-box; nay, there's snuff in't; – here, will you have any? – O good! How sweet it is. – Mr Tattle is all over sweet, his peruke is sweet, and his gloves are sweet, and his handkerchief is sweet, pure sweet, sweeter than roses. – Smell him, mother, madam, I mean. He gave me this ring for a kiss.   [II i]

This has little to do with Hobbes, Locke, Mycenean villages, Christian allegory, or moral uplift. But it is good theatre. The whole circle of actors upon the stage are drawn into the comedy: Miss Prue in triumphant rustic naïvety now launched into the way of the world, about to take snuff (the most unladylike of habits), and remembering, almost, to call her stepmother madam; the ladies themselves recoiling from the odious snuff-box; sweet Mr Tattle overwhelmed (perhaps) with embarrassment at Miss Prue's profession of his arts and proclamation of his seductive charms. Moreover, even Henry James does not always achieve a limpidity of expression to match this passage from Congreve; and, whatever the sexual insights to be gained in the woods near Wragby, D. H. Lawrence cannot always express the grossness of sensuality in prose at the same time so physically suggestive and comically ridiculous. Miss Prue is indeed gross and trivial, but, surely, as a stage creation, she is not dull.

Although the judgement of stage drama in relation to the novel is of limited viability, the comparison with James, at least, is valuable. James found Congreve 'insufferable', but perhaps envy resides in proximity, for both were writers whose foremost concern was with the perfecting of their art. Praise has always been lavished by Congreve's admirers on the harmonies of his prose, but this concern for the lustre of language was merely one aspect of his Augustanism – his determination as a self-conscious dramatic craftsman to polish to its highest lustre matter traditionally given; not to make things new, but to make them with greater elegance. Hence, since his material is in its origin literary, from Terence, from Jonson or Molière, from the whole European tradition of classical comedy, he is a writer not concerned with holding the mirror up to his own society, which provides merely the local colouring for traditional stage action, but rather with holding the mirror up to Nature: that idealised world of neo-classical literary aspiration which art strove to create, although the Augustan usually claimed merely to imitate. The aim of the dramatist was to realise, in the artifact, perfect form, to create a world of ideal or universal types – what Lamb calls, in the sloppy language of Romantic criticism, first Utopia, and then a 'dream' world. When Congreve was not up on a high horse trying to defend himself from Collier by claiming a moral justification for his satire[1] – his defence everyone agrees is feeble – he writes as an artist, not as a moralist. He envies Terence because his material was given him (from Aristotle via Menander); and thus Terence, in his drama, could concentrate upon 'purity' of style, and 'justness' (conformity to type) of manners.[2] Congreve speaks in his own work of the problem of displaying and arranging each character, 'how much of it, what part of it to show in light, and what to cast in shades; how to set it off by preparatory scenes, and by opposing other humours to it in the same scene.'[3] He makes characters in order to display various extravagant 'humours' (dominant traits), or 'affectations' in manners or eccentricities in speech, but he does not explore the moral consciousness. He represents Nature; he is not a social historian. He does not see his plays as intellectual or epistemological dilemmas, but as artifacts in a traditional 'kind', the genre 'Comedy' as practised by his great predecessors.

Love for Love is probably the closest to 'pure' art of all his comedies. The triangle lover-mistress-hostile father was old even to Thespis. Terence would have called Jeremy, Davus. Miss Prue, the not so innocent country maid; Mrs Frail, the ageing woman eager for marriage, are Restoration stock in trade. Even sailor Ben has his forefathers. The astrologer, Foresight, the most famous of Congreve's humour characters, is a fabrication from literary theory. Social history may tell one something about the status of astrology in Congreve's day (even Dryden, a member of the Royal Society, cast horoscopes); in the debunking of Foresight one may see something of the effect of the Enlightenment upon literature; and in the satire on false science one may find a rational purpose in the comedy – but Foresight is an imaginative fabrication, a creation of literary fantasy working from literary theory, a type, not a character one *recognises*, or if one recognises, only in the most general manner. The art is in the making of a stage personality which is projected; in providing a vehicle for the actor. There is no illusion that this is a real person whose inmost mind we come to know, perhaps better than he knows himself. It is extrovert and extravagant art, not introverted and morally exploratory:

FORE. (*Looking in the glass*) I do not see any revolution here. Methinks I look with a serene and benign aspect – pale, a little pale – but the roses of these cheeks have been gathered many years. Ha! I do not like that sudden flushing – gone already! Hem, hem, hem! faintish. My heart is pretty good – yet it beats; and my pulses, ha! – I have none – mercy on me! Hum – yes, here they are. Gallop, gallop, gallop, gallop, gallop, gallop, hey! Whither will they hurry me? Now they're gone again. And now I'm faint again; and pale again, and hem! and my hem! – breath, hem! – grows short; hem! hem! he, he, hem!

SCAN. It takes; pursue it in the name of love and pleasure.   [III i]

If this were 'real' it would not be comic. Foresight is tormented by hypochondria while his wife is seduced before his face. But if this is not Lamb's 'Utopia of gallantry', it is nonetheless the make-believe world of the theatre. If the audience will not laugh at *this*, it is doubtful if the Catos of the pit will laugh at anything. It is, of course, very simple fare to offer to readers nourished by the complexities of modern academic analysis. So too is Ben's wooing of Miss Prue as through a loud hailer across the room; or, in Mozart, Leporello wooing Donna Elvira in the guise of Don Giovanni; or, in Shakespeare, Bottom with the head of an ass, loved by Titania. Sometimes one wonders whether, if we are not prepared to be like children, we should stay away from the theatre altogether. If *Love for Love* occasionally seems to impinge on serious matters, it returns swiftly to the world of fantasy again. Here, for instance, is Foresight sounding almost as if he were really angry:

I defy you, hussy! But I'll remember this, I'll be revenged on you, cockatrice; I'll hamper you. – You have your fortune in your own hands, but I'll find a way to make your lover, your prodigal spendthrift gallant, Valentine, pay for all, I will.

But it is thus that Angelica rejoins:

Will you? I care not, but all shall out then. – Look to it, nurse; I can bring witness you have a great unnatural teat under your left arm, and he another; and that you suckle a young devil in the shape of a tabby-cat by turns; I can.

This is high fantastical. It explodes at once into farce as nurse is overwhelmed:

A teat, a teat, I an unnatural teat! O the false slanderous thing! Feel, feel here, if I have anything but like another Christian (*Crying*) or any teats but two that han't given suck this thirty years.   [II i]

It is, of course, the stage weeping of the nurse that provides the comic climax to the exchange.

Even the most serious of ethical poets have observed that it is pleasant to play the fool on occasion, and this is what Angelica is doing, and Congreve, and, one hopes, the audience. It is this low epicureanism which the high seriousness of Puritanical morality cannot stomach, this flippant Cavalier sophistication which while it persists in enjoying art with the naïve acceptance of a child, insists on seeing it as a game. Foresight's anger is a stage anger. Nor, later, will he be a cuckold, because he is *not* married to Mrs Foresight. Miss Prue has only a stage maidenhead to lose to sweet Mr Tattle of about as much substance as the fair form of the amorous Titania. Even in the more corrupt world of *Don Giovanni*, no one credits that the hero goes to hell. Why else, by a self quotation, should Mozart remind us before the splendid horrors of the talking statue, that this is just another of his operas? Like all magic arts, the theatre belongs to charlatans.

But there is more to Congreve than polish, stage-craft, and high fantasy. Those who have admired him have sometimes called him a poet, not only for his care and refinement in the handling of language, but because there are in the plays suggestions of more general meaning beyond the local comic situation, and which carry one from the humour of situation and dialogue towards deeper, and sadder, concerns. The overtones are there in Foresight's speech first quoted: 'Methinks I look with a serene and benign aspect – pale, a little pale – but the roses of these cheeks have been gathered many years', or in the conclusion of the nurse's outburst, 'Feel, feel here, if I have anything but like another Christian or any teats but two that han't given suck this thirty years.' At another time, in a different place, this would not move laughter. It is the voice of pathos from behind the comic mask. We find it in Pope, or Mozart, or Watteau, whose Harlequin, Columbine and Clown, Pater wrote, like tragedians in motley, are able 'to throw a world of serious innuendo into their burlesque looks, with a sort of comedy which shall be but tragedy seen from the other side.'4 Yet, equally characteristic of Congreve, is the melancholy voice of disenchantment; for instance, Angelica's, 'Security is an insipid thing, and the overtaking and possessing of a wish discovers the folly of the chase. Never let us know one another better; for the pleasure of a masquerade is done when we come to show faces.' It could be a comment on Watteau, and it is coming close to the tragi-comedy of *The Way of the World*. It is no more than an element in the texture of the comedy, but it runs throughout. Here, for instance, is Valentine on Angelica (or Harlequin on Columbine, the names are indifferent):

VAL. You're a woman, one to whom heaven gave beauty when it grafted roses on a briar. You are the reflection of heaven in a pond, and he that leaps at you is sunk. You are all white, a sheet of lovely spotless paper, when you first are born; but you are sure to be scrawled and blotted by every goose's quill. I know you; for I loved a woman, and loved her so long that I found out a strange thing: I found out what a woman was good for.
TAT. Aye, prithee, what's that?
VAL. Why, to keep a secret.   [IV i]

The honied cadences of this bitter-sweet cynicism are obvious and even facile, but the total effect is not easy to describe, for the final bathetic fall, suspended over Tattle's interjection – one is tempted to use a musical analogy – seems like an evasion. Whatever it is that Valentine is thinking, the intrusion of Tattle leads him to repress. There is something that he avoids, but what it is remains a mystery. This is characteristic of Congreve. His comedy is, as it were, suspended. One move more and we might actually feel the texture of life, but then, whatever we would have, it would not be comedy. His art is a deliberate flirtation with experience, and its triumph is to tantalise with the appearance of life while denying the substance. In this he is like James, but is closer to what Pater called the 'marvellous tact of omission' in Watteau. There might be more than the game and the dance if Congreve did not cling to his style like a mask.

Whether this is maturity or mere frivolity, the kind of achievement we should admire in comic art, or a shirking of moral responsibility, probably only taste can decide. Perhaps, judged by the mature standard of those who use James as a measure of what is dull and trivial, Congreve is wanting, although judged by the mature standard of a Millamant, Isabel Archer sometimes appears little more than a goose. Nonetheless, those for whom art is a moral medicine should probably stay away from Congreve. . . .

SOURCE: extract from Introduction to Kelsall's edition of *Love for Love* (London, 1969), pp. xiv–xix.

NOTES

[Revised and renumbered from the original – Ed.]

1. *Amendments of Mr Collier's False and Imperfect Citations* (1698)   [excerpted in Part One above – Ed.]
2. Dedication of *The Way of the World*.
3. *Concerning Humour in Comedy* (1696)   [excerpted in Part One – Ed.]
4. Walter Pater, *Imaginary Portraits* (1887; 4th edn, London, 1901), p. 6.

William Myers   'A Partial Synthesis of Lockean Ideas' (1972)

[The discussion here is related to the general argument on Plot and Meaning in William Myers's excerpt in section 1 of Part Three – Ed.]

. . . [An almost] wilful castration of his plots derives from Congreve's firm commitment to modern rather than traditional concepts of society, if not of man, [and this] is plainly evident from his careful elaborations of Lockean arguments in *Love for Love*. Sir Sampson is thus cleverly set up as private-life James II, a bungler who claims a divine right to dispense with laws: 'What, [he cries] I warrant my Son thought nothing belong'd to a Father, but Forgiveness and Affection; no Authority, no Correction, no Arbitrary Power; nothing to be done, but for him to offend, and me to pardon' [II i]. This seems to be a direct satire on Dryden's arguments about Mercy and Prerogative in *The Hind and the Panther*:

> The god-head took a deep consid'ring space:
> And, to distinguish man from all the rest,
> Unlock'd the sacred treasures of his breast:
> And mercy mix'd with reason did impart;
> One to his head, the other to his heart:
> Reason to rule, but mercy to forgive:
> The first is law, the last prerogative.[1]

Sir Sampson, however, clearly illustrates the fact that, superior as mercy and prerogative may be to reason and law in theory, arbitrary power cannot in practice be limited to merciful acts. The need for 'Writings of Settlement and Joynture', for Lockean constitutional government which secures a man's rights in law to his property and so to his peace, remains.

But for Congreve it is not just a matter of property. Ben and Prue suggest that there are other grounds why men should unite into commonwealths. They are, to use a term of Mr Norman Holland's, 'pre-social' figures, though Ben is not so much the 'essentially good'[2] figure of Holland's account, as simply an attractively spontaneous egoist. By being outside the world he and Prue are denied full opportunities for developing and humanising their faculties and appetites. Prue has sexual needs she can do nothing about in her 'natural' isolation, and Ben lacks minimal family feeling – hence his gross inquiries after his dead brother's health [III i]. Their behaviour and their fate in effect explain and justify Valentine's worldliness, even if he does end up with nothing but debts and bastards to show for it. And though such a defence of worldliness in terms of privileged emancipation and personal development might superficially be thought more appropriate in a World based on Hobbist rather than Lockean assumptions, Valentine, in fact, finds these ideas very useful in exposing the weakness of his father's claims. He insists that Sir Sampson has a duty to provide for him not as that notional lay-figure, a Son, but as the complicated, passionate, witty adult which Appetite and Circumstance have created. Poor Sir Sampson's blustering assertions in response to this about 'the lawful Authority of a Parent' [II i] – so reminiscent of the patriarchal arguments of Sir Robert Filmer, Locke's unimpressive aunt sally – might have force in the crassly conceived commonwealths of heroic drama, but in the substantial World of *Love for Love* they are bound to fail. For it is the World, as Valentine points out, which has stirred up his 'Reason, Thought, Passions Inclinations, Affections, Appetites, [and] Senses' [II i], and Sir Sampson cannot cancel his relations with his son merely by having him 'Uncase, Strip, and go naked out of the World as you came into't' [II i]. Fathers and societies give to sons and subjects far more than a merely material basis for life; and it is precisely because the social contract has thus more important implications than that of merely preserving property that it cannot be left to the mercy of royal or paternal whimsy.

The World of *Love for Love* is, then, a rather more sophisticated concept than the World as represented by Lord Touchwood's house in *The Double-Dealer*, and it is so because Congreve has been able to achieve a partial synthesis of Lockean ideas and more traditional notions of personal values. His problem is, however, that because his social order is based on contract, and not, as it was according to traditional arguments, on necessity or divine dispensation, his World creates opportunities for Mrs Frail and Tattle as well as arguments for Valentine. For no matter how humanely based the latter's case may be, the World as such remains a system of 'writings of Settlement'. To live exclusively in it, therefore, is to inhabit a waste land, where impulse can only become perverse, where virtue is irrelevant, and marriage a mere contract. The importance of Ben and Prue is the way they expose the diseased artifice of Tattle and Mrs Frail's worldliness, while at the same time, by the very crudity of their naturalness, they block any retreat by Valentine or the audience into a false pastoralism. Valentine has therefore to project himself into what Holland calls a 'suprasocial' level of experience, and by renouncing his inheritance, abandon the World and events there in an act of 'real madness, that lifts him above ordinary social realities'.[3]

In doing so he becomes, like Mellefont, an early version of *le jeune homme moyen sensuel* who wins his woman by suffering, not by action, and who is 'neither . . . an absolute Wit, nor a Fool' [v i]. He represents an advance on Mellefont, however, because whereas *The Double-Dealer* pretends that Mellefont is a wit, Valentine publicly renounces the wit's traditional role of mastering the World. Congreve's sense of the relationship between his notions of social order and his sense of the potentialities of the individual is becoming clearer and more explicit. What is unclear, however, is whether he realised what a death-blow Valentine's gesture would deal to the kind of play that he was committed to writing, in which the action is central to the meaning. What we have to decide, therefore, is how serious, as a theatrical gesture, and a judgement on society, this reversal in the Fifth Act of *Love for Love* of the traditional assumptions of Restoration comedy is meant to be. Is it, like Tony Lumpkin's victory in *She Stoops to Conquer*, merely a deftly minor deviation from the norm, or, like the radical unconventionality of *The Beggar's Opera*, is it meant to shock us into a major reappraisal of our convictions both about society and the literature which images it?

There is much to support the latter view, especially the violence of some of the language and the grotesqueness of some of the imagery. But an examination of the climax of this element in the play, Valentine's survey of contemporary manners in his mad speeches, indicates clearly enough that the satire is pictorial, Hogarthian, belonging rather to pamphlet or canvas than to the stage. It is not part of a co-ordinated dramatic attack on folly and vice. Indeed after the puritanical severity with which Congreve tried to organise and concentrate his effects in *The Double-Dealer*, *Love for Love* seems an almost irresponsibly relaxed play. Not that it is unsophisticated. The First Act is technically very adroit, while the business which results in the marriage of Tattle and Mrs Frail is as well-managed as anything in *The Country Wife*. But Ben's sing-song, the shifting of scenes, and moments of conscious theatrical naïvety, such as Angelica's discovery that Valentine is feigning madness, are nearer in spirit to the lightheartedness of Dryden's *Marriage à-la-Mode* than to the intensity of purpose one finds in Etherege or Gay. Foresight's astrology is relevant in this connection. He may not be an anachronism, but as a personality in the World of the Act of Settlement, Newtonian physics, and the Bank of England, he is a triviality, a figure of fun, not of serious social comment or analysis. That he is an acceptable element in the play is a sign of how urbanely relaxed it is about its own correctness and seriousness, but it is precisely this elegant carelessness which makes Valentine's gesture in the Fifth Act, at any rate in terms of formal innovation, a relatively minor matter. There is certainly nothing radically challenging to the assumptions of Etherege and Wycherley in Angelica's triumph, which in performance looks simply like a pretty piece of theatre that works because the play has never given the impression of concentrated seriousness.

Angelica is thus in one sense at the centre of the play's success, but she is also the reason why that success is a minor one. Etheregean comedy and Lockean social theory have at least one thing in common, they are intolerant of the unexplained. Divine right is to the merchant banker what a *deus ex machina* is to the neoclassical critic, and simply on a mechanical level Angelica's control over her own fortune offends against the ideal of an action which produces out of itself the means by which its dilemmas are resolved. It is always possible for her to intervene and end the action arbitrarily. This is, of course, a conscious decision on Congreve's part – it is an aspect of the play's commitment to personal rather than contractual relationships. Angelica can thus be said to embody Congreve's difficulty with a Lockean plainness and intelligibility, at any rate in the personal sphere:

Wou'd any thing, but a Madman complain of Uncertainty? [she asks] Uncertainty and Expectation are the Joys of Life. Security is an insipid thing, and the overtaking and possessing of a Wish, discovers the Folly of the Chase. Never let us know one another better; for the Pleasure of a Masquerade is done, when we come to shew Faces. [IV i]

We may not take this quite at its face value since in the final scene a Madman does unmask and reveal the limitations of Uncertainty. But because he is mad – in Norman Holland' terms invested with 'suprasocial' knowledge – Valentine's gesture, at least in terms of the worldly logic of the plot, is the opposite of plain and intelligible. And even if we accept that it has a meaning, the route to this 'suprasocial' condition of mind remains obscure. On the one hand, it would seem the achievement is entirely Valentine's, that Angelica's behaviour has driven him to madness and a new level of sincerity, in which case he is the teacher and she the taught. On the other hand, her triumphant air of having arranged everything suggests that from the beginning she has occupied a 'suprasocial' position herself. Unfortunately her declared motives for deceiving Valentine support both views. On the one hand, she seems merely to be playing ('if I don't play Trick for Trick, may I never taste the Pleasure of Revenge' [IV i], and on the other to be genuinely testing whether Valentine has been acting merely 'for mercenary Ends and sordid Interest' [IV i]. Her behaviour is thus dramatically unaccounted for, as gratuitous a factor in the scheme of things as her control over her fortune and Sir Sampson's claims to authority. The only difference, indeed, between their two forms of wilfulness is that Congreve knows that the audience will laugh at Sir Sampson's because he is coarse and brutish, and enjoy Angelica's because she is witty and pretty. He has failed therefore to excise the factor of gratuitousness from his plot and his image of the world, and has thereby offended simultaneously against the canons of neoclassical order and the ideal of rationally constituted, rather than gratuitously ordained, social arrangements. Angelica's sprightliness is clearly intended as an answer to crass Lockean materialism, but because it is simply thrust into the play, and not tested dramatically, it is as much a sentimentality as Bevil Junior's virtue, even if it is more urbanely conceived and presented with greater theatrical flair.

Love for Love, then, may have a more sophisticated grasp of some of the problems involved, but finally it demonstrates once again the profound incompatibility between newly developed notions of social order and a significant comic action in the Jonsonian tradition. . . .

[In the next section William Myers's enquiry is continued in regard to *The Way of the World* – Ed.]

SOURCE: extract from 'plot and meaning in Congreve's Comedies', in Brian Morris (ed.), *William Congreve* (London, 1972), 79–84.

NOTES

[Reorganised and renumbered from the original – Ed.]

1. *The Hind and the Panther*, I, 256–62: *The Poems and Fables of John Dryden*, ed. James Kinsley (Oxford, 1962).
2. Norman N. Holland, *The First Modern Comedies* (Cambridge, Mass, 1959), p. 174.
3. Ibid., p. 164.

Harold Love   'The Rake Reforming'
(1974)

... When we first see Valentine in Act I he is in every sense a creature of the town. He has exhausted his money in his pursuit of Angelica (the interpretation of the other characters would be no doubt that she has milked him of it) but without securing any profession of love in return. This is hardly surprising: his extravagant spending has been an attempt to buy her and she has been perfectly aware of this and is not prepared to be for sale. His next plan, and one that is open to much the same objections, is to shame her:

> Well; and now I am poor, I have an opportunity to be reveng'd on 'em all; I'll pursue *Angelica* with more Love than ever, and appear more notoriously her Admirer in this Restraint, than when I openly rival'd the rich Fops, that made Court to her; so shall my Poverty be a Mortification to her Pride, . . . [I i]

Valentine is still in this speech picturing Angelica as a quarry to be hunted, not as a human equal to be loved. It is also clear that his courtship is not directed at her alone, but is simultaneously a performance put on to gain the approbation of the town. In compensation for these imperceptive and rather narcissistic attitudes, we are also made aware of an agreeable impulsiveness, a determination to make the best of whatever his situation offers, and a general openness to new possibilities, which raise him well above the usual pitch of the town. (Being unable to afford breakfast he has been edifying himself with a study of the Stoics.) He still has a chance to change. A visit from the nurse of one of his illegitimate children gives him a chance to display generosity in the limited modern sense by somehow finding her some money and his residual ill-nature by a quip about infanticide. The next visitors are Trapland, a creditor, accompanied by two officers, and, on another errand, Valentine's father's steward. Between them the choice is put to Valentine of accepting his father's proposal for the payment of his debts, which is to surrender his right in the family inheritance, or to go to prison. Valentine consents, as the arrangement will also permit him to leave his lodgings and go in search of Angelica, although here Scandal is pessimistic about his chances:

SCAN. A very desperate demonstration of your love to *Angelica:* And I think she has never given you any assurance of hers.

VAL. You know her temper; she never gave me any great reason either for hope or despair.

SCAN. Women of her airy temper, as they seldom think before they act, so they rarely give us any light to guess at what they mean: But you have little reason to believe that a Woman of this Age, who has had an indifference for you in your Prosperity, will fall in love with your ill Fortune; besides, *Angelica* has a great Fortune of her own; and great Fortunes either expect another great Fortune, or a Fool.   [I i]

From the town's point of view his reasoning could hardly be faulted.

In the following act we receive our first sight of Angelica and are given no reason to question Scandal's diagnosis of her 'airy temper'. She comes in to demand her uncle's coach, ridicules his harmless obsession with astrology, taunts him openly with his wife's infidelity, confesses to spying on him through a keyhole, and threatens to denounce him to the magistrates as a wizard. None of this is at all serious, but there is still a strong air of gratuitous bullying about it. Our hero has not given very many signs of promise, and neither at this stage does our heroine. Valentine is a town rake and she, to all appearances, is little better than a town miss, superbly adroit in the skills of social manipulation, and not above keeping these skills razor-sharp by a little practice in the domestic circle. What is not clear is whether the purpose of this formidable conversational armoury is offensive or defensive, whether there is an Araminta behind the mask or just another Belinda.

When we see Angelica next she is together for the first time in the play with Valentine and once again she is giving nothing away:

ANG. You can't accuse me of Inconstancy; I never told you, that I lov'd you.

VAL. But I can accuse you of Uncertainty, for not telling me whether you did or no.

ANG. You mistake Indifference for Uncertainty; I never had Concern enough to ask my self the Question.   [III i]

Later in the play, at the moment of self-revelation in Act v, we are to discover that she did love him after all; but in the present scene there is no sign of this. And it is not hard to fathom the reasons for Angelica's wariness. Living in a world of Tattles and Frails, she has had to learn to handle their weapons even better than they do themselves. To be in love is to be in a position of vulnerability. The rule of the town is to take advantage of the vulnerable. To be in love, and to reveal this love, is to invite the person you love to take advantage of you. The only safe course, therefore, is to conceal love under the affectation of indifference or dislike. This was Tattle's first lesson to Prue, and an identical principle guides Angelica's behaviour towards Valentine. The problem with Valentine is not simply that he is a town rake and lives by the assumptions of a town rake: that love is a hunt or pursuit, that women are mercenary simpletons to be bought or tricked into submission, that 'He alone won't Betray in whom none will Confide/And the Nymph may be Chaste that has never been Try'd'. If that were all that there was to him, Angelica would not have fallen in love with him in the first place. Valentine in fact has a number of very good and un-town-like instincts. He is not, for instance, interested in money for its own sake but only as a means of helping him to Angelica. (Though this still, of course, makes him guilty of the assumption that she is available to be bought.) His real trouble is that he insists on interpreting other people's behaviour, including Angelica's, according to the cynical principles of the town and Scandal. He is therefore in the grip of two wrong images, one of himself and one of Angelica, each reinforcing the other. For Angelica to reveal the wrongness of his image of her, which would not be hard as it is largely of her own creation, would be of no use until he had learned to interpret such an action according to principles other than those of the Age. It is only when he has made the break-through of his own accord and come to see himself in completely new terms that it will be safe for her to reveal that she is not what he thought she was. It is this which Angelica is trying to explain to him when at the end of the scene he asks her whether she is going to 'come to a Resolution' and she replies 'I can't. Resolution must come to me, or I shall never have one.' It is Valentine who has to find both their ways out of the vicious circle.

At this stage in the play, however, the probability of such a break-through does not seem very high. The immediate task of Scandal and Valentine is to test the genuineness of Angelica's indifference, with the aim, should they find any evidence of feigning, of exploiting the revealed vulnerability as ruthlessly as possible. Scandal, whose power to fathom the masks and stratagems of the town has already been presented for our admiration in Act I, is clearly of the opinion that there is more to her behaviour than meets the eye. Taking up her 'I never had Concern enough to ask my self the Question' quoted earlier, he inserts a sly hint of his disbelief:

SCAN. Nor good Nature enough to answer him that did ask you: I'll say that for you, Madam.

ANG. What, are you setting up for good Nature?

SCAN. Only for the affectation of it, as the Women do for ill Nature.

[III i]

Scandal's insight here amounts to nothing more than the normal town assumption that things are probably the reverse of what they seem, or, as Tattle enlarges, 'All well-bred Persons Lie! . . . you must never speak what you think: Your words must contradict your thoughts. . . .' In reply to this, Angelica is rather surprisingly prepared to concede that he may be right but challenges him to persuade Valentine of this. For Angelica knows that Valentine has no real understanding of her and to this extent cannot seriously threaten her. And Valentine, again rather surprisingly, is perfectly prepared to confess to his ignorance both of her and mankind: 'I shall receive no Benefit from the Opinion: For I know no effectual Difference between continued Affectation and Reality.' This passage is sometimes quoted out of context as if it were a statement of Congreve's personal attitude towards social role-playing, but this is not so.[1] The point of the lines is to show the inadequacy of Valentine's understanding both of himself and of others, for there *is* a difference between reality and continued affectation, a difference which Angelica understands perfectly because it is something she has to live with all the time.

The same issues, along with one or two new ones, inform the comedy of the subsequent scene between Angelica, the two men, and Tattle. Tattle embodies the values and expectations of the town in their purest state. Where Valentine had felt unable to distinguish between continued affectation and reality but was not prepared to deny that there was such a difference, Tattle is so far gone as to have mistaken his own affectations for reality. His conversation is a long romance on the theme of his prowess as a lover. At the same time, as we saw in Act I, he is inordinately proud of his reputation for discretion. This is partly an effect of his desire to be thought a wit and partly a technique of seduction in its own right, on the principle that women would be more inclined to have affairs with a man who could be relied on to keep it a secret. At the present juncture he is exhibiting his accomplishments, secrecy among them, for the benefit of Angelica. The fun of the scene lies in the careful manœuvring by which Valentine and Scandal set his two reputations at odds with each other, a subtle exercise in the art which Wilkinson calls 'enjoying the fool'.[2] In trying to defend his reputation for secrecy he is forced to assert that he had 'never had the good Fortune to be trusted once with a Lady's Secret'. This brings the objection from Angelica 'But whence comes the Reputation of Mr *Tattle*'s Secresie, if he was never trusted?', putting him in the position of having to betray his reputation in order to defend it . . . [Cites Tattle's speeches, III i]. Tattle's narcissistic male egotism is exactly what Angelica is trying to protect herself from. However, his situation is also relevant to hers in another way. As he has destroyed his reputation for secrecy in defending it; so she is still in the position where to reveal her love to an unregenerate Valentine would be to resign herself for ever to the role of conquered quarry. Hers is a genuine secrecy, unlike Tattle's fraudulent one, but is just as self-defeating.

By this time Scandal has a strong suspicion that Angelica is more kindly disposed than she would have the men believe. When he exits it is with the promise to Valentine 'I've something in my Head to communicate to you' – presumably the pretence of madness which is to be Valentine's last and most daring throw in his attempt to confound his father and to extract a capitulation from Angelica on his terms rather than hers. Angelica is the first to call on him after his supposed condition has been proclaimed, and on her entrance comes close to betraying her real feelings. 'She's concern'd, and loves him' is Scandal's diagnosis. But Scandal has forgotten, or perhaps never realised, that she is quite as brilliant a penetrator of pretence as himself, and he betrays his own game by an unguarded wink to Jeremy. Having gauged the true situation, Angelica's responsibility is to repay trick with trick, which she does by denying outright that she loves Valentine and then announcing on the basis of excellent London reasons that she will not see him after all:

But I have consider'd that Passions are unreasonable and involuntary; if he loves, he can't help it; and if I don't love, I can't help it; no more than he can help his being a Man, or I my being a Woman; or no more than I can help my want of Inclination to stay longer here . . .   [IV i]

Angelica here is doing no more than give the men the treatment appropriate to the role in which they insist on casting her. She sweeps out leaving Scandal undisturbed in his belief in the weathercock nature of 'this same Womankind'. Later she will be back to put Valentine through his paces more thoroughly.

Angelica resents the situation because it shows that Valentine is still seeing the world in terms of Scandal's bitter satiric vignettes at the close of Act I, among them 'Pride, Folly, Affectation, Wantonness, Inconstancy, Covetousness, Dissimulation, Malice, and Ignorance' as the image of a 'celebrated Beauty'. But it is now Valentine's turn to grow satirical: his 'madness' takes the form of ringing denunciations directed at such targets as lawyers, citizens, and elderly husbands; when he comes to address Angelica, however, the tone changes and the accents of simulated madness give way to a perfectly composed beauty:

ANG. Do you know me, *Valentine?*
VAL. Oh very well.
ANG. Who am I?
VAL. You're a Woman, – One to whom Heav'n gave Beauty, when it grafted Roses on a Briar. You are the reflection of Heav'n in a Pond, and he that leaps at you is sunk. You are all white, a sheet of lovely spotless Paper, when you first are Born; but you are to be scrawl'd and blotted by every Goose's Quill. I know you; for I lov'd a Woman, and lov'd her so long, that I found out a strange thing: I found out what a Woman was good for.
TAT. Aye, prithee, what's that?
VAL. Why to keep a Secret.
TAT. O lord!
VAL. O exceeding good to keep a Secret: For tho' she should tell, yet she is not to be believ'd.   [VI i]

The speech is one of the few in the play where Congreve's language achieves a genuine richness of poetic implication, yet once again the images are expressions of an imperfect understanding: Angelica had asked Valentine if he knew her, and he reveals very clearly in his reply that he knows only the false self she shows to the town. He does not see that the scrawls and blots are of his own imagination: that were he to leap, he would not be sunk at all. Yet the closing lines do suggest that he has intimations of a truth unknown to him before the experiment with madness. Angelica has indeed kept a secret, two secrets in fact: that she is in love with him, and that she is not the person he and the town take her for. He is beginning to know this without knowing that he knows.

There is still, however, a long way to go. Angelica is not yet won; she is still resentful of the contemptuous shallowness of his artifices; and when he trustingly confesses the stratagem, she will not yield an inch in return. His request is that, as he puts off his pretence of madness, so she should suspend her affectation of disregard:

> Nay faith, now let us understand one another, Hypocrisie apart, – The Comedy draws toward an end, and let us think of leaving acting, and be ourselves; and since you have lov'd me, you must own I have at length deserv'd you shou'd confess it. [IV i]

This is too simple altogether. For one thing it shows that he still regards courtship as a matter of trickery and charades. So Angelica repays him in kind by pretending that she still believes him to be mad and treating his protestations of sanity as a madman's self-delusion. She is also quick to take him up on his reasons for adopting the stratagem:

> VAL. . . . my seeming Madness has deceiv'd my Father, and procur'd me time to think of means to reconcile me to him; and preserve the right of my Inheritance to his Estate; which otherwise by Articles, I must this Morning have resign'd: And this I had inform'd you of to Day, but you were gone, before I knew you had been here.
>
> ANG. How! I thought your love of me had caus'd this Transport in your Soul; which, it seems, you only counterfeited, for mercenary Ends and sordid Interest.
>
> VAL. Nay, now you do me Wrong; for if any Interest was considered, it was yours; since I thought I wanted more than Love, to make me worthy of you.
>
> ANG. Then you thought me mercenary – But how am I deluded by this Interval of Sense, to reason with a Madman? [IV i]

Valentine's frankness has been returned with a town miss's trick which, of course, he knows to be a town miss's trick. But he is also to be given a clue to the secret which still eludes him. Before she leaves, Angelica speaks to him in words which have some of the elegiac quality of his own mad language, and which are her most explicit statement of her sense of the situation:

> VAL. You are not leaving me in this Uncertainty?
>
> ANG. Wou'd any thing, but a Madman complain of Uncertainty? Uncertainty and Expectation are the Joys of Life. Security is an insipid thing, and the overtaking and possessing of a Wish, discovers the Folly of the Chase. Never let us know one another better; for the Pleasure of a Masquerade is done, when we come to shew Faces; But I'll tell you two things before I leave you; I am not the Fool you take me for; and you are Mad and don't know it. [IV i]

In returning him the unmasking image Angelica is conceding what is after all a central fact of the play – that the world of masks, of illusion, of inconstancy, of trickery, of unceasing psychological combat, of the rake's pursuit and the woman's hypocritical refusal, the world in which 'Love hates to center in a Point assign'd,/But runs with Joy the Circle of the Mind', is in its way an exciting, testing world. Valentine has thoroughly enjoyed his life in it, and so far he has resisted all her attempts to make him leave it. But now that Angelica has seen beyond it she is not to be drawn back. For all its dazzle and movement it is a world in which it is impossible to trust or to love. The relationship of Angelica and Valentine has been conducted along the lines prescribed by the world and behind the masks of its making. When Valentine asks her to take off her mask it is in the expectation of finding a face beneath which will be not very different from the mask. Appreciating this, Angelica is only being fair in warning him that 'the Pleasure of a Masquerade is done, when we come to shew Faces'. If they were to live their lives according to the town's terms there would always have to be some kind of mask in place. But what if the face beneath the mask were itself a mask and the face beneath that second mask one that Valentine had never dreamed of? If this were so it is possible that she might after all not be a fool, which is the rake's basic assumption about the women he pursues by trick and bribe, and that Valentine might well be led into actions which by all the standards of the town (and when the moment comes Scandal is to use exactly this word) are 'mad' ones. If she does not succeed in enlightening him she is at least able to puzzle him. 'She is harder to be understood than a Piece of *Ægyptian* Antiquity, or an *Irish* Manuscript; you may pore till you spoil your Eyes, and not improve your Knowledge' [IV i]. Yet he has at least recognised that there is a mystery and that his 'Lesson' must have a 'Moral'; which is a start. And at the close of the scene he is even prepared to query one of the dicta of the hitherto infallible Scandal.

By the time we see him again he has discovered the answer which, all things considered, is a very simple one. For Scandal's principle of 'trust to no one' he has substituted another – 'if you do trust, trust absolutely' – and his trust is rewarded. At the very moment he is about to give assent to the deed of disinheritance, Angelica tears the earlier bond and in the same breath renounces the marriage with Sir Sampson. What is it that he has discovered to bring about this change? His preparedness to sacrifice himself is the most obvious thing; but this is itself the fruit of a deeper awareness. The solution is in her answer to the question he asks her before he proceeds to sign to his own undoing:

'Tis true, you have a great while pretended Love to me; nay, what if you were sincere? still you must pardon me, if I think my own Inclinations have a better Right to dispose of my Person, than yours. [v i]

The notion that other people's persons should be in their own disposal, and not one's own, is not particularly original, but the difficulty that Valentine has had in reaching it should caution us against imagining it to be self-evident. For the whole system of the town had been built on an explicit denial of it. Valentine has at last emerged from the delusion, and through this from his poverty. Ironically enough the second part of the benison has been brought about by the most arrant town trick of all – and its perpetrator has been Angelica.

SOURCE: extract from ch. 4, *Congreve* (Oxford, 1974), pp. 72–81.

NOTES

[Reorganised and renumbered from the original – Ed.]

1. [Ed.] See Congreve's own remarks on this topic in excerpt II of section 2 in Part One, above.]
2. D. R. M. Wilkinson, *The Comedy of Habit* (Leyden, 1964), p. 84.

Peter Holland 'Continued Affectation and Reality: Effectual Difference Explored' (1979)

[The ensuing discussion follows on from the 'Text and Performance' excerpts in section 1 of Part Three, above – Ed.]

. . . *Love for Love* uses only two locations, Valentine's chamber (Acts I and IV) and a room is Foresight's house (Acts II, III and V). Valentine's chamber is no longer the place from which the rake sallies forth to conquer the world. Instead it is a refuge from a world that is pursuing him for money. The same pattern had been used by Dryden as early as *The Wild Gallant* (acted 1663) but now, thirty years later, the device represents the rake in full retreat, not only from the pressures of his creditors but also from himself. Valentine, unlike Loveby, has to change dramatically and completely if he is to pass the test and win Angelica. The libertine is now only a memory, proved true only by his bills and his bastards. Even while Scandal indulges in rakish promiscuity, he is juxtaposed with Tattle. Valentine's description of Scandal's manner applies equally well to Tattle. The rake and the fop are, like Brisk and Careless, increasingly indistinguishable:

> ANG. Perswade your Friend, that it is all Affectation.
> VAL. I shall receive no Benefit from the Opinion: For I know no effectual Difference between continued Affectation and Reality.
> [III i]

The entire play can be seen as being constructed around the exploration of that difference.

While the hero is vulnerable at home, he is even more so outside of it. Valentine goes to visit Angelica and she is out; he tries to persuade Sir Sampson and fails (though, as he says, it 'at least look'd well on my side'). Valentine's fall, his final rejection of the ethic by which he had lived, is as usual accomplished in the dupes' world. But that world itself has by then been shown to be more than foolish; it is also inverted, a clear case of the world upside-down, as even Foresight knows,

> When Housewifes all the House forsake,
> And leave good Man to Brew and Bake,
> Withouten Guile, then be it said,
> That House doth stond upon its Head . . .   [II i]

Old men try to be young rakes; women rule the men; the world is topsy-turvey.

The two sets thus provide their own polarity in the play, a theatrical structure of alternates that a play moving conventionally within the genre would seek to reconcile. But *Love for Love* in the end rejects both: the two contrasted worlds are equally unacceptable. It is not surprising, lacking any clear basis of place, that Valentine should not be sure what he ought to be and that Angelica should go through the play like a witty angel, mysterious and impossible to pin down.

But the alternating sets indicate a certain theatricality in the play. Throughout the play a tension is created in the adoption of a convention or device, as a means of hiding the self, of ignoring the truth. Later in the action Tattle and Frail are tricked into marriage by their over-eagerness but also, as it appears on stage, by their willingness to be theatrical and marry in disguise, assuming incorrectly that Valentine's madness and Angelica's compliance represent reality not theatrical affectation. The marriage springs from their own character but also, in its place in the sequence of the play, by their theatricality, their role-playing. . . .

The clearest example of this excessive theatricality comes in Act IV. Structurally the scene of Valentine's feigned madness is placed in the corresponding position to the scene between Mellefont and Lady Touchwood played out for Lord Touchwood's benefit. Both are 'scenes' in a double sense, scenes in the play and also scenes acted out to other characters, hypocritical feigning. They are plays within plays, examples of the characters' willingness to take up a role for their own ends. Like the one in *The Double-Dealer*, this scene is emphasised as a scene by the use of the discovery, in this case by the servant Jeremy.

Mr *Scandal* is with him, Sir; I'll knock at the Door.
(*Goes to the Scene, which opens and discovers* Valentine *upon a Couch disorderly dress'd,* Scandal *by him.*)   [IV i]

The discovery is . . . particularly common in tragedy. By 1695, it was also part of the increased use of the scenic stage, the use of scenery as environment, as part of a fictional world, that was combined with a move away from acting on the forestage. This can be seen in *Love for Love* in Act II which opens on to '*A Room in* Foresight's *House*' with Foresight and his servant discovered. In Act IV, the discovery of a tableau, particularly of someone lying on a couch, is a direct invocation of the world of Restoration tragedy. Thus Tate has Lear discovered 'a Sleep on a Couch'.[1] Valentine's madness is a parody of the vatic mad scenes throughout Restoration tragedy. The direct satire is coincidental, an indication of the parodic status of the scene. The madman has no true place in contemporary comedy. Significantly, the mad-scene in

Durfey's *The Richmond Heiress* (1693) had also had false madmen and used the pretended aberration as an excuse for satire. The use of the stage in *Love for Love* immediately indicates to the audience that the discovery is a transposition from another mode, from a serious drama. Valentine makes the device work theatrically but against Angelica it is a complete failure.

The 'performance' shows the extent of the difference between Mellefont and Valentine at this stage. Mellefont is a naïve victim of the pretence; Valentine is the victim of his own ingenuity, as Angelica wilfully misunderstands him. Valentine's failure is marked by his own misjudgement over the type of 'play' he is in. Increasingly frustrated by Angelica's actions, he demands abruptly that the disguise, the continued affectation' be abandoned even though he has not indicated that he does love sincerely:

Nay faith, now let us understand one another, Hypocrisie apart, – The Comedy draws toward an end, and let us think of leaving acting, and be our selves; and since you have lov'd me, you must own I have at length deserv'd you shou'd confess it. [IV i]

But a comedy does not end with the fourth act, nor can this one end with Valentine still acting. It is the conscious theatricality of his device that disqualifies him from success at this stage. Angelica's reluctance to commit herself is confirmed by the way Valentine attempts to force an admission of love. Neither she nor the audience can be sure exactly what type of rake Betterton is playing. They cannot be sure that his conversion is genuine, that his love is sincere.

In Act v then, it is the turn of Angelica to use a trick, a stage-managed manoeuvre, to put Valentine in the position from which he must make the crucial decision. Although the play has questioned the validity of the theatrical gesture, Angelica's device is justified both by her own nature, accepted as virtuous by the audience, and by the change of tone that accompanies the resolution. There is nothing else in the play like the language Valentine uses for his generous gesture of defeat:

SCAN. 'S'death, you are not mad indeed, to ruine your self?
VAL. I have been disappointed of my only Hope; and he that loses hope may part with any thing. I never valu'd Fortune, but as it was subservient to my Pleasure; and my only Pleasure was to please this Lady: I have made many vain

Attempts, and find at last, that nothing but my Ruine can effect it: Which for that Reason, I will sign to – Give me the Paper. [v i]

The passage has an oddly flat quality. There is nothing extravagant and heroic, nothing theatrical about the statement or the gesture. Instead it convinces as a demonstration of sincerity and generosity through a purity of tone which Restoration comedy had usually managed without. Certainly the speech convinces Angelica absolutely. The contrast with the immediately preceding revelation of Tattle's marriage to Mrs Frail is sufficient not only to show the audience how to judge Valentine, but also to convince Scandal. Scandal moves away from his alignment with Tattle-ish foppery and towards a belief in sincerity.

The play as it unfolds clearly demonstrates Congreve's use of the design to chart a changing evaluation of character. The audience learns how to separate theatrical action from sincere action. The stage intrigue is associated with affectation and excess – unless it is as clear as Angelica's. Any excess of plotting now works against the character. . . . Congreve does not evidence distrust in the theatre in attacking theatricality and associating it with foolishness. Rather, he works through it, using it as a means of transcending the convention in order to reconnect the play with the audience's perception of society. As Valentine learns that dramas have a fifth act, so *Love for Love* moves through its own classicism of construction. Valentine's generosity is proved by a repudiation of the intrigue that has brought on his disaster. He resolves the design and plot of the play by abandoning plotting.

Source: extracts from *The Ornament of Action* (Cambridge, 1979), pp. 229–30, 230–2, 232.

NOTE

[Renumbered from the original.]

1. Nahum Tate, *The History of King Lear* (1681), p. 51.

4. *THE WAY OF THE WORLD*

Kathleen M. Lynch   'Modes of Laughter' (1926)

. . . Millamant's personality is not exhibited simply through sparkling rejoinders, inspired, from moment to moment, by the wit of her associates. Unlike other characters in Restoration comedy, she has a gift for interpreting a situation as a whole and moulds her caprices to suit the temper of the occasion, of which she at once assumes full control. She has an advantage over Mirabell in possessing an alert sense of humour, which enables her to laugh at his 'love-sick face' and sententious phrases and gaily expose the weak spots in his lover's self-conceit. She begs of him in merry concern: 'Ha! ha! ha! what would you give, that you could help loving me?' And poor Mirabell can only reply: 'I would give something that you did not know I could not help it.'

Millamant's very flippancies are charged with meaning. It is plain that her excessive gaiety is forced. She talks very fast and is afraid of pauses, fearful lest the realities of love may somehow rudely intrude upon the pretty decorum of this *beau monde*. The social mode makes no allowance for the sympathies of lovers. In those inarticulate silences that check now and again the flashing current of her raillery, Millamant is wistfully pleading with Mirabell to accept her love without the shame of a confession, and to permit her to remain in appearance imperious, brilliant, heartless, the finest of fine ladies.

We are so vividly assured of Millamant's personality that the comic contrast between her real and her artificial self becomes remarkably distinct and thought-provoking. One recalls Meredith's wise aphorism:

You may estimate your capacity for comic perception by being able to detect the ridicule of them you love without loving them the less; and more by being able to see yourself somewhat ridiculous in dear eyes, and accepting the correction their image of you proposes.[Essay on Comedy (1877), p. 133.]

In the light of the first half of Meredith's aphorism we estimate Millamant. By relying on this type of friendly laughter, Congreve and other comic dramatists of his age are able to cherish and protect their ideal characters.

The type of laughter evoked by Millamant is obviously not called forth by the majority of Congreve's characters. For one Millamant and one Cynthia we have a host of Froths and Witwouds. Millamant and Cynthia themselves laugh at the Froths and Witwouds, because the latter, when judged by the best Restoration standards, are guilty of false wit and false affectation. In contrasting true people of fashion and these pretenders to fashion, Congreve continually emphasises the double standard of Restoration comedy. . . .

SOURCE: extract from *The Social Mode of Restoration Comedy* (New York, 1926, pp. 204-5).

Kenneth Muir 'Millamant's Witty Quotations' (1965)

. . . Hazlitt thought Millamant was 'nothing but a fine lady', and Meredith said she was 'a type of the superior ladies who do not think'.[1] Both critics were surely mistaken. Millamant's wit, like that of Rosalind and Beatrice, is a sign of intelligence; and although affectation and coquetry usually indicate a frigid temperament, Millamant's affectation is the cloak of affection, and her coquetry conceals a nature capable of a whole-hearted love. She can act the fine lady to perfection, she can pose as a woman who makes wit the be-all and end-all of her life, but fundamentally she is a sensitive girl in an insensitive society. This is made perfectly clear when just after the bargaining scene she confesses to her friend: 'Well, if *Mirabell* should not make a good Husband, I am a lost thing – for I find I love him violently.' It was made clear, too, for Congreve's original audience, by the poems he puts into his heroine's mouth just before her surrender. Suckling's lines –

> There never yet was woman made,
>   Nor shall, but to be curs'd;

– are part of a poem which pretends to discuss women's promiscuity, but which goes on to imply the inconstancy of men. Millamant then quotes the first stanza of another of Suckling's poems:

> I prithee spare me, gentle Boy,
> Press me no more for that slight Toy,
> That foolish Trifle of an Heart;
> I swear it will not do its part,
> Tho' thou dost thine, employ'st thy Power and Art.[2]

Suckling goes on to explain that he calls out for the last course before the rest, and as soon as the woman capitulates he hurries off to new conquests:

> Men rise away, and scarce say grace,
> Or civilly once thank the face
> That did invite, but seek another place.

Millamant's fourth quotation is from Waller's 'The Story of Phoebus and Daphne, Applied';[3] and Mirabell, entering in the middle of a couplet, completes it, thereby showing that he understands the allusion and knows the reason for Millamant's hesitation 'upon the very Verge of Matrimony'.

Millamant's quotations – the aptness of which proves that she has 'genuine intelligence' – come at the end of nearly a century of argument on the subject of 'platonic' love. This was stimulated by the fashionable cult introduced by Henrietta Maria and by the realisation by many of the poets that absolute licence made conquests unsatisfying. So we have Suckling proclaiming that 'Fruition's dull' and that

> 'Tis expectation makes a blessing dear;

Henry King tells us that it is impossible to

Enjoy our Love and yet preserve Desire;[4]

and Cowley tells his mistress that she would be a fool to yield:

> Much of my *Veneration* thou must want,
> When once thy *kindness* puts my *ign'rance* out;
> For a *learn'd Age* is always least devout.[5]

On the other side of the debate there were numerous poems attacking platonic love, from Donne who ridiculed those who ignored the 'right, true end of love' to Suckling who exclaimed, this time ironically:

> Oh, what a stroke 'twould be! sure I should die,
> Should I but hear my mistress once say ay.[6]

Congreve was writing more than a generation after the Cavalier poets, and he revived for his own purposes, in a more licentious society, the theme that possession involves the decay of desire, and hence of love. In the world of Restoration comedy – and to some extent in the society reflected by that comedy –it was assumed that men and women were naturally promiscuous. But whereas Etherege cheerfully accepted this state of affairs, Congreve's main concern was always with the comparatively sensitive who were seeking for a more satisfactory relationship between the sexes. His heroines are fully aware of the fact that love is not supposed to outlast the honeymoon, and they all shrink from marriage until their gallants have undergone a period of probation. Cynthia, observing the behaviour of the Froths and of her own father and stepmother, asks Mellefont: 'What think you of drawing stakes, and giving over in time?' Angelica, living in the same house as Mrs Foresight who cuckolds her husband, Mrs Frail whose name expresses her reputation, and Miss Prue who tries very hard to be seduced, and loving the prodigal Valentine, naturally hesitates before committing herself to matrimony – he may be after her fortune. Millamant knows that her cousin is Mirabell's cast-off mistress, and that she is treated badly by her husband. This is sufficient to account for her behaviour. . . .

SOURCE: extract from 'The Comedies of William Congreve', in

Harris and Brown (eds), *Restoration Theatre* (London, 1965), pp. 232–4; reproduced in Muir's *The Comedy of Manners* (1970).

NOTES

[Revised and renumbered from the original – Ed.]

1. Hazlitt, *Lectures on the English Comic Writers* (edition of 1910), p. 74; Meredith, *Essay on Comedy* (edition of 1927), p. 41. [Excerpted, from both authors, in Part Two, above – Ed.]
2. Suckling, in R. C. Howarth (ed.), *Minor Poets of the Seventeenth Century* (London, 1931), pp. 195, 198.
3. *Poetical Works of Waller* (ed. Gilfillan, London, 1857), p. 22.
4. Henry King, in George Saintsbury (ed.), *Minor Poets*, vol. III, p. 209.
5. Cowley's *Poems* (edition of 1903), p. 98.
6. Suckling, op. cit., pp. 83–4.

Maximillian E. Novak   'Villainy Humanised' (1971)

. . . Fainall's confrontation with Marwood is one of the most brilliant scenes in the play, for they are lovers like Laclos's Valmont and Merteuil in *Liaisons Dangereuses* or James's Osmond and Merle in *Portrait of a Lady*; it suggests a near tragic vision of love among the hateful. Their interview says everything that can be said about those who have wit without morals, who have passion without the capacity for love, and who are evil without losing our admiration. Marwood urges Fainall to follow his wife, pretending that she is interested in upholding his honour; but he accuses her of being jealous of seeing his wife with Mirabell and confesses that he deliberately allowed his wife to make advances to his friend so he might enjoy Marwood securely. As evidence of Marwood's jealous love for Mirabell, he offers her betrayal of Mirabell's plots to Lady Wishfort; when Marwood argues that she did it for the sake of friendship, he laughs at the friendships of women.

But, at this point, Fainall makes a slip; he accuses her of betraying his wife, her supposed 'Friend', and puts himself in the position of upbraiding Marwood for her fidelity to him. Provoked, Marwood says that she will not forgive his scorn and threatens to reveal all to his wife and the world – how he ruined her, wasted her fortune, and destroyed her honour. Somewhat shaken by this threat, Fainall reminds her that, by preventing Mirabell from carrying off Millamant, she lost him half of Millamant's fortune, which would have gone to his wife. 'And wherefore did I marry', says Fainall, 'but to make lawful Prize of a rich Widow's Wealth, and squander it on Love and you?' By this act he has suffered much, he argues; for he has had the humiliation of abandoning his libertine code by marrying – worst of all, by marrying a widow who hates him enough to wish him dead.

The reconciliation of Fainall and Marwood is a masterpiece of Congreve's mimetic art. Fainall holds Marwood's hands as she struggles to run off:

FAIN. You know I love you.

MARW. Poor dissembling! – O that – Well, it is not yet –

FAIN. What? What is it not? What is it not yet? It is not yet too late –

MARW. No, it is not yet too late – I have that Comfort.

FAIN. It is, to love another.

MARW. But not to loath, detest, abhor Mankind, my self and the whole treacherous World.

FAIN. Nay, this is Extravagance – Come, I ask your Pardon – No Tears – I was to blame. I cou'd not love you and be easie in my Doubts – Pray forbear – I believe you; I'm convinc'd I've done you wrong; and any way, ev'ry way will make amends; – I'll hate my Wife yet more, Damn her, I'll part with her, rob her of all she's worth, and we'll retire somewhere, any where, to another World, I'll marry thee – Be pacify'd – 'Sdeath they come, hide your Face, your Tears – You have a Mask, wear it a moment. This way, this way, be persuaded.

[II i]

The sudden depression into which Mrs Marwood falls was conventional enough for the time and particularly common in roles written with Mrs Barry in mind, but what is so moving in this scene is the way Congreve humanises the emotions of his villains. Fainall's resolution to rob his wife of all she has rises at least partly from a desperate longing to appease his mistress. And his final solution – to retire to another world where they may marry – is curious in view of the title of the play. In his daydreams. Fainall conceives a solution to his life that lies outside the world of manners and morals with which he must deal successfully if he is to gain his ends. . . .

Marwood and Fainall have the last scene in the third act, and a comparison between this and the melodramatic encounters between Maskwell and Lady Touchwood in *The Double-Dealer* is a good index to Congreve's growth as a writer of comedy. Fainall has been informed how Mirabell had cuckolded him 'in Embrio' before he even married, and his tone is both angry and witty as he comes to see himself as a 'Rank Husband . . . all in the Way of the World'. Marwood soothes his anger and urges her lover to wrest Mrs Fainall's fortune and half of Millamant's from Lady Wishfort. Satisfied that they have both been wronged and content with their plans for revenge, Fainall and Marwood change the tone of their dialogue to a self-mocking wit that is their basic mode of communication. They agree that, since marriage is an honourable institution, cuckoldom must be the same; and Fainall guarantees to provide for Marwood in the event that Foible tries to destroy her reputation. As for accepting Marwood's insistence that she hates Mirabell, Fainall is willing to do so as an act of faith; and he renounces jealousy as the condition of husbands, a status which he disavows from this point forward, closing with a moral tag: '*All Husbands must, or Pain, or Shame endure; The Wise too jealous are, Fools too secure*' [IV i]. Congreve allows his villains wit and, within the milieu of libertine ethics, a kind of honesty that is appealing. There is always something sympathetic about a man who can ease his anguish through wit and humour; Fainall's failure in marriage and his cynicism provide a test and balance for Mirabell's hopes in his marriage to Millamant.

SOURCE: extracts from *William Congreve* (New York, 1971), pp. 143–4, 148–9.

William Myers   'A New Function for Vice and Folly' (1972)

[The discussion here is related to the general argument on Plot and Meaning in William Myers's excerpt in section 1 of Part Three, and linked to the closing observation, on the incompatibility between comic action in the Jonsonian tradition and new notions of social order, in the excerpt on *Love for Love* in section 3 above – Ed.]

In . . . *The Way of the World* . . . Congreve . . . unmistakably seeks to bring his view of public order and his sense of private values into a coherent and optimistic dramatic relationship, to put on public display a decorum which, in a distinctively classical manner, imposes order with equal grace and effectiveness on the social, the personal and the aesthetic spheres. Thus Vice and Folly not only suffer public defeat in this play; they themselves acknowledge their own unsuitability for life in the World. Fainall is at least as fierce as Manly in his denunciation of it. In the very scene in which he proclaims that he has 'a Heart of Proof, and something of a Constitution to bustle thro' the ways of Wedlock and this World', he suggests to Mrs Marwood that they 'retire somewhere, any where to another World' [II i], while at the end of the Third Act he proclaims his own anti-social isolation: 'I am single; and will herd no more with 'em'. Lady Wishfort, too, wishes to escape from social realities by retiring with Mrs Marwood 'to Desarts and Solitudes' [v i]. The social implication of Fainall's anarchic individualism is finally revealed when, having failed to manipulate the law to his own advantage, he resorts to sheer force and demands that Lady Wishfort simply withhold her consent to any match Millamant might wish to make. Such behaviour is to be expected from a man who has learnt his manners 'from his *Czarish* Majestie's Retinue' [v i], that is from Peter the Great's courtiers who accompanied the Czar on his visit to England in 1697, and demonstrated the civility of autocracies by wrecking John Evelyn's gardens at Sayes Court. Barbarity and Absolutism are indistinguishable in Congreve's view, and must finally be excluded from the civilised World.

Mirabell, on the other hand, is the perfect worldly man. If *Love for Love* was moving towards the dishonesties of *The Conscious Lovers* on the question of the relation of public to private success, *The Way of the World* sharply changes direction . Mirabell's role, in Mr Van Voris's words, is that of 'the Machiavellian poet as maker of society' who knows that personal dilemmas can be resolved 'only within the reformed circle of the World'.[1] Congreve was far from reluctant to have a man of the world instead of a moderately sensual juvenile as his chief character, and Mirabell obviously embodies his conviction that man becomes himself not passively, by education or self-denial, but in the full and active exercise of his powers. The humanism of the play is thus firmly centred in Mirabell's discernment, a discernment which is impressive precisely because it has the measure of its own limitations: 'for a discerning Man', Mirabell admits, he is 'somewhat too passionate a Lover'; for he likes Millamant 'with all her Faults; nay, like[s] her for her Faults' [I i]. In this play wit is not its own justification.

Millamant is the crucial test of Mirabell's humanism because, like Harriet in *The Man of Mode*, her chief and legitimate preoccupation in a World dominated by appetite and entailed estates is her own freedom. She has the sense to see that this, and not the virtue that Angelica in *Love for Love* professes to believe in, is the principal issue between Mirabell and herself, and that the problem is reciprocal: 'What wou'd you give, that you cou'd help loving me?' she asks him. 'I would give something that you did not know, I cou'd not help it' [II i], he replies. Her mistake, however, in this situation of mutual vulnerability, is to try to defend herself by deploying her beauty and power of refusal with the ruthlessness of an absolute monarch: 'One's Cruelty is one's Power [she insists], and when one parts with one's Cruelty, one parts with one's Power; and when one has parted with that, I fancy one's Old and Ugly' [II i]. In her heart, however, she knows that this maiden sprightliness leads to a shrinking not only from the prospect of growing Old and Ugly in the future, but from love in the present. In a striking echo of Harriet's feelings about Dorimant in *The Man of Mode*, she admits to Mrs Fainall, 'Well, If *Mirabell* shou'd not make a good Husband, I am a lost thing; – for I find I love him violently' [IV i].

In the proviso scene, therefore, she exchanges the arbitrary vivacities of the virgin, which anyway sparkle mainly with fear, for liberty of a maturer, more rational, more modern kind. Her emphasis, however, is still on freedom – 'To have my Closet Inviolate; to be sole Empress of my Tea-table . . .' [IV i] – and it is Mirabell's capacity as a modern man of the world to reconcile these legitimate demands with the ideal of intelligible and plain relations which is thus put to the test in this scene. Significantly he demands of Millamant that there should be no closet intrigues in their home, but honourably open manners and conduct. His most important contribution to their agreement, however, comes at the end when he promises to be 'a tractable and complying Husband', and calls on Mrs Fainall 'to be a witness to the Sealing of the Deed' [IV i]. The fact that Mrs Fainall does so willingly, and urges Millamant to be frank in her love for Mirabell, is a sign of how civilised this play is compared with *The Man of Mode*. The basis for this new civility is a sort of written constitution of marriage. Each forswears arbitrary power, Millamant as a beauty, Mirabell as a husband. Lockean notions of order have at last been brought into sensitive relation with a full and humane sense of the complexity of the individual's freedom.

The problem is that the action has nothing to do with this resolution. Like the two previous comedies, *The Way of the World* has a lively but meaningless plot in the Fifth Act. As a result of Mirabell's Deed, and the off-stage collusion between the characters which it makes possible, events on the stage cease to be crucial to the wellbeing of the people involved. The audience is merely deceived (along with Fainall, Marwood and Lady Wishfort) into thinking that they are, and that the resolution of the purely practical problems in the play is directly related to the virtue or vice, wisdom or folly of the protagonists. It is not.

Van Voris tries to get round this by arguing that *The Way of the World* offers as an alternative to the crudely doctrinaire Toryism of Collier's *Short View* a special vision of natural disorder which can only be controlled by the creation of successful fictions. 'This capacity for control, and not the divine power worshipped by Collier, nor the property of the parsimonious Locke, nor the absolute power of Leviathan, gives the world its stability in its necessary revolutions.'[2] Mirabell thus becomes the master pragmatist of the play, and his drawing-up of the Deed, an act of wit in a large and representative sense. For if the chaos which threatens public order is the same as that which threatens private peace, the artifice which secures us from the one must also secure us from the other. Mirabell's cleverness in securing Mrs Fainall's property is thus neatly merged with the artifice with which he and Millamant 'meet and bargain to create a new unity . . . a marriage that will extend the moment and artfully slow the fractures of time'.[3]

Persuasive as this is as an account of Congreve's probable convictions, it remains the case that no dramatic connection is established between the Deed and the proviso scene. They just happen to be achievements of the same man, but it would have been perfectly possible for Mirabell and Millamant to have reached moral agreement while Fainall proved the cleverer at shuffling documents. Mirabell's personality is thus finally irrelevant to the plot of the play, which means that no dramatic connections are established between its humanism and the way of the world. This becomes obvious if we consider Mirabell's relations with Mrs Fainall before the action begins. There was no absolute reason, since she had an adequate fortune, why he should not have married her himself. He could not plead that he did not love her since he was quite prepared to involve her in a brutally loveless marriage with Fainall, to which she consented only out of fear and because she loved him more than he loved her. It is impossible therefore to associate his cleverness in having the original deed drawn up with the genuinely civilised relationship he achieves with Millamant.

There is, however, one way in which it is possible to save something of Van Voris's case. His basic position is that for Congreve man's sole protection against the anarchic fractures of time is 'a cultivated stance before that chaos'.[4] It follows that a successful conjuring trick, which merely suggests coherence without earning it in Jonsonian fashion by an exhaustive exploration of actuality and illusion, may be the only way a Congreve play can really be in earnest about life. 'Like drama', Van Voris argues, 'the World shapes and controls *by fictions* its necessary durations'.[5] Why should not *The Way of the World*, therefore, simply create opportunities for the audience as well as the players to adopt a cultivated stance and give credence to the fiction that Mirabell embodies a humane solution to the play's problems? They could then sustain for a time ideals which are clearly desirable, but which have no other basis in reality than our ability wilfully to believe in them.

I confess that I find such a view of *The Way of the World* both attractive and in important respects true to the spirit of the play. But if the text does invite us to create our own response to the events and people it depicts, I would prefer, finally, rather to confront its incoherence than to make use of the opportunities it offers, certainly in performance, for self-deception however cultivated. Such an approach to *Love for Love* might very well be acceptable, but the greatness of *The Way of the World*, for me, lies in the fact that even though Congreve was trying to give it that classical perfection of a plot meaningful because it was pure which he had first pursued in *The Double-Dealer*, he was none the less ready to be inclusively honest about the nature of modern social relationships at whatever cost to his ideal of correctness. He was prepared, in other words, to let his own mind become a battlefield in the war between a great literary past and an irresistible historical present.

It is the meticulous honesty of much of *The Way of the World* which is so impressive. Thus Congreve doesn't assume, as Steele was to do later, that virtue and prosperity are such manifestly distinct categories that their independent operation can be taken for granted. Millamant, unlike Bevil Junior, controls only half her estate, and a close if complicated connection is established between the degree to which she is financially independent and the degree to which she can be considered morally accountable. In the very first scene Fainall says to Mirabell of Millamant's behaviour the previous night:

FAIN. You were to blame to resent what she spoke only in Compliance with her Aunt.

MIRA. She is more Mistress of her self, than to be under the necessity of such a resignation.

FAIN. What? tho' half her Fortune depends upon her marrying with my Lady's Approbation?

MIRA. I was then in such a Humour, that I shou'd have been better pleas'd if she had been less discreet.   [1 i]

Millamant's partial independence financially thus explains but does not entirely excuse her lack of moral independence. In both spheres she has still to be finally set free. The great weakness of *Love for Love*, therefore, Angelica's gratuitous emancipation from all problems of fortune and character, is avoided in *The Way of the World*. The play acknowledges that society and personality deeply interpenetrate each other, and that virtue, wisdom, wit, success, and the positive laws of the commonwealth all derive their meaning and value from each other.

For reasons I have attempted to outline, however, it inevitably fails to create a coherent image of these relationships, in spite of all the 'toil' Congreve admitted went into writing it. The labour of imposing a Jonsonian order on the recalcitrant facts of modern life is particularly obvious in the tensions between form and content in the language of the play. Notoriously, Congreve's style is either frigidly laboured or triumphantly graceful, depending on your point of view; but for me it is precisely the fact that it is both which is so impressive. The stylistic tensions in Mirabell's and Fainall's speeches are an extraordinarily detailed and subtle record of that struggle between Renaissance humanism and modern life which it is my contention Congreve experienced in writing the play. These tensions are particularly marked in its sudden moments of real grossness. Van Voris remarks of Congreve's language:

When the movement of the play is down and away from the sublime and the beautiful toward the fractured and the explicit, an image is the swiftest way to get there. Congreve used a stylistic device he took from Wycherley, who knew well how an image can upset a public pose. But because Congreve had a firmer concept of verbal beauty, he also had a firmer grasp of what was ugly.[6]

This ugliness has profound social implications in Congreve's World precisely because it can upset the public pose, that urbanely sceptical pragmatism which makes possible the assumption that life is in truth orderly. Gross language, moreover, is frequently linked to folly and vice in the man who uses it. In *The Double-Dealer*, for instance, the Froths indulge their taste for it and thereby expose themselves as well as the people they are sneering at to ridicule. In *Love for Love* the note of brutality is more persistent, even though the play as a whole is more lighthearted. The grossness of Tattle is particularly discordant, though Valentine's mad speeches also provide some notable examples of ugliness. It is in *The Way of the World*, however, that grossness of language acquires a major significance by being systematically linked to ugliness of thought and action. As a result Fainall and Marwood become far more impressive figures of melodramatic evil than Maskwell and Lady Touchwood, in *The Double-Dealer*. Out of the semi-sadistic elegance of Fainall's first speech about himself, for instance – 'I'd no more play with a Man that slighted his ill Fortune, than I'd make Love to a Woman who undervalu'd the loss of her Reputation' [i i] – there emerges before long the stylistically and morally less controlled nastiness of

If I had kept my speed like a Stag, 'twere somewhat, – but to crawl after, with my Horns like a Snail, and out-strip'd by my Wife – 'tis Scurvy Wedlock,
[iii i]

and this in turn leads to the uncontrolled grossness of his actions and ideas as well as of his images in the final scene:

You thing that was a Wife, shall smart for this. I will not leave thee wherewithall to hide thy Shame; Your Body shall be Naked as your Reputation.   [v i]

Marwood, too, has access to a supply of verbal nastiness ('Here comes the good Lady, panting ripe' [iii i]) which she uses to the full in her gleeful description to Lady Wishfort of divorce proceedings.

It is the fools rather than the knaves, however, who indulge in the most extravagantly unpleasant images [as in this exchange between Petulant and Witwoud]:

PETU.   Stand off – I'll kiss no more Males, – I have kiss'd your *twin* yonder in a humour of reconciliation, till he (*hiccup*) rises upon my stomack like a Radish. . . . I'll go sleep.

WITW. Do, rap thy self up like a *Wood-louse* and dream Revenge – [IV i]

Congreve exploits this tendency of folly to indulge in verbal ugliness and extravagance to greatest effect in and through the figure of Lady Wishfort in the Fifth Act. In the wildness of her language she is given a presence and significance quite independent of the unfolding plot, though, of course, as the only person on stage except Fainall and Marwood who does not know its outcome in advance, she is also the central personage in the dénouement. Lady Wishfort's folly involves, among other things, a total inability to focus fully on the reality of what is happening around her. When pressed by Fainall to agree never to marry, for instance, she remains capable, in the midst of her own and her daughter's distress, of a remark as absurd as 'but in Case of Necessity; as of Health, or some such Emergency' [v i]. Lady Wishfort's indulgence in unrealities opens a seam of language which had not been heard in the theatre since Jonson, and which, indeed, was impossible in plays like *The Man of Mode* or *The Country Wife*, concerned as they were with the functioning of wit in that narrowly conceived World, the *beau monde*, rather than the broadly based London of Jonson. For in the World as it was conceived of by the dramatist of the 1670s, even the foolish and the vicious, Sir Fopling and Mrs Loveit, had to retain a degree of self-restraint if they were to contribute seriously to a credible study of the relevance of wit and virtue to social survival and personal happiness. But once it is assumed that man's place in society is secured and sustained, not by the exercise of wit, but through established laws and contracts – and this is the assumption of the Fifth Act of *The Way of the World* – folly can safely acquire an almost Dickensian grotesqueness. Lady Wishfort's account of her daughter's upbringing isn't believable even as an exaggeration of the truth. It is a superbly comic extravaganza, effective precisely because its excess is superfluous, because we don't need it to clarify our sense of motive, to carry the action forward, or to enrich our awareness of theme. It is magisterially irresponsible of Congreve to have his characters speak in this way, to give a frightened middle-aged woman a line like 'Out *Caterpillar*. Call me not Aunt, I know thee not' [v i]. But it is wildness of this kind which makes the last Act of *The Way of the World* so impressive. It opens up the play, gives an urgency to the problem of folly and corruption which would be quite impossible in the world of Etherege where decorum of a kind has always to be maintained. But Lady Wishfort's remoteness from the discipline of correctness either of speech or action, opens up a vision of the world beneath the World far more disturbing than anything in the first scene of *The Man of Mode*:

> begon, begon, begon, go, go, – that I took from Washing of old Gause and Weaving of dead Hair, with a bleak blew Nose, over a Chafeing-dish of starv'd Embers and Dining behind a Traverse Rag, in a shop no bigger than a Bird-cage, – go, go, starve again, do do   [v i]

Only supreme folly could allow such a collapse of the cultivated stance and such a revelation of the psychological, moral and material horrors of the abyss.

This disturbingly comic extravagance, like Fainall's brutally effective ruthlessness, cannot, however, finally be separated from the undoubted weakness of the plot. They are all products, if not equally inevitable ones, of the Lockean social premises of the play. Congreve's greatness is that he does not evade the resulting contradictions. Certainly his loyalty to traditional forms cannot be attributed merely to neo-classical pedantry since, provided the dramatist was content to produce a casually minor piece, writing a classical play was to remain possible for another seventy years. Congreve, however, as Dryden's heir, was interested in the major issue of how Man functions best in the World. It was left to him, therefore, to illustrate, against all his inclinations, in what ways the kind of plot Etherege produced no longer worked as a vehicle for a large and significant imitation of human life. This concern with the main issues, however, also made possible his discovery of a new function for figures of vice and folly in comedy. Merely to establish in and through the action that one issues in the other had lost its relevance in a World governed by plain and intelligible property rights. But precisely because decorum in such a World is not an absolute requirement for worldly prosperity, a Lady Wishfort or a Fainall can expose, even if only momentarily, the deeply disturbing possibilities of uninhibited humanity, unrestrained by any need for a complex social conformity. Jacobean tragedy and the heroic play had, of course, already exploited the idea of uninhibited man, but never in the context of everyday, commonsense, prudential living. Congreve has suddenly found a way of bringing the anarchic extravagance of melodrama into striking conjunction with the ordinariness of comedy.

First in the figure of Maskwell, then more tellingly in the figure of Fainall, he offers a much more impressive, potentially more explosive, image of anti-social man than anything in Etherege or Wycherley, while in Lady Wishfort he gives us a character whose greatness lies in the fact that, like Falstaff, though by very different means, she can make us laugh at the same time as she makes us feel appalled. It is not, indeed, an exaggeration to say that *The Way of the World* is a necessary experiment in the process that leads to Lovelace in *Clarissa*, Blifil in *Tom Jones*, and even Bill Sykes in *Oliver Twist*. Precisely as a failure, as a work which does not resolve its own internal tensions according to the conventions on which it is relying for its main effects, it belongs to the mainstream of our literature, as more perfectly plotted plays, by Farquhar, Goldsmith and Sheridan, do not.

SOURCE: extracts from 'Plot and Meaning in Congreve's Comedies', in Brian Morris (ed.), *William Congreve* (London, 1972), pp. 84–92.

NOTES

[Reorganised and renumbered from the original – Ed.]

1. W. H. Van Voris, *The Cultivated Stance: The Design of Congreve's Plays* (Dublin, 1965), p. 132.
2. Ibid., p. 130.
3. Ibid., p. 142.
4. Ibid., p. 22.
5. Ibid., p. 130 (italics mine).
6. Ibid., pp. 159–60.

Harriet Hawkins   'The Audience's Dilemma' (1972)

. . . However baffled, boorish, bombastic or befuddled the individual characters in *Love for Love* may be, we in the audience remain superior and secure in our possession of privileged information concerning them.

We are fully aware of all their intentions and pretensions. We are thus spared the dilemmas involved in determining motives, we are safe from the uncertainties about other people which confront us in ordinary life, and which confront Valentine and Angelica up there on the stage.

In *The Way of the World* Congreve deliberately confronts his audience with precisely the same dilemmas faced by his characters. The contrasts to his mode of presentation in *Love for Love* make it even more evident that in the opening scenes of his last comedy Congreve departs from his previous practice to lead us into a comic world where we ourselves are not sure just what is going on, where we are uncertain who may be related to or in love with whom, and where we wonder whether the people we meet are honourable or dishonourable. Such insecure responses are unusual responses to the expository scenes of a Restoration comedy, but they certainly are familiar enough in ordinary social experience. Reading or seeing *The Way of the World* for the first time, one feels like an outsider at a smart cocktail party who overhears snatches of conversation, the implications of which he does not fully understand ('When you are weary of him, you know your remedy'); who classifies the guests in certain ways only to learn later that his initial classifications were all wrong, that Miss Y, who he had decided was in love with Mr X, is actually the mistress of Mr Z, or that the witty and elegant man who seemed so amusing is a vicious cad. Obviously this sort of gradual process of discovery is not the usual expository way of Restoration comedy. We learn all we need to know about the natures of Dorimant, Loveit, Ben, Horner and Lady Fidget in the first five minutes of our acquaintance with them. But a continuing process of discovery is the usual way of the social world we all live in.

In his title, Congreve insists that he imitates life, but his peculiar method of imitating social life in *The Way of the World* is more frequently encountered in the novel, or in modern drama (in Henry James, Proust or Chekhov) than in Restoration comedy. In this play characters who only gradually reveal their true natures to us, who only gradually reveal their true attitudes towards each other, are set off against other characters (Witwoud, Petulant, Lady Wishfort) who continue to behave in accord with our first impressions of them. And rather like Lady Wishfort herself, we in the audience frequently must modify our own original reactions to several characters and situations. Sir Wilfull, whom everybody automatically classifies as a stock boor from the country who is ruder than Gothic, turns up on the side of the Truewits in the end. Millamant, the proud and ostensibly heartless heroine, gradually reveals a certain vulnerability and fear. Fainall's great elegance and dry wit prove to be the masks of malice. At first glance, Mrs Fainall appears identical to Marwood, a bitter and jealous woman who has been scorned, but she later becomes a very sympathetic figure. And our final responses to such characters are cumulative in a peculiar way, since Congreve gives us a series of partial perspectives on them that combine in a comprehensive response which frequently assimilates the previous ones. For instance, our appreciation of Sir Wilfull's generosity does not preclude continuing laughter at his boorishness. Similarly, enjoyment of Fainall's witty cynicism remains even when he behaves with extreme cruelty, and our pity for Lady Wishfort's serious predicament does not stop our laughter at her bombastic discomfiture:

LADY W. This is most inhumanly Savage; exceeding the Barbarity of a *Muscovite* Husband.
FAIN. I learn'd it from his *Czarish* Majestie's Retinue, in a Winter Evenings Conference over Brandy and Pepper, amongst other secrets of Matrimony and Policy, as they are at present Practis'd in the *Northern* Hemisphere. [v i]

Thus where other Restoration comedies frequently simplify audience responses for the sake of comic intensity (perhaps by eliminating sympathy for their comic targets), Congreve complicates our responses throughout *The Way of the World*. And our complicated, sometimes uncertain, responses are the clear result of the play's form and the accurate reflection of its meaning, given a world where our responses to people and situations inevitably grow more complex when more is known about them. Since the plot hardly moves at all, the movements of the play really are the progressive revelations of character, the movements of the characters into new relationships with each other, and the movements of our own progressive understanding of the various characters and their situations. All this is an elaborate way of saying that Congreve first presents us with apparently simple surfaces, with stock types and situations, and then he takes us beneath the surfaces and behind the masks. What, this play asks, may hide behind the stereotypes of comic and social forms? And when dramatic and social forms that once served to reveal character have become dramatic and social ends in themselves, why can they not serve equally well to conceal character? Congreve's last comedy is all about the forms of language and manners, about the forms of wit. It is a graceful, elegant, unsentimental, comic and incisive exhibition of what these forms may conceal and what they may reveal. And this play's extraordinary way of first defining its own form as that of a typical Restoration comedy, and then proceeding to escape from its own definition, contributes both to its success and to its difficulty. For when it sets the norms and forms of contemporary drama and contemporary society against each other, *The Way of the World* ceases to be even a typical Congreve comedy. It was not what his own audience expected. There is no Miss Prue, no Tattle, no Ben. Motives, rather than cleverness, define true wit. Indeed, the formulas of witty language prove to be of no help at all, since (precisely because they are formulas) just about anybody can master them. A Fainall can speak as brilliantly as a Mirabell. Mirabell's servant can easily adopt the lingo fit for a suitor to Lady Wishfort. Similarly, the forms of manners provide no basis for distinction if a Marwood can impeccably observe the forms of friendship until it suits her convenience to abandon them. But a closer look at Congreve's presentation of his key representatives of True and False Wit, and a glance at the manners and mannerisms of Millamant can get us nearer to the elusive essence of this play as manifested in its language and in its heroine.

Until the surprising dénouement of *The Way of the World*, Fainall appears to be an equal match for Mirabell. He is expert with language, perceptive, always amusing. And however hollow his wit may appear under scrutiny, it certainly sounds like the real thing.

FAIN. You are a gallant Man, *Mirabell*; and tho' you may have Cruelty enough, not to satisfie a Lady's longing; you have too much Generosity, not to be tender of her Honour. Yet you speak with an Indifference which *seems to be affected; and confesses you are conscious of* a Negligence.

MIRA. You pursue the Argument with a distrust that *seems to be unaffected*, and *confesses you are conscious* of a Concern for which the Lady is more indebted to you, than your Wife.   [I i, emphasis mine]

In retrospect, when we know the play, we can admire the stiletto of Mirabell's wit as he parodies Fainall, skilfully forestalls further prying, and hints at the love affair between Fainall and Marwood.[1] But this is possible only in retrospect, only on a second reading or viewing of the play. Likewise, an understanding of Fainall's reference to Mirabell's 'gallantry' requires information about Marwood's character which is withheld at this point in the action. And there are other reasons why we may be initially confused by this interchange. 'Seems to be' is equated with 'confesses you are conscious' in both speeches. To say what they think is in fact the case, each character points out what 'seems to be' the case. Mirabell speaks with indifference, but Fainall decides that the indifference 'seems to be affected', and thus concludes that Mirabell is conscious of having neglected Marwood. 'What is', these speeches imply, may be the opposite of what it seems to be, or it may in fact be what it seems to be. Everything depends on whether the emotion expressed is affected or unaffected. But all this goes by like lightning. On a first reading we cannot know how to interpret this preliminary sparring because we simply do not have enough information about these characters, or about their true relationship with each other, or about their relationships with Marwood and Mrs Fainall. We can tell that both characters are attempting to probe the truth behind the surface of appearance. We can tell that the two characters sound very much alike, and that they each claim to know a lot more about each other than we know. But, for all we know at this point in the play, the two characters are equally clever rakes who appear to be confidants. Mirabell has just described his own calculated courtship of Lady Wishfort, and Fainall makes clear his cynicism about marriage in general. Fainall's name is not even much help here, for if a character named 'Scandal' can turn out to be a pretty good friend to Valentine, a character named 'Fainall' might turn out to be simply an affected rake who is the confidant and foil of the hero. Certainly Mirabell and Fainall appear to be at one in their scorn for Witwoud. Anyway, throughout their initial encounter, the similarities between the two characters are far more evident than their differences.[2]

The parallels between Mirabell and Fainall continue into the second act, when each character walks off with a lady who is involved with the other. Fainall pairs off with his mistress, Marwood, who really loves Mirabell; and Mirabell walks with his former mistress, who is married to Fainall. Then, even as we learn of Fainall's infidelity, we learn that Mirabell himself contrived the Fainall marriage to suit his own convenience. And when Fainall admits that he married for money, we are reminded that Mirabell himself is not indifferent to Millamant's great fortune. Nevertheless, throughout the comedy, we are gradually made aware that while both characters share certain goals, and certain modes of speech and behaviour, the motives and judgement behind their actions differ sharply. In retrospect, the two characters may be seen to define opposite visions of the way of the world from the very beginning:

FAIN. For a *passionate Lover*, methinks you are a *Man* somewhat too *discerning* in the Failings of your Mistress.

MIRA. And for a *discerning Man*, somewhat too *passionate* a *Lover*; for I like her with all her Faults.   [I i, emphasis mine]

Here Fainall accuses Mirabell of departing from the conventional forms of courtship which would acknowledge no flaws in the beloved. Mirabell neatly exposes the hollowness of this stereotyped idealism by reversing Fainall's key adjectives and nouns to define a love which is more honest, more realistic, and far more genuine than any courtly pose ever could be. But Mirabell's point is not all that obvious at a glance. It is only obvious upon reflection. To illustrate the verbal subtlety that characterises *The Way of the World* it is helpful to contrast Mirabell's reversal of Fainall's words with the more immediate comic effect of the same rhetorical technique ('When the words of a sentence are turned upside down, or as I may say, repeated backward')[3] as it appears in other plays. By giving the original placement of words to one character, and the reversal of the same words to another, Restoration comic playwrights commonly use this device to organise their witty repartee. For example, in *The Country Wife*, Wycherley deftly exploits the technique to expose Lady Fidget's hypocrisy and to illustrate Horner's keen wit:

LADY F. . . . *affectation* makes not a Woman more odious to them than *Virtue*.

HORNER. Because your *Virtue* is your greatest *affectation*, Madam.

Wycherley's exchange of wit is funnier than Congreve's and its impact is much more obvious. Horner's attack is direct, and he emerges the clear verbal winner when he takes Lady Fidget's contraries and identifies them. And in *The Old Batchelor* Congreve explicitly calls our attention to his delicious use of this rhetorical device when he reverses the proverbial conclusion, '*Marry'd* in *haste*, we may *repent* at *leisure*', to argue that

> Some by Experience find those Words misplac'd:
> At *leisure marry'd*, they *repent* in *haste*.
>   [v i, emphasis mine]

Amusingly, two of the key words, 'Marry'd' and 'repent', maintain the same chronological order, and this implies an unchangeable relationship between them. The significant difference lies only in the chronological 'haste' or 'leisure' of the inevitable repentance.

Clearly Mirabell's reversal of Fainall's terms 'passionate Lover' and 'discerning Man' is less overtly hilarious than either of the earlier examples of the same technique. Still, the conclusion which Mirabell reaches by this reversal comes as a striking surprise, as a kind of revelation, both to him and to us. Few passionate lovers in any period admit faults in their beloved, and hardly any of them sit down and deliberately make catalogues of the faults of their ladies. In fact, ever since Ovid, this sort of catalogue has been prescribed as one of the 'remedies of love', and Mirabell frankly admits that he originally intended to concentrate on Millamant's faults in order to cool his passion for her. But his ultimate acceptance and understanding of Millamant, with all her faults, also reveals Mirabell's full acceptance and understanding of himself.

Nevertheless, Fainall refuses to collapse in defeat: 'Marry her, marry her', he says, 'be half as well acquainted with her Charms, as you are with her Defects, and my Life on't, you are your own Man again' [I i]. Fainall's line is very funny, and it also rings true to the usual treatment of marriage in Restoration comedy, where sexual or emotional familiarity breeds contempt and where love is thus possible only at a safe distance. In fact, on the basis of Fainall's conclusion, and on the basis of conventional Restoration comic practice, even so perceptive a comic writer as Thackeray predicts that 'When Mirabell is sixty, having of course divorced the first Lady Millamant, and married his friend Doricourt's granddaughter out of the nursery – it will be his turn; and young Belmour will make a fool of him.'[4] Of course Thackeray's prophecy misses Congreve's distinction between the 'ways of wedlock and this world' that are advocated by and embodied in Fainall, and the more honest and more honourable ways that are discovered and devised by Mirabell and Millamant. But Congreve himself always makes it very clear that in the world of this play good marriages (like true wits) are very rare. They are the exception rather than the rule. Fainall's own marriage of convenience is the play's example of the rule. And given the example of wedded life set by the Fainalls, Millamant's reluctance to 'dwindle into a wife' is easy to understand.

In his famous and influential attack on Restoration comedy, L. C. Knights summons Millamant to face severe judgement because of her lack of 'intelligence'. But one of the witnesses that Mr Knights calls for the prosecution of Restoration comedy can serve as an excellent witness in Millamant's defence.[5] In his *Advice to a Daughter*, Halifax gives us an excellent perspective on Millamant's situation, and on her artifices. Writing in the witty style of a fatherly Mirabell, Halifax graphically describes the dangers of the contemporary social scene: 'It is time now to lead you out of your *House* into the *World*. A dangerous step; where your Vertue alone will not serve you, except it is attended with a great deal of *Prudence*: You must have *both* for your *Guard*, and not stir without them; the Enemy is abroad, and you are sure to be taken, if you are found stragling' (pp. 95–6). For self-protection, his daughter (like Millamant) must remain aloof. Indeed, cautious 'Reserve' is 'a *Guard* to a *good Woman*, and a *Disguise* to an *ill one*. It is of so much use to both, that those ought to use it is an *Artifice*, who refuse to practice it as a *Vertue*' (p. 116). 'Reserve', when it becomes the external basis for judgement of virtue, will serve quite adequately as a cover for vice. How then does one distinguish between virtue itself and vice disguised as virtue when both involve exactly the same outward manifestations? How does one distinguish between true wit and its artful imitation? How does one distinguish between true sincerity and sincere acting? Congreve poses these problems through the prose style and characterisation of a comic world where a Mirabell and a Fainall may sound, dress and act alike. Thus Millamant quite rightly conceals her love from Mirabell and from the world. Maintain Mirabell's elegance, but pervert his motives, and you get – Fainall.

Millamant is also threatened in her dealings with women, and the song 'If there's delight in love 'tis when I see/That Heart which others bleed for bleeds for me' is a clever means of disguising her feelings and, simultaneously, exposing the prying and dangerous Marwood. It is a defence, and it certainly should not be interpreted as the summing up of Millamant's philosophy of life. In the proviso scene, Millamant explicitly insists on the substance, as opposed to the forms, of a good marriage. 'I'll not be call'd Names', she says, while one remembers the hypocritical endearments of the Fainalls. And, she goes on,

Good *Mirabell* don't let us be familiar or fond, nor kiss before folks, like my Lady *Fadler* and Sr *Francis*: Nor goe to *Hide-Park* together the first *Sunday* in a New Chariot, to provoke Eyes and Whispers; And then never to be seen there together again; as if we were proud of one another the first Week, and asham'd of one another for ever After.   [IV i]

Given the examples of contemporary matrimony in Restoration comedy we hardly need a battery of Restoration authorities to justify the extreme caution of Congreve's heroines, Angelica and Millamant. But Halifax's comments on the husbands his own daughter might face definitively substantiate their fears that most Restoration wedding ceremonies were (for upper-class brides) entrances into narrow, if gilded, cages. Halifax frankly warns his daughter that her husband may turn out to be unfaithful, drunken, covetous, ill-humoured, weak, or incompetent, and he gives practical, realistic advice on how to cope with each of these melancholy prospects. For instance, 'when your *Husband* shall resolve to be an *Ass*', you must be very undexterous if you 'do not take care he may be *your Ass* . . . do like a wise *Minister* to an easie *Prince*; first give him the Orders you afterwards receive from him' (pp. 59–60). In any event, his daughter should not expect happiness from marriage, and Halifax fills his advice on marriage with poignant warnings: 'You are therefore to make the best of what is *setled* . . . by *Law*, and not vainly imagine, that it will be *changed* for your sake' (p. 32). 'I will conclude this Article with my Advice, that you would, as much as Nature will give you leave, endeavour to forget the great *Indulgence* you have found at home. After such a gentle Discipline as you have been under; every thing you dislike will seem the harsher to you' (pp. 66–7). And before she recovers her cool poise, Millamant herself reaches something of the same conclusion, 'If Mirabell should not prove a good husband, I am a lost thing.'

Of course we know that Mirabell will be a good husband, but it is nevertheless not surprising that Millamant's confession of love comes only after reflection, and is accompanied by fear. And Millamant has, in fact, been afraid all along. Throughout the comedy she constantly breaks off her sentences, a stylistic device which contemporary playwrights used to reveal 'some affection, as either of sorrow, bashfulness, fear, anger or vehemency':[6] 'Well, I won't have you *Mirabell* – I'm resolv'd – I think – You may go – Ha, ha, ha' [II i]; 'Well then – I'll take my death I'm in a horrid fright – *Fainall*, I shall never say it – well – I think – I'll endure you' [IV i]. This nervous style is characteristic of Millamant throughout the play, and the nervousness behind all her bravura and arrogance seems fully justified. Except in the scenes with Mirabell, whom she is not quite ready to trust, she is surrounded by impossible relatives (her fortune and future are in the hands of Lady Wishfort) and a protective convoy of fools. Nevertheless, Congreve's young heroine handles her difficult economic, personal, and social situations without ever losing humour, poise, self-control, or charm.

Millamant's plight reflects Congreve's dramatic concern with the problems of experiencing genuine emotion and still behaving with due decorum within a world of artificiality. *The Way of the World* thus brings us full circle from *The Man of Mode*, which was concerned with various methods of suppressing emotion in order to behave with brillant artificiality. Still, neither Millamant nor Mirabell throws good sense or good manners to the winds for the sake of sheer, unmitigated passion. Mirabell sees to it that the financial situation is well in hand, and Millamant sees to it that she can maintain as much autonomy and glamour as possible even after marriage. This measure of control, this degree of calculation, seems inevitably necessary in any world where some degree of artifice and a large degree of economic and social realism are necessary in order to survive (but where the expression of emotion beyond artifice is equally necessary in order to live richly and fully instead of merely managing to exist by duly observing the proper forms). . . .

SOURCE: extract from *Likenesses of Truth in Elizabethan and Restoration Drama* (Oxford, 1972), pp. 126–36.

NOTES

[Reorganised and renumbered from the original – Ed.]

1. In their exchanges Mirabell frequently gets the last word. As Dryden said, 'there may be much acuteness in a thing well said; but there is more in a quick reply.'

2. The original casting of the play may have contributed to the confusion between the two characters, since Betterton, who customarily played the hero, played Fainall.

3. See John Smith's definition of *epanodos* in *The Mysterie of Rhetorique Unveil'd* (1673), p. 90.

4. Thackeray, *The English Humourists of the Eighteenth Century*, ed. George Saintsbury (Oxford, 1908), p. 516. [Excerpted in Part Two, above – Ed.]

5. L. C. Knights, in 'Restoration Comedy: The Reality and the Myth', *Explorations* (London, 1946), p. 136, calls George Savile, Marquess of Halifax, an 'extremely handsome representative of his age' and uses the prose of the *Character of Charles II* as a touchstone by which to condemn Restoration comedy as irrelevant to the best thought of its time. [Knight's essay is

excerpted in section 1 of Part Three, above – Ed.] But see Halifax, *The Lady's New-years Gift: or Advice to a Daughter* (London, 1688) for a perfect gloss on *Love for Love* and *The Way of the World*; page numbers of this edition are cited in my text.

6. John Smith's definition of *aposiopesis*, op. cit., p. 142. See also *Sir Martin Mar-all* in *Works of John Dryden*, ed. John Loftis and Vinton A. Dearing, vol. IX (Berkeley, Cal., 1966):

> *Lady Dupe* [I will] seem to strive to put my passion off, yet shew it still by small mistakes.
> *Mrs Christian* And broken Sentences.   [1 i 94–6]

Anne Barton   'A Blush May Spell Disaster' (1978)

. . . Congreve knew that very little of *The Way of the World* (1700) was 'prepared for that general taste which seems now to be predominant in the palates of our audience' (Dedication to the Earl of Montague). It was his fourth comedy and, although he was still a comparatively young man, he never attempted to write another. Congreve is now usually described as the greatest of the Restoration comic dramatists. All of his plays, however, were conceived and staged after the Glorious Revolution of 1688, during the reign of William and Mary, for a London audience far more subdued and conservative than that of Etherege and Wycherley. The man who wrote *The Way of the World* was, in some ways, a dramatist trying to turn back the clock, to evoke the comedy of a vanished, libertine society of which he had himself never been part. At the same time, he could not help but be affected by those movements of taste and alterations in moral and social attitudes which had declared themselves during the decade of the 1690s. *The Way of the World* is a brilliant compromise between an old order and a new. In its own time, it was not very successful – indeed, as Congreve felt, was scarcely understood. Subsequently, it has suffered by being valued more for the attractiveness of some of its individual acting parts (notably those of Millamant and Lady Wishfort) than for its overall achievement as a play. This is unfortunate, because *The Way of the World* is, in fact, one of the greatest of English comedies: a work that is finely wrought and witty, but also remarkably honest and humane.

It is a play which makes fierce demands upon a theatre audience. Not for Congreve that casual shuffling off of the demands of exposition which Shakespeare, for instance, could afford, precisely because his interests lay elsewhere. 'What's the new news at the new court?' Oliver asks Charles the Wrestler at the beginning of *As You Like It*. And the answer effectively and lucidly tells the theatre audience what it needs to know about the relationship which exists between several of the main characters, and about the situation in which we will find them. Congreve, on the other hand, makes us enter the world of the play and grapple with its complexities on terms remarkably like those he affords to the characters themselves. He even insists that the time span of the action is precisely equivalent to the number of hours we have spent in the theatre watching it unfold. Everywhere he is concerned to point out how much the way of this comic world, for all its heightened quality, is really the way of our own.

There is a sense in which the plot of this comedy – the legacy hunt which sets most of the principal characters in chase of Lady Wishfort's money – is comparatively simple. Far more difficult to comprehend is the pattern of relationship, both formal and unacknowledged, which binds these people together in groupings so intricate and closely-knit as to be claustrophobic. Statements like 'He is half brother to this Witwoud by a former wife, who was sister to my Lady Wishfort, my wife's mother. If you marry Millamant, you must call cousins too' are characteristic of the play. Everybody in *The Way of the World* appears to be the half-brother, nephew, cousin, niece or mother of somebody else. And, at the same time that we are struggling to master this kinship structure, the plain facts of who is related or married to whom, Congreve is also demanding our attention for another and even more complicated system of association: one which is secret rather than public, irrational and extremely dangerous. This second skein of relationship is not only different from the first: it is always threatening to blow the family system sky-high, to contradict and annihilate its patterns. In some cases, it comes close to succeeding.

In the world's eyes, Mrs Fainall is Fainall's wife and Lady Wishfort's strictly brought-up daughter. But she is also, and more passionately, Mirabell's former mistress, and it is Mirabell who defines her as a person and brings out what is best – if also most agonised – about her. Fainall, the husband of this heiress, is engaged in a clandestine affair with

Mrs Marwood: a lady who is trying not only to keep that disreputable association hidden from the world, but to prevent her lover from recognising that, really, Mirabell is the man she loves. Mirabell, the focus of so many women's desires, has himself paid public, false addresses to Lady Wishfort, in order to conceal his real passion for Millamant – who, in her turn, encourages the (again) public addresses of fools in the hope of concealing an intense, private feeling for Mirabell of which she is, for complicated reasons, afraid. Fainall and Mirabell, the two wits and men about town, pose as friends but are secretly one another's enemy. A discrepancy between acknowledged and unacknowledged relationships creates the real plot of this play. At its most explosive, it guides our response to the Fainall/Marwood/Mrs Fainall/Mirabell imbroglio. At its most comic level, it governs the absurd behaviour of Witwoud, whose antipathy to his country half-brother Sir Wilfull is so great that he tries to pretend, in public, that they have never met. But everywhere we look, the relationships of the heart – people's real emotional responses – are at odds with those acknowledged, surface ties of love and friendship which are recognised by society.

A dramatic structure like this demands an alert audience, urging upon it just that kind of unremitting observation, shrewd speculation and judgement which might be described as the most characteristic occupation of the people in the play. In this civilised but ferocious world not even the tremor of an eye-lid goes unremarked. A blush may spell disaster, involuntarily revealing a weakness otherwise concealed. Despite their intelligence, despite their mastery of the social game, these people remain at the mercy of their own bodies, victims not only of uncontrollable physical desires, but of slight but revealing physical reactions over which not even their formidable sophistication can exercise any control. At various crucial points in the play, a rush of blood to the cheeks gives away what Millamant, Mrs Fainall and Mrs Marwood would dearly love to hide. Lady Wishfort, under her layers of white varnish, cannot blush. But she can no more suppress her fifty-five year old lust than she can stop the ageing of her face. Her daughter Mrs Fainall, repressed as a child, married off young to a man tellingly called Mr Languish, has rushed as a widow into the arms of Mirabell, who never pretends that he has really loved her. Millamant employs a defensive screen of fools to keep Mirabell at bay, because she is worried about the effects of time and habit upon love, but she remains haunted by the man and by her own desire for him. All the women in the play are caught, in different ways, in a war between body and mind. Lady

Wishfort, Mrs Marwood and Mrs Fainall have already suffered a costly defeat in this combat. Only Millamant ends the comedy with some chance of emerging victorious. This is partly because of her own intelligence and understanding of the situation, but also because of the nature of her lover, Mirabell.

Towards the end of the play Millamant finally confesses what she has known all along: 'If Mirabell should not make a good husband I am a lost thing – for I find I love him violently.' In this guarded social world a public confession of this kind is as startling as Mirabell's own insistence that he would have Millamant give herself to him 'over and over again' – that his wife should never become something to be taken for granted, but always a person in her own right, to be approached with interest and sensitivity. The famous 'proviso' scene in which Mirabell and Millamant try to define the nature of their marriage and the ways of keeping it alive and honest cannot provide a lasting solution. But at least it creates an intelligent understanding between equals. If any marriage in this society can work, it will be this one. And Congreve suggests that it may, after all, be possible to unite the two kinds of relationship which have appeared in the comedy hitherto as so divergent: the way of the world with the way of the heart. Mirabell and Millamant cannot opt out of society. They can, however, engage in the social game in a spirit poles apart from that of aspiring half-wits like Petulant. They are not malicious. They respect one another. And they can also cut across the whole elaborate and artificial scale of social values in order to see that Sir Wilfull Witwoud, for all his folly and ineptitude, is an honest man and that this fact matters. At the end of *The Way of the World*, as at its beginning, Sir Wilfull is ridiculous in his manners, his speech and his heavy country boots. Yet he has formed a pact with the lovers, and Mirabell can say of him as he could not of Fainall, 'Sir Wilfull is my friend'. There could be no more striking affirmation of that deepening and extension of Restoration values which it was the special greatness of Congreve to have created.

SOURCE: from programme note to the Royal Shakespeare Company's production of *The Way of the World*, 1978.

Patrick Lyons   Subjective Love (1981)

Once endings are evidently artistic, Byron pointed out with some glee, there is room to doubt whether their conclusions have any practical application; that passion can weary and 'love and marriage rarely can combine' is not countered or challenged when weddings are the stopping-place as well as the goal of comedies:

> All tragedies are finished by a death,
> All comedies are ended by a marriage.
> The future states of both are left to faith,
> For authors fear description might disparage
> The worlds to come . . .   [*Don Juan*, III 9]

Equal scepticism not only pervades *The Way of the World*, but actually shapes its ending: faith finds no footholds, as disaster is averted only by self-interest combining with legal acumen, and then the conventions of comedy are glanced at mockingly as Witwoud exclaims in surprise 'are you all got together like Players at the end of the last Act?' With nothing to bar his union with Millamant, Mirabell hesitates:

> LADY W. Well Sir, take her, and with her all the Joy I can give you.
> MILL.   Why do's not the man take me? Wou'd you have me give my self to you over again?
> MIRA.   Ay, and over and over again; for I wou'd have you as often as possibly I can. (*Kisses her hand.*) Well, heav'n grant I love you not too well, that's all my fear.   [v i]

While it is in part delicacy that stays his eagerness, uncertainty here coexists beside gallantry, with neither triumphing. The dance that follows has its immediate potential to image harmony undermined in advance by Foible's disconcerting reminder that the musicians were to have played for Lady Wishfort's public humiliation. The dance is broken off with Lady Wishfort 'ready to sink under the Fatigue', Mrs Fainall's future still a worry to her. And, although Mirabell returns her deed to her, leaving Mrs Fainall's erring husband penniless and the fortune in her control, it comes with cold enough comfort, hedged about with qualification: 'It may be a means well manag'd to make you live easily together.' More dismayingly, Mirabell then closes the play in couplets offering only stern warning and no cheery promise:

> From hence let those be warn'd, who mean to wed:
> Lest mutual falsehood stain the Bridal-Bed:
> For each deceiver to his cost may find,
> That marriage frauds too oft are paid in kind.   [v i]

However successful Mirabell may have been, he is far from being absorbed in contentment, much less in rapturous abandon. Unlike *Love for Love*, there is no miracle, only dissonances that reach back and prolong the moody restlessness of the play.

But for happiness to guarantee a future of love safe from all risks would run contrary to all that Congreve's knowing heroines can find to say about happiness. Most bored, and most intolerant, Angelica in *Love for Love* is also the most forthright; asking

Wou'd any thing but a Madman complain of Uncertainty? Uncertainty and Expectation are the Joys of Life. Security is an insipid thing, and the overtaking and possessing of a Wish, discovers the Folly of the Chase. Never let us know one another better; for the Pleasure of a Masquerade is done when we come to shew Faces; . . .   [*L. for L.*, iv i]

Millamant says as much, as teasingly, dismissing Mirabell's attempt to state for certain where they stand: 'if you are so tedious, fare you well' [ii i]. Like Cynthia in *The Double-Dealer*, whose observation 'that tho' Marriage makes Man and Wife One Flesh, it leaves 'em still Two Fools' [ii i] held her back from marrying, Millamant has seen nothing to encourage her in married couples. Public endearments are too brash to trust ('as Wife, Spouse, My dear, Joy, Jewel, Love, Sweetheart and the rest of that Nauseous Cant, in which Men and their Wives are so fulsomely familiar'). Protestations of feeling betray only hollowness in their over-insistence ('There is not so Impudent a thing in Nature, as the sawcy look of an assured man, Confident of Success'). Fashionable songs supported and championed this preference for uncertainty: 'Love hates to centre in a point assign'd', according to the song Valentine calls for; and the same sense that happiness happens, but cannot be relied on, appeared in songs from other writers. Rochester concluded one song:

> If I, by Miracle, can be
> This life-long Minute true to thee,
> 'Tis all that Heav'n allows.

But however modish these recognitions of transcience and instability, they turn up in the talk of Congreve's characters with more ruefulness, even with open regret, as when Mrs Fainall and Mrs Marwood acknowledge "tis an unhappy Circumstance of Life, that Love shou'd ever die before us: and that the Man so often shou'd out-live the Lover' [II i]

No new certainty, nor even rashness, appears in the betrothal of Mirabell and Millamant: his feelings have been plain to her from the start of the play; and, as Fainall angrily points out to Mrs Marwood, Millamant would have 'stollen' into elopement had not the first attempt to trick her aunt been exposed. What has changed is that the half of Millamant's fortune which they stood to lose unless Lady Wishfort agreed to their marriage, is now to be theirs. On the conspiracy to gain this all the plotting hinges. What is extraordinary is that this is totally unnecessary. Throughout the complex movements of intrigue on intrigue, it is again and again insisted that only half her fortune is at stake. That it is 'the Moiety of her fortune' is mentioned four times by Fainall, once by Mirabell (when explaining the scheme to Mrs Fainall, his ex-mistress), once (not very clearly) by Mrs Fainall, and once by the maid Mincing, who is hugely impressed at the magnitude of that moiety ('such a vast sum as Six Thousand Pound'). Fainall is hard up, and so money matters to him, but the reason for stressing that but a moiety is at stake (Congreve could have, had he wished, made matters simpler by putting her entire fortune in Lady Wishfort's hands) can only be to imply a gratuitous element in the conspiracy to secure it. Millamant is hardly mercenary – she never mentions money, the half-fortune already hers being ample to supply independent needs. Mirabell is far from impecunious; his personal servant is prepared to marry at his bidding on the promise of a farm, and he would know his master's ability to provide better than most could. When Congreve wished characters to be seen as economically dependent, he made this explicit: Mellefont, Maskwell, Silvia, Valentine are all, like Fainall, unquestionably cut-of-funds. It is only Lady Wishfort, in wilful and splenetic self-deceit, who can imagine

Mirabell in beggary. All that has been won is a bonus, and it is awarded to a couple who neither need it nor bother to gloat over it.

The dedication to the play draws attention to the 'care and pains' that its composition took. What the carefully placed financial details tell is that the action is driven by an unnecessary conspiracy to overcome an obstacle of no importance. With no real hindrance to their marriage, Mirabell and Millamant choose to invent an impediment against which to strive and scheme gratuitously.[1] Both know love to be dangerous and so occupy themselves with delaying love. She would be 'solicited to the very last, nay and afterwards'; he would not have her surrender for once and for all but 'over and over again'. Instead of what Angelica termed 'over-taking and possessing', they opt for that subjective passion which shuns finality, the kind of love that thrives on unfulfilment and separation.

Subjective love rooted in unattainability has a long and respectable literary history.[2] In mid-seventeenth-century England, however, the cavalier poets had assimilated it to the psychology of desire, as a commonplace of poems 'against fruition' that make prolonged anticipation a spur for jaded appetites. To re-energise subjective love as a kind of passion valid in itself, Marvell had to stress its oddity and present it as something specialised and extraordinary, as in his 'The Definition of Love':

> My love is of a birth as rare
> As 'tis for object strange and high:
> It was begotten by despair
> Upon Impossibility.

But if this is unusual, it is no more so than Marvell made the other possible kinds of passion to which he gave entire poems. Strangeness equally characterises narcissistic celibacy in 'The Garden', where the solitary soul appears preening as a bird that 'combs its silver Wings', or the energetic beat-the-clock coupling at the ending of 'To his Coy Mistress', or the masochism delighted in by 'The Unfortunate Lover', glad to bleed because 'he saies, a Lover drest / In his own Blood does relish best'. Subjective love, like these other varieties, appears in the only way love could appear in Marvell's poetry, as an extreme of experience at once ludicrous and intense, exclusive in its commitment to its own outer limits. Not until later in the century did other treatment seem possible.

New possibilities for subjective love appear in Nathaniel Lee's remarkable play *The Princess of Cleve* (*c.* 1681), described by its author as 'Farce, Comedy, Tragedy or meer Play'.[3] (It derives, of course, from Mme de La Fayette's celebrated work, *La Princesse de Clèves*, 1678.) Towards the close the Princess, by this point widowed, encounters the Duke of Nemours, who is still prepared to offer her the love she had (reluctantly, but honourably) refused while her (unwanted but constant) husband was alive. Remembering how her husband's passion had continued keen when she had been without answering ardour, she rejects Nemours on the grounds that

> 'Tis Obstacle, Ascent, and Lets and Bars
> That whet the appetite . . .   [VII 172–3]

When Nemours protests that he can love her forever, she answers with bitter realism:

> Why this sounds well and natural till you're cloid
> But Oh! when once satiety has pall'd you,
> You sicken at each view, and ev'ry glance
> Betrays your guilty Soul, and says you loath her.
>   [v iii 181–4]

In Lee's French source, this was effectively the ending, subjective love dissolving into poignant renunciation,[4] but Lee made his play continue with less bleakness, more brutality. Although the Princess departs protesting 'you shall never see me more', Lee's Nemours immediately comments to a friend 'she Lyes, I'll wager my State, I Bed her eighteen months three weeks hence, at half an hour past two in the Morning', and the play ends on his cynical pledge to marry one of his cast-off mistresses to 'convince the World of the Ingenuity of my Repentance'. What is interesting here is that subjective love does not appear obsessive and stifling – as in Mme de La Fayette's novella – but as a possible and valid reading of experience. It may, as Nemours suggests, be a mask that intensifies the lust it would disguise, or it may be that his fascination with the Princess of Cleve proves him to be in thrall to a subjective love his bravura will not admit to. The options are open.

It is widely agreed that Lee's model for Nemours was the Earl of Rochester, and in some of Rochester's poetry subjective love became compulsively central.[5] In 'The Mistress', which first appears in a collection of 1691 published by Tonson (who was to publish Congreve's work), Rochester dwells on the power of absence to sustain intensity in passion – developing his wife's jest, 'You grow constant through despair', until subjective love becomes an inescapably necessary absurdity, as time and transcience ensure that 'none but dull delights endure'. Pitting love-in-absence against violent surrender, his logic grows tight. The poem opens on an apparent promise of boundless pleasure –

> An Age, in her Embraces past,
>   Would seem a Winters Day;

– but its wintry aspect is extended until this seems a yielding to ruin:

> Where Life and Light, with envious hast,
>   Are torn and snatch'd away.

Instead of present and immediate love, love-in-absence is proposed, not for comfort but because then 'how slowly Minutes rowl'; love is, through absence, prolonged in time and not burnt up suddenly:

> For then no more a Soul but shade,
>   It mournfully does move;
> And haunts my Breast, by Absence made
>   The living Tomb of Love.

The implicit absurdity is then, self-reflexively, brought forward for comment as, accepting this shady idiom as the mad raving of love-sickness, its very lunacy becomes its justification; the very pangs of jealousy brought on in separation amount to a reliable experience:

> Fantastick Fancies fondly move . . .
>   But Pain can ne're deceive.

Because consummation's suddenness seems shockingly outside the movement of time, the more enduring hurt that separation generates seems preferable because it does give a sense of love continuing in time: a conclusion that is at once inescapable and hardly bearable. A similar concern with subjective love as a productive tension, outlasting passion that dissolves in satiety, places it within the alternatives explored in *The Way of the World*.

The importance of love in the play emerges through the way characters are grouped, in satiric contrast and counterpoint. Content to plan his travels and sometimes to get drunk, Sir Wilfull courts Millamant because his aunt commands him, as, for the same reason, he leaves the drawing-room to pull off his boots. His younger brother Witwoud admires her so far as that is fashionable – being country-bred, it takes him all his attention to be fully foppish. All the other characters who count pursue love variously, so that love is central in any production of the play to the degree that the Witwoud brothers are ridiculous.

For the affected wits, love is a decoration, an ornament to be displayed, to win prestige. It is to be flaunted in public, not experienced. But although Petulant dresses as a trull to call on himself in chocolate-houses, he exposes only his preoccupation with projecting an image he would deem impressive. Recognisable as a charade, his pursuit of love only betrays his capacity for self-delusion, laughably: Witwoud remarks that he would 'not finding himself, sometimes leave a letter for himself'. Self-evasion likewise marks Lady Wishfort's attempt to stage her meeting with Sir Rowland and display more desirableness than her niece. Most lucid in the excitement of rehearsal, she betrays what her charade would mask – 'I am an old peel'd wall' – her agitation mounting as she evades her own evident unattractiveness. What is disturbing is her need for unreality, for self-deception more desperate than Petulant's, quickening to life only with panic. The outcome of her posturing is to make her ridiculous to herself, Foible's 'Property', 'a botcher of second hand Marriages, between Abigails and Andrews' [v i].

Alert in advance to the vulnerability love brings, the truewits prefer secrecy to ostentation. As their jests recognise, love is an experience subject to time's corrosive passing ('that were like enquiring after an old fashion, to ask a Husband for his Wife'), as Mrs Fainall has learned the hard way. Having, she admits, 'loved with Indiscretion', she has had no option but to marry a man she hates, at Mirabell's suggestion, when she feared herself to be pregnant as a result of what had been their passionate love. Because love passes in time, it leads to loss; putting matters generally she can say that when men 'cease to love (we ought to think at least) they loath; they look upon us with Horror and Distaste; they meet us like the Ghosts of what we were, and as from such, fly from us' [II i]. She exhibits, in her resignation, the painful fact that love declines, while Mrs Marwood and Fainall show the course of that decline. Their meeting in the second act begins with Fainall jealous at the restlessness he detects in Marwood: in blocking Mirabell's pretended advances to Lady Wishfort, she had betrayed her own fascination with his charms, threatening Fainall's security. As his inquisition sharpens, her ease with him is in turn shaken, and he gains the upper hand as rage drives her to weeping. What is left for them to share is conspiracy, and so the decay of their love is not final. But they are noticeably less intense and less passionate in their later scenes together, as love has dwindled to comradeship in adversity, following the course that Cynthia in *The Double-Dealer* had feared:

I swear it never does well when the Parties are so agreed – For when People walk Hand in Hand, there's neither overtaking nor Meeting: We hunt in Couples where we both pursue the same Game, but forget one another, and 'tis because we are so near that we don't think of coming together.   [*D.-D.*, IV i]

When Mirabell and Millamant do meet during the play, they do not declare their love to each other directly. Although Mirabell can confess it to Fainall, ruefully, he dodges her 'what do you say to me' [II i]; and Millamant, with dreadful irony, only confesses to his former mistress 'if Mirabell shou'd not make a good husband, I am a lost thing – for I find I love him violently' [IV, i]. Their commitment being to delay, the play can only allow them rare meetings. In their second encounter on stage, as they lay down provisos for marriage together [IV i], it is particularly noticeable that neither envisages how they will be when married. Their attention centres on how they will *not* live, and they employ negative language ('let us be . . . as well bred as if we were not marri'd at all'), and lay down conditions either for continuing to live as they already do independently or for not imitating the behaviour they have observed in married people. Their provisos are defensive, and show strong unwillingness to envisage any modification in the course of time, any change that mutual living might bring. Their subjective love amounts in this respect to a bulwark against experience, against presence and against time, yet vital in the continuous tensions it generates for them.

Congreve's ending, then, has Lee's variety and Rochester's compulsive insistence on necessary, even hurtful, absurdity. Fainall and Mrs Marwood lose the opportunity to 'retire somewhere, anywhere to another world', but it is hard to say whether Millamant and Mirabell are truly better off – they face a change their imaginations cannot compass, that this play cannot describe. Their subjective love may offer different pleasures from the secretive mutual loves more vulnerable to decay – either is preferable to empty posturing – but therein lurks cruelty that comes close to sadism: baiting Lady Wishfort is near to an attack by the strong against the weak. If a production is to find champions for continued love, Foible and Waitwell, as free from nauseous cant as Millamant could wish, are the likeliest candidates, with hardly time for mutual endearment and nothing to deter 'Iteration of Nuptials'. But this is a matter for the actors to decide (Foible and Waitwell have no exchanges in the last act). The text Congreve left offers no assurances or comforts, and its power lies rather in the searchingness with which it explores the kinds of love it dramatises.

SOURCE: First published in this Casebook.

NOTES

1. Freud claimed that this approach to love became necessary whenever sexuality was unrestricted. In the second of his 'Contributions to the Psychology of Love' (1912), he added that 'the psychical value of erotic needs is reduced as soon as their satisfaction becomes easy. An obstacle is required in order to heighten libido; and where natural resistances to satisfaction have not been sufficient men have at all times erected conventional ones so as to be able to enjoy love.' See *Pelican Freud Library*, vol. 7 (London, 1977), pp. 256–7.

2. The pervasiveness of subjective love in Western literature is surveyed by Denis de Rougemont, *Passion and Society*, 2nd, revised edition (London, 1956).

3. In his dedication of the play to Charles Sackville, Earl of Dorset (to whom Congreve was to dedicate *Love for Love*). See *The Works of Nathaniel Lee*, edited by T. B. Stroup and A. L. Cooke (New Brunswick, 1955), vol. II, p. 153. Other passages quoted from the play follow the line-references of this edition.

4. This aspect of Mme de La Fayette's work is discussed with particular sensitivity by Barbara Wright in the introduction to her edition of Eugène Fromentin's *Dominique* (Oxford, 1965), pp. xxviii–xxix.

5. Rochester's preoccupation with absence-games is further discussed by Anne Barton in her British Academy lecture on his poetry, *Proceedings of the British Academy*, LIII (1967), pp. 47–69, esp. pp. 68–9.

PART FOUR

Twentieth-Century Productions

Virginia Woolf 'Too Full-Hearted to be Witty' (1921)

Love for Love at the Lyric Theatre, Hammersmith, 1921

I suppose it must happen that gentlemen with cellars come to fight shy of the old bottles in the corner. The labels slung round their necks testify to their age and to their ancestry. But the dust is thick, the wax all cracked, and Heaven knows whether the fluid within is not by this time gone sour and cloudy. So it is with the old books with famous names. The occasion comes for tasting them. We make all ready, poke the fire, adjust the light, rub the glasses, and then gingerly open *Love for Love, a Comedy*, written by Mr Congreve and first produced on April 30th, 1695, at the New Theatre, in Little Lincoln's Inn Fields. But it has kept uncommonly well. Try a sip with me. 'Well, if he be but as great a sea-beast as she is a land-monster, we shall have a most amphibious breed – the progeny will be all otters,' 'To your element, fish; be mute, fish, and to sea. . . .' Don't you agree that this is infinitely better stuff than they make nowadays? In God's name, why does one ever read anything else? – so pleasant is it to shake out a good, wholesome laugh now and again. Yet *Love for Love* is not a jolly play; nor is it a profound play; nor a poetical play; there is nothing that disturbs the social conscience or sends us stumbling up to bed thinking of the sorrows of the world. The nearest we can come to a description of our state at the finish is that we have drunk good wine. We are slightly tipsy. We are about to say something very witty. The maid who brings in the cocoa is about to do something very coarse. Write a letter to make an appointment with the dentist and the sentence, with its two or three round oaths, will be (or will momentarily appear) as beautifully turned as the legs of a Sheraton table.

The truth is that *Love for Love* is much simpler than the kind of play we write nowadays. That is part of the reason why we seem to breathe sea air and look for miles and miles into the distance. There were then two fit topics for conversation – love and money. Both are frankly talked about with the natural relish of people who are not distracted by other concerns, but have kept a sort of virgin energy for the two prime objects of life. They take them much too seriously to muffle them up in decent ambiguity. Further, it is a very small society, acquainted with each other's language so that the pellets of repartee which they are for ever discharging fly straight, hit hard, and yet have about them an extraordinary distinction. They have been at this game for so long that they talk as well as noblemen now shoot pheasants. Whether this is not better perceived in reading than in acting is, I think, an open question. At the Lyric Theatre, Hammersmith, last week there were a good many words dropped or fumbled, and Congreve never wrote a speech that did not balance with a kind of tremulous vitality. Knock out a word and the sentence tumbles like a house of cards.

But at the Lyric Theatre things happened rather against expectation. Reading, relishing the wit, getting the effect of the give-and-take of repartee, tend to make for hardness and concentration. It was natural to expect that the same words spoken by living men and women would warm and blossom, and that there would be drawn to the surface other subtleties of character which scarcely come to the top in reading. Yet as the play went on one came to wonder whether the life which was so capably and admirably breathed into figure after figure was the life of the period.

Miss Vivian Rees, for example, acting Angelica, the mother of Peacock's women, the grandmother of Meredith's, was charming to look at, charming to hear, but when it came to flaunting Angelica's philosophy – 'Uncertainty and expectation are the joys of life. Security is an insipid thing; and the overtaking and possessing of a wish discovers the folly of the chase. Never let us know one another better; for the pleasure of a masquerade is done, when we come to shew our faces' – when it came to the wildness and rashness and rakishness of this, Miss Vivian Rees was altogether too demure. If we had been fancying that Scandal somehow represents a kind of chorus, a point of view from which all this heartlessness and brazen morality could be seen shaded and in perspective, Mr Holloway scarcely supported our venture. Indeed the character who came out best was Sir Sampson Legend. To begin with, Mr Roy Byford is a superb figure of a man. To go on with, it seems likely that our natural taste for the burly humour and the florid figures of the past has been nourished, and is even now kept alive by the humour of the music-halls. For the rest, we are too good-hearted or too full-hearted to be witty. Give us wit, and we broaden it into farce.

SOURCE: review in *New Statesman* (2 April 1921).

James Agate 'The Highest Pitch Known to Classic Comedy' (1924)

The Way of the World in Nigel Playfair's Production,
Lyric Theatre, Hammersmith, 1924

Charles Lamb did a world of mischief when he put before his most famous essay the title *On the Artificial Comedy of the Last Century*. Sitting at this performance of the greatest prose comedy in the English language, I could not, for the life of me, see anything artificial in the personages beyond their inessentials – dress, speech, and polite notions. Manners change, but not the man who wears them. If Lady Wishfort is artificial, then so, too, is Falstaff. I see equally little reason why Congreve's hot-handed widow should be so superfluous to demand the time of day, except for the causes assigned to that other gormandiser. Wishfort is all appetite, and as real as any canvas of old Hogarth or modern page of Zola. One of her kind attends dinner parties to this day, less her candour and wit.

Millamant, too, could go into any novel of Meredith, *mutatis mutandis*, having regard to the topics which a more generous age has conceded to the sex. Wit of Millamant's order is imperishable, for the simple reason that her creator gave her a mind. Lamb's celebrated excuse for compunctionless laughter is that these creatures never were. The truth is that they are, and always will be. 'The effect of Congreve's plays', says Hazlitt, 'is prodigious *on the well-informed spectator.*' It is easy to pronounce as artificial a world of which you are ignorant; in the Hebrides *Our Betters* would doubtless be dubbed fantastic. There are more Wishforts and Millamants about town to-day than there are Hedda Gablers. Mirabell is a poseur, but he does not date one-tenth as much as Wilde's Lord Wotton. And as for Sir Wilfull Witwoud, one of his kidney sold me a horse no later than Wednesday last. Congreve, in a word, was the natural well from which Sheridan, Wilde and our own Somerset Maugham have drawn their 'natural table-waters'. Without, alas, quite so much naturalness.

How is the piece played at Hammersmith? For all it is worth, is the answer; and perhaps just a teeny-weeny bit popularised. We could do without that business with the chandelier and the bewigged orchestra. The play is keyed up to the highest pitch known to classic comedy. It may be that Mr Playfair was afraid to trust us with the pure distillation of the Comic Spirit; it is much more probable that he recognised that in Miss Margaret Yarde he had a Wishfort who must prove a moral and physical eruption in – to use Prince Hal's phrase – flame-coloured taffeta. It was a first-class performance, striking alike to eye and ear. The simpering of this hag-ridden beldam would have brought down the comminations of a Lear. There was cut-and-come-again, you felt, in the way of grotesque, unbridled fancy. Sobriety could not hold the stage against this monstrously comic obsession. And therefore was sobriety not attempted.

But what of Millamant? Almost everything, is our answer this time. Never can actress have spoken the epilogue with less belief in its aptness.

> There are some critics so with spleen diseased
> They scarcely come inclining to be pleased

was not true of those who on Thursday came to see, not only the old piece, but the speaker of the epilogue fulfil prophecy. Let me not mince matters. Miss Edith Evans is the most accomplished of living and practising English actresses. . . .

Her Millamant is impertinent without being pert, graceless without being ill-graced. She has only two scenes, but what scenes they are of unending subtlety and finesse! Never can that astonishing 'Ah! idle creature, get up when you will' have taken on greater delicacy, nor 'I may by degrees *dwindle* into a wife' a more delicious mockery. '*Adieu*, my morning thoughts, agreeable wakings, indolent slumbers, all ye *douceurs*, ye *sommeils du matin, adieu*' – all this is breathed out as though it were early Ronsard or du Bellay. And 'I nauseate walking', and 'Natural, easy Suckling!' bespeak the very genius of humour. There is a pout of the lips, a jutting forward of the chin to greet the conceit, and a smile of happy deliverance when it is uttered, which defy the chronicler. This face, at such moments, is like a city in illumination, and when it is withdrawn leaves a glow behind.

One fault I find, and one only. Millamant's first entry bears out Mirabell's announcement: 'Here she comes, i' faith, full sail, with her fan spread and her streamers out.' The actress makes her appearance something lapwing fashion, a trifle too close to the ground. It is possible, too, that Mrs Abington gave the whole character a bigger sweep. Miss Evans conceives her as a rogue in porcelain, and keeps her within that conception. Walpole, one feels sure, would have had civil things to say of this performance of which the perfect enunciation is one of the minor marvels.

The Mirabell of Mr Robert Loraine was a trifle on the sober side, but showed distinction if a trifle too much heart. The part was beautifully spoken, and the actor used only the suavest and most gentle notes in his voice. He listened exquisitely. Miss Dorothy Green made great music of her lines, and Messrs Playfair and Norman enjoyed themselves hugely.

Source: review in the *Sunday Times* (10 Feb. 1924); reprinted in Agate's *The Contemporary Theatre* (London, 1924), pp. 302–6.

Sir Nigel Playfair 'Comedy of Manners Burlesqued' (1925)

On his Production of *The Way of the World*,
Lyric Theatre, Hammersmith, 1924

. . . *The Way of the World* is the greatest of all comedies of manners – a kind of comedy which Congreve himself defined in his dedication to the Earl of Montague in saying that his idea was 'to design characters which should appear ridiculous, not so much through a natural folly as through an affected wit: a wit which, at the same time that it is affected, is also false'. At the same time, it was a sort of reply to Jeremy Collier's attack on 'the immorality and profaneness of the English stage'. Its first unlucky production was in 1700 at the Lincoln's Inn Fields Theatre, where *The Beggar's Opera* afterwards appeared. The best possible cast was secured for it, including Betterton, Mrs Barry, and Mrs Bracegirdle (the secretly adored of Congreve).

You will readily see that in attempting to produce it again I had far greater need of faith than in the case of *The Beggar's Opera*, for whereas *The Beggar's Opera* had never failed to make the fortunes of all who handled it, *The Way of the World*, in spite of the eulogies of the critics, had never failed to lead to bankruptcy. This I put down largely to its extremely complicated action – 'a jungle of passionless intrigues' – which an ordinary audience finds hard to follow; and what an ordinary audience finds hard to follow it rejects altogether. I therefore burlesqued the plot considerably, and treated it as a joke. As [A. B. Walkley] said in *The Times*, it was 'a rattling, jaunty, jigging, almost jazzing revival. The play is fantasticated.' That seemed to me the only thing to do; and I think I was justified in the result.

But no, that is hardly fair. I think, in discussing the character of Polly, I have mentioned how the character of Millamant ran away with its author; and that indeed is the case. What started as a comedy of manners is suddenly rapt from our sight in one of the most blinding visions of character that have ever been dramatised. And it was that which gave Miss Evans her real chance. The Millamant of that last final surrender to Mirabell is something far more than the Millamant who comes 'full sail, with her fan spread, and her streamers out, and a shoal of fools for tenders': it is a woman wittier, more fascinating, and more tender, probably, than has ever been seen off the stage or elsewhere on it. Here is no 'character rendered ridiculous by its affected wit': here is a character rendered sublime by the poignancy and the sincerity of its wit. And I repeat that there never has been on or off the stage a woman so sublime in the same way as Millamant: no one reading the play can fail to see this, and it is a most extraordinary tribute to Edith Evans that she was able to take on her shoulders the weight of such an enormous conception, and play it almost as if the conception were purely her own rather than the author's.

Nobody could find fault with Miss Evans – indeed, nobody tried; though the rest of the cast were not altogether so kindly treated. Miss Margaret Yarde's Lady Wishfort was a frequent bone of contention; and though one critic gave her the palm for the piece, several others considered that she made it too farcical. But why, in heaven's name, shouldn't she? She made it an outstanding piece of acting, and a piece of acting which fitted in perfectly well with the rest of the production. Even if it was not, perhaps, entirely Congreve's Lady Wishfort, it was a performance which justified itself simply and solely by its own excellence. Miss Yarde is in an unique position among contemporary actresses: she lights up any play in which she appears for a few moments, and yet there is hardly any play in which a part for her of any magnitude can be found! And except for Lady Wishfort, she has hardly ever had a chance of giving scope to her peculiar and inimitable gifts. . . .

SOURCE: extract from *The Story of the Lyric Theatre, Hammersmith* (London, 1925), pp. 183–5.

Sir John Gielgud   'In a Naturalistic Style'
(1943)

On his Revival of *Love for Love* in Wartime

. . . Playfair always contrived in his productions to give a decorative, pleasing series of pictures without undue elaboration. This was partly imposed on him by the fact that he worked in such a small theatre with a very low budget. . . .

My problem in doing a West End revival of *Love for Love* in 1943 was intensified by the prospect of playing in very large theatres, both in London and in the provinces, and of trying to make the wordy, classical text seem alive and truthful to audiences unfamiliar with this type of dialogue. I was lucky enough to cast the play extremely happily despite war conditions, and I discussed with Leon Quartermain, who was to play Scandal, how best to set about the direction of it. We both felt that if the actors would all play realistically – and were also stylish enough to wear their clothes and deport themselves with elegance – there was no reason why we might not play the play in a naturalistic style, with the 'fourth wall down' as it were. This was in direct opposition to anything I had even seen, for, in Playfair's productions, the asides were delivered (as no doubt they were in the eighteenth century) directly to the audience, and there was no attempt at localisation in the settings, which were merely drop scenes and wings, and served as a background (but not as a home) for the characters in the play.

Of course I am quite prepared to see a revival of *Love for Love* which is directed in a completely different way from mine, for Congreve himself certainly pictured the play without realistic scenery, and with the asides spoken to the audience, just as Shakespeare always pictured his apron stage and balcony.

Rex Whistler . . . sketched two settings which were exactly of the kind that I had imagined for the play. Valentine's lodgings, a crowded, panelled room, full of junk, furniture, pictures and statuary; and, in contrast, the hall of Foresight's house, with a Thornhill mural and lofty ceiling, arched doorways, and almost empty of furniture. Jeanette Cochrane, who designed the costumes, insisted on absolute accuracy in the cut of the clothes, and, in Whistler's enforced absence, supervised every detail of the furnishings of the scenes and details of the accessories. . . . Nigel Playfair will be chiefly remembered in our theatre for his great influence in popularising eighteenth-century revivals. . . . His scenery was decorative rather than realistic, and there was a minimum of furniture and accessories. I found the final effect too much like a revue for my own taste. . . .

Edith Evans's performance as Millamant [in Playfair's *The Way of the World* of 1924 – Ed.] was probably the finest stylised piece of bravura acting seen in London in the last fifty years. Her economy and grace of movement, her perfectly sustained poses, the purring coquetry of her voice with its extraordinary subtlety of range, was inimitably captivating. . . . When a leading player achieves a consummate style in a classical revival, the whole performance is naturally affected. . . . Yvonne Arnaud, a brilliantly farcical actress . . . brought such skill and experience to the part of Mrs Frail in my *Love for Love*, that the whole cast seemed to discover and develop the right gusto and style from her example. . . . It is true that nearly all of us were a good many years too old for the characters we represented but, fortunately, this did not seem to worry anybody who saw the play. . . .

SOURCE: Extracts from *Stage Directions* (London, 1963), pp. 63–4, 67–8, 64, 70).

Irving Wardle 'By Far the Best Production I Have Seen' (1978)

The RSC's Production of *The Way of the World*
Aldwych Theatre, 1978

While living human beings have for years been invading the plays of Farquhar and Vanbrugh, Congreve remains the last fortress of artificial comedy. Neither the National Theatre's *Way of the World* nor Prospect's recent Edwardian version dared to scratch the gilded façade; and it has been left to John Barton and the RSC to examine our greatest prose comedy for traces of sober meaning.

The result is by far the best production I have ever seen, although I doubt whether it succeeds exactly as Mr Barton intended. The plot is famously incomprehensible. But instead of skating over it for the sake of the marvellous separate scenes, this production begins by challenging the spectator to make sense of it. Fainall introduces Sir Wilfull as 'half brother to this Witwoud by a former wife, who was sister to my Lady Wishfort, my wife's mother'. John Woodvine speaks this straight out to the house, almost with a wink: he gets his laugh, and he also leaves you determined to try to sort things out. Thereafter the ramifications of the intrigue are all most carefully accentuated, and the plot takes shape with startling coherence. What it does not do is to develop into the kind of moral fable which seems intended from the icy treatment of the closing speech on marriage frauds. What we get is a superlative treatment of the individual scenes, linked rather better than usual.

The most conspicuous novelty among the performances is Michael Pennington's Mirabell. Gielgud has succeeded, and others have tried with less success, to pass off this character as Millamant's equally dazzling partner. But where Millamant lives through her lines, Mirabell lives mainly through the words of others; and Mr Pennington never competes with her. Instead he relaxes into a cool acceptance of his own power, and concentrates on the lover rather than the intriguer. He knows he will win in the end, and waits quietly at the centre of the whirling dance of fools and fops until the delicious bird enters his net. The unnerving thing about Mr Pennington's performance is its apparent sincerity.

The marriage scene remains the jewel of the production, and the high point of Judi Dench's wonderful Millamant, a piece of high-precision sexual engineering constructed from languishing cries, bubbling laughs, instantaneous mood transitions, always in motion with a train like a matador's cloak, designed at once to exert invincible attraction and evade capture. One masterstroke among many is her final compliance with Mirabell: 'I hate your odious provisos.' Even Edith Evans delivered this skittishly: Miss Dench lingers caressingly over it.

As her grotesque erotic counterpart, Beryl Reid achieves extraordinary variety as Lady Wishfort without the usual coarsening of the character. There is a certain level of decorum beneath which Congreve's old harridan does not sink, whether taking her fan to the drunken Sir Wilfull (treated for once with real respect by Bob Peck), or belabouring the treacherous Foible (Eliza Ward) with a hefty stick. The pathos is there as well as the absurdity: expressed in the precipitous slips of her genteel vowels. The performance is full of robust invention: 'Nothing so alluring as a *levée* from a couch', she declares, vainly struggling to get up.

These characters, together with David Lyon's Waitwell and Marjorie Bland's poisonous Marwood, are creatures with recognisable passions. But they also supply the traditional pleasures of the play in their handling of those decorative spurts of verbal invention that grow like luxuriant foliage from the central stem. Roughly set (with forestage doors) and splendidly dressed by Maria Bjornson, the production also teaches the National Theatre's *Country Wife* a lesson in the effective use of direct address.

SOURCE: review of the Royal Shakespeare Company's production, *The Times* (30 Jan. 1978).

SELECT BIBLIOGRAPHY

THEATRE HISTORY AND BIOGRAPHY

For theatre history relative to Congreve the standard works of reference are: E. L. Avery *et al.* (eds), *The London Stage, 1660–1880* (Carbondale, Ill., 1960–68, and London), and P. H. Highfill Jnr *et al.* (eds), *A Biographical Dictionary of Actors, Actresses, Musicians, Dancers, Managers and Other Stage Personnel in London, 1660–1800* (Carbondale, Ill, 1973–).

For Congreve biography the most thorough work is John C. Hodges, *William Congreve: The Man* (London, and New York, 1941). Professor Hodges has also compiled a list of books in *The Library of William Congreve* (New York, 1955) and edited *William Congreve: Letters and Documents* (London, and New York, 1964).

The playwright's immediate milieu is evoked vividly by Kathleen M. Lynch, *A Congreve Gallery* (Cambridge, Mass., 1951; reissued London, 1968).

CRITICISM

Along with works cited in this Casebook, the following offer critical discussion of Congreve's plays.

(a) *Studies Relating Congreve to Larger Literary Topics*

Virginia Ogden Birdsall, *Wild Civility: English Comic Spirit on the Restoration Stage* (Bloomington, Ind., 1970; and London).

Donald Bruce, *Topics of Restoration Drama* (London, 1975).

Ian Donaldson, *The World Upside-Down: Comedy from Jonson to Fielding* (Oxford, 1970; new edn 1974).

T. H. Fujimura, *The Restoration Comedy of Wit* (Princeton, N. J., 1952).

G. Wilson Knight, *The Golden Labyrinth: A Study of British Drama* (London, 1962; and New York).

John Loftis, *Comedy and Society from Congreve to Fielding* (Stanford, Calif., 1958).

Margaret Lamb McDonald, *The Independent Woman in the Restoration Comedy of Manners* (Salzburg, 1976).

Martin Price, *To the Palace of Wisdom: Studies in Order and Energy from Dryden to Blake* (New York, 1964).

J. H. Smith, *The Gay Couple in Restoration Comedy* (Cambridge, Mass., 1948).

James Sutherland, *English Literature of the Late Seventeenth Century* (Oxford, 1969).

D. R. M. Wilkinson, *The Comedy of Habit* (Leyden, 1964).

(b) *Studies Centrally Concerned with Congreve*

Malcolm Kelsall, *Congreve: 'The Way of the World'* (London, 1981).

Paul & Miriam Mueschke, *A New View of Congreve's Way of the World* (Ann Arbor, Ill., 1958).

W. H. Van Voris, *The Cultivated Stance: The Design of Congreve's Plays* (Dublin, 1965).

Aubrey Williams, *An Approach to Congreve* (New Haven, Conn., 1979)

The collection of papers read to a conference at York and edited by Brian Morris, *William Congreve* (London, 1972) from which excerpts are included in this Casebook, also contains John Barnard's important reply to claims by Aubrey Williams that Congreve's comedies were designed to illustrate the working of Christian Providence.

(c) *Essays and Articles*

John Barnard: see above

Brian Corman, ' "The Mixed Way of Comedy": Congreve's *The Double-Dealer*', *Modern Philology*, 71 (1974), 356–65; and '*The Way of the World* and Morally Serious Comedy', *University of Toronto Quarterly*, 44 (1975), 199–212.

Charles H. Hinnant, 'Wit, Propriety and Style in *The Way of the World*', *Studies in English Literature*, XVII (1977), 373–86.

Paul J. Hurley, 'Law and Dramatic Rhetoric in *The Way of the World*', *South Atlantic Quarterly*, 70 (1971), 191–202.

Anthony Kaufmann, 'Language and Character in Congreve's *The Way of the World*', *Tulane Studies in Language and Literature*, 15 (1973), 411–27.

Sue L. Kimball, 'Games People Play in Congreve's *The Way of the World*', in Donald Kay (ed.), *A Provision of Human Nature: Essays in Honor of Miriam Austen Locke* (Birmingham, Al., 1977).

Charles A. Lyons, 'Congreve's Miracle of Love', *Criticism*, VI (1964), 331–48.

Marvin Mudrick, 'Restoration Comedy and Later', in W. K. Wimsatt (ed.), *English Stage Comedy* (New York, 1955).

Susan J. Rosowski, 'Thematic Development in the Comedies of William Congreve: The Individual in Society', *Studies in English Literature*, XVI (1976), 387–406.

Darwin Turner, 'The Servant in the Comedies of William Congreve', *College Language Association Journal*, 1 (1958), 68–74.

John Wain, 'Restoration Comedy and its Modern Critics', *Essays in Criticism*, VI (1965), 367–85.

Gerald Weales, 'The Shadow on Congreve's Surface', *Educational Theatre Journal*, 19 (1967), 30–2.

NOTES ON CONTRIBUTORS

Parts One and Two

Edmund Burke(1729–97): political theorist, statesman and man of letters; his most important non-political work is *A Philosophical Enquiry into the Sublime and the Beautiful* (1756).

Fanny Burney (1752–1840): pioneer of the 'domestic' novel, with *Evelina* (1778), *Cecilia* (1782), *Camilla* (1796) and *The Wanderer* (1814); her diaries and letters illuminate literary and Court life.

Colley Cibber (1671–1757): actor, playwright and Poet Laureate (1730–57); a controversial figure in literary and theatre circles, Pope made him the chief butt of the final version of the *Dunciad*.

Jeremy Collier (1650–1726): Non-juring clergyman, imprisoned for pamphleteering in support of the exiled James II, and notorious for supporting a plot to assassinate William III.

John Dennis (1657–1734): playwright and critic; his critical writings include *The Advancement and Reformation of Modern Poetry* (1701), *The Grounds of Criticism in Poetry* (1704) and *An Essay on the Genius and Writings of Shakespeare* (1712).

John Dryden (1631–1700): Poet Laureate (1668–89), dramatist and literary critic; his critical writings, which include the *Essay of Dramatick Poesie* (1668), the Dedication to *Examen Poeticum* and prefaces to his plays, are milestones in the development of literary criticism in England.

Oliver Goldsmith (1730–74): poet, novelist, playwright and essayist; his critical writings include *An Enquiry into the Present State of Polite Learning* (1759).

William Hazlitt (1778–1830): essayist, literary critic and political writer; his critical writings include *A View of the English Stage*, *Lectures on the English Comic Writers*, and *The Characters of Shakespeare's Plays*.

Bevil Higgons (1670–1735): historian, critic and poet, one of the literary circle at Will's Coffee-house in Bow Street.

Mrs Elizabeth Inchbald (1753–1821): novelist, dramatist and actress.

Samuel Johnson (1709–84): poet, novelist, critic, lexicographer, dramatist and editor of the works of William Shakespeare with its notable Preface (1765).

LORD KAMES, Henry Home (1696–1782): Scottish judge, psychologist and critic; his *Introduction to the Art of Thinking* (1761) and *Elements of Criticism* (1762) had a strong influence.

CHARLES LAMB (1775–1834): essayist and critic; his discernment did much to advance appreciation of Shakespeare and to revive interest in the older school of English dramatists.

LORD MACAULAY, Thomas Babington Macaulay (1800–59): historian, statesman, critic and poet.

GEORGE MEREDITH (1828–1909): novelist and poet; of his novels *The Egoist* (1879) and *Diana of the Crossways* (1885) have been most esteemed; *Modern Love* (1862) is now regarded as an outstanding poem of the nineteenth century.

ALEXANDER POPE (1688–1744): poet and critic, he exercised a powerful influence on the literary outlook of his day, notably by his didactic poem *Essay on Criticism* (1711) and his satirical writings, including the *Dunciad* (1728, 1729 and 1743).

RICHARD BRINSLEY SHERIDAN (1751–1816): playwright and politician.

ADAM SMITH (1723–90): professor of Logic (1751) and of Moral Philosophy (1752) at Glasgow University; in addition to his epoch-making *Inquiry into the Nature and Causes of the Wealth of Nations* (1776), he wrote and lectured on philosophical and literary topics, including *Theory of the Moral Sentiments* (1759).

THOMAS SOUTHERNE or Southern (1659–1746): playwright and friend of Dryden and Congreve; author of several comedies, it is for his tragedies *The Fatal Marriage* (1694) and *Oroonoko* (1695) that he is most remembered.

JONATHAN SWIFT (1667–1745): Dean of St Patrick's Cathedral, Dublin; poet, satirist and political writer, and a member of the literary circle of Pope and Gay.

WILLIAM M. THACKERAY (1811–63): novelist and essayist; his *English Humourists of the Eighteenth Century* (lectures delivered in 1851, published in 1853) is a keynote work of mid-Victorian literary criticism.

VOLTAIRE (1694–1778): French poet, dramatist, critic, satirist and historian; from his exile in England (1726–29) derive the *Lettres Philosophiques or Lettres sur les Anglais,* in which he applies the canons of classical French criticism to earlier and contemporary English writers.

HORACE WALPOLE, 4th Earl of Orford (1717–97): man of letters and connoisseur, author of *The Castle of Otranto* (1764); his reputation, for students of literature and history, rests today mainly on his unrivalled correspondence.

PARTS THREE AND FOUR

JAMES AGATE (1877–1947): dramatic critic, especially for the *Sunday Times* from 1923 until his death; in addition to collections of theatre reviews, he published several autobiographical volumes (*Ego*).

ANNE BARTON (also writing as Anne Righter): Fellow of New College, Oxford, and formerly Hildred Carlile Professor of English, Bedford College, London; in addition to work on Wycherley, Rochester and Byron, she has written extensively on Shakespeare, including (as Anne Righter) *Shakespeare and The Idea of the Play* (1962).

F. W. BATESON (1901–78): he lectured in English in the University of Oxford, and was founding editor of *Essays in Criticism* and editor of the *Cambridge Bibliography of English Literature*.

BONAMY DOBRÉE (1891–1974): he was Professor of English in the University of Leeds and general editor of the *Oxford History of English Literature*; his many publications include *Restoration Tragedy* and *Modern Prose Style*.

SIR JOHN GIELGUD: actor and producer; his publications include three volumes of theatrical and literary memoirs, *Early Stages* (revised edn 1974), *Stage Directions* (1963) and *Distinguished Company* (1972).

ANTHONY GOSSE: Professor of English at Bucknell University, Lewisburg, Pennsylvania.

HARRIET HAWKINS: Professor of English at Vassar College, New York; her publications include *Likenesses of Truth in Elizabethan and Restoration Drama* (1972) and *Poetic Freedom and Poetic Truth* (1976).

NORMAN N. HOLLAND: Professor and Director of the Center for the Psychological Study of the Arts, State University of New York at Buffalo; his publications include *The First Modern Comedies* (1967), *Shakespearian Imagination* (1968) and *The Dynamics of Literary Response* (1969).

PETER HOLLAND: Fellow of Trinity Hall, Cambridge; his publications include *The Ornament of Action* (1979).

MALCOLM KELSALL: Professor of English Literature, University College, Cardiff; he has published several studies on eighteenth-century literature and edited a number of works, including Congreve's *Love for Love*, Otway's *Venice Preserv'd* and Sarah Fielding's *The Adventures of David Simple*.

L. C. KNIGHTS: formerly (1965–73) King Edward VII Professor of English Literature in the University of Cambridge, and now Emeritus Professor; his many publications include *Some Shakespearean Themes* (1959), *An Approach to Hamlet* (1960), *Drama and Society in the Age of Jonson* (1937), *Public Voices: Literature and Politics with Special Reference to the Seventeenth Century* (1971), *Explorations* (1946), *Further Explorations* (1965) and *Explorations 3* (1976).

CLIFFORD LEECH (died 1977): he was Professor of English, University of Toronto, and general editor of the 'Revels Plays' series of drama texts; his writings on the drama range from Shakespeare to Eugene O'Neill.

HAROLD LOVE: Professor of English Literature, Monash University, Victoria, Australia; his publications include *Restoration Literature: Critical Approaches* (1972), *Congreve* (1974) and the *Penguin Book of Restoration Verse* (1968).

KATHLEEN M. LYNCH: American critic and scholar; her publications include *The Social Mode of Restoration Comedy* (1926; reissued 1967), *Congreve Gallery* (1951; reissued 1968) and an edition of *The Way of the World* in the Regents Restoration Drama Series (paperback 1965).

PATRICK LYONS: lectures in English Literature in the University of Glasgow.

KENNETH MUIR: formerly (1951–74) King Alfred Professor of English Literature, University of Liverpool, and now Professor Emeritus; widely known for his studies on Shakespeare, Wyatt, Milton, Keats and other poets; editor of *Shakespeare Survey* and of the Casebook on *The Winter's Tale*.

WILLIAM MYERS: lectures in English Literature in the University of Leicester; his publications include *Dryden* (1973).

MAXIMILLIAN E. NOVAK: Professor of English, University of California at Los Angeles; his publications include studies of Defoe and of Congreve, and an edition of Thomas Southerne's *Oroonoko*.

SIR NIGEL PLAYFAIR (1874–1934): actor and theatre-manager; noted for his management (1918–32) of the Lyric Theatre, Hammersmith.

IRVING WARDLE: drama critic of *The Times*.

VIRGINIA WOOLF (1882–1941): novelist and critic; her main critical writings are collected in the two volumes of *The Common Reader*.

INDEX

Page numbers in **bold type** denote essays or extracts in this Casebook. Entries in SMALL CAPS denote characters in plays. Each of Congreve's comedies has a separate entry in the alphabetical listing; all other plays and literary works are listed under the respective authors.